Human Rights Matters

D1636754

Stanford Studies in Human Rights

Human Rights Matters

Local Politics and National Human Rights Institutions

Julie A. Mertus

Stanford University Press
Stanford, California

Stanford University Press
Stanford, California

Printed in the United States of America on acid-free, archival-quality paper

Library of Congress Cataloging-in-Publication Data

Mertus, Julie, 1963–
   Human rights matters : local politics and national human rights institutions / Julie A. Mertus.
       p.   cm. — (Stanford studies in human rights)
   Includes bibliographical references and index.
   ISBN 978-0-8047-6093-5 (cloth : alk. paper) — ISBN 978-0-8047-6094-2 (pbk. : alk. paper)
   1. Human rights advocacy—Europe—Case studies.   2. Human rights—Europe—Case studies.   3. Europe—Politics and government—1989–   I. Title.
   JC599.E9.M47 2009
   323.094—dc22

                              2008032675

Designed by Bruce Lundquist
Typeset at Stanford University Press in 10/14 Minion Pro

Contents

Acknowledgments

THIS BOOK would not have been possible without the support of the Fulbright Associations of Denmark and the United States and the Danish Institute for Human Rights. I thank Marie Mønsted, the executive director of the Denmark-America Foundation and Fulbright Commission, for her strong support of my somewhat unusual research proposal; and Barbara Lehman, the Fulbright Program coordinator in Copenhagen, for help with logistics and, most important, for her willingness to share in my excitement for the research. At the Danish Institute for Human Rights, the list of people who had a hand in making my stay pleasant and productive is too long to mention by name, but I am particularly grateful to Hans Otto-Sano and Lone Groth-Rasmussen for their support throughout the entire process. I am also thankful for my "new family" in Copenhagen—especially Muborak and Preban—for taking me in and supporting me, not only with a place to stay but also with home-cooked meals and late night card games.

I thank all of the many people who agreed to be interviewed for this project (the list of interviews in the back of the book is not inclusive of all those who gave their time in this manner, and I apologize for inadvertent omissions). Special thanks go to Emir Kaknjasevic in Bosnia-Herzegovina for his superhuman logistical support; Catherine O'Rourke and Christine Bell in Northern Ireland for everything from a warm place to stay to the most intense interviewing schedule I have ever attempted; and Caroline Fetscher in Berlin for literally opening her home to me and for remaining patient as I bumbled my way up the learning curve. Other colleagues who have shared their homes and their expertise with me on this project include Marianne Schulze in Vienna, Chandra Sriram in London, and Belinda Cooper in New York.

I am indebted to C. Raj Kumar and Sonia Cardenas for their fine work on national human rights institutions, which helped to kindle my interest in the subject at the outset and to point me to Europe for field research (because they were already embarking on studies of NHRIs in Asia and Latin America). For specific substantive input and editorial advice, I would like to thank Brian Burdekin, Nancy Flowers, Michael Goodhart, Todd Landham, Anja Mihr, Catherine O'Rourke, Tazreena Sajjad, Marianne Schulze, and Frauke Seidensticker. Janet Lord read the entire draft on more than one occasion and offered numerous inputs. Stephanie Brophy was tasked with the final formatting and production of the final manuscript and I am incredibly grateful for her good work. At Stanford University Press, I am grateful to Kate Wahl for undertaking this project and for the entire production, editing, and marketing staff at Stanford who worked so carefully on this project, including Carolyn Brown, Joa Suorez, and Mimi Braverman.

My home university, American University, also warrants specific mention. This book would not have been possible without a faculty research grant and sabbatical. Thank you Dean Louis Goodman and Professor Abdul Aziz Said for your faith in me. Also, through American University's Center for Global Peace, I have been involved in NHRI support in the Middle East. This opportunity has significantly enhanced my understanding of the proliferation of NHRIs, and I am tremendously appreciative of the work of my colleagues on this project, spearheaded by Carol O'Leary and Betty Sitkah and including Mary Gray, Kathy Guernsey, and Christopher Argyris.

Above all, I am incredibly thankful for Janet Lord's support at each stage of this project, and I dedicate this book to her.

Abbreviations

ABA/CEELI	American Bar Association/Central European and Eurasian Law Initiative
AI	Amnesty International
BiH	Bosnia-Herzegovina
CAJ	Committee for the Administration of Justice (Northern Ireland)
CDU	Christian Democratic Union (Germany)
CEDAW	Convention on the Elimination of All Forms of Discrimination Against Women
CERD	United Nations Committee for the Elimination of Racial Discrimination
CESCR	United Nations Committee on Economic, Social, and Cultural Rights
CPP	Conservative People's Party (Denmark)
CRC	United Nations Committee on the Rights of the Child
CSCE	Conference on Security and Cooperation in Europe
ČSSD	Czech Social Democratic Party
CSU	Christian Social Union (Germany)
DACORD	Documentation and Advisory Center on Racial Discrimination
DAMES	Danish Center for Migration and Ethnic Studies
DCISM	Danish Center for International Studies and Human Rights
DIHR	Danish Institute for Human Rights
DIIS	Danish Institute of International Studies
DPP	Danish People's Party

DR	Danish Broadcasting Corporation
DUP	Democratic Unionist Party (Northern Ireland)
DUPA	Danish Academy for International Affairs
DUPI	Danish Institute for International Affairs
ECHR	European Convention on Human Rights
ECNI	Equality Commission for Northern Ireland
ECOSOC	United Nations Social and Economic Council
ECPT	European Committee for the Prevention of Torture and Inhuman or Degrading Treatment or Punishment
ECRI	European Commission Against Racism and Intolerance
ENAR	European Network Against Racism
ERRC	European Roma Rights Center
EU	European Union
FRG	Federal Republic of Germany (West Germany)
GDP	Gross domestic product
GDR	German Democratic Republic (East Germany)
HDZ	Croatian Democratic Union of Bosnia and Herzegovina
ICC	International Criminal Court
ICERD	International Convention on the Elimination of All Forms of Racial Discrimination
ICESCR	International Covenant on Economic, Social, and Cultural Rights
IDPs	Internally displaced persons
IRA	Irish Republican Army
ITPF	International Police Force
LP	Liberal Party (Denmark)
MSLA	Ministry of Labor and Social Affairs (Czech Republic)
NATO	North Atlantic Treaty Organization
NGO	Nongovernmental organization
NHRI	National human rights institution
NIHRC	Northern Ireland Human Rights Commission
ODS	Civil Democratic Party (Czech Republic)
OHCHR	United Nations Office of the High Commissioner for Human Rights

OHR	United Nations Office of the High Representative
OSCE	Organization for Security and Cooperation in Europe
PSNI	Police Service of Northern Ireland
RMAP	Rights-Based Municipal Assessment and Planning Project
SD	Social Democrats (Denmark)
SDA	Party of Democratic Action (Bosnia-Herzegovina)
SDLP	Social Democratic and Labour Party (Northern Ireland)
SDS	Serb Democratic Party
SPD	Social Democratic Party (Germany)
SPP	Socialist People's Party (Denmark)
UN	United Nations
UNDP	United Nations Development Program
UNHCR	United Nations High Commission for Refugees
UDHR	Universal Declaration of Human Rights
UNICEF	United Nations Children's Fund
UUP	Ulster Unionist Party (Northern Ireland)
WTO	World Trade Organization

Chapter 1

Operationalizing Human Rights
at the Local Level

O NE PHENOMENON is widely celebrated as the key to making human rights matter: the worldwide proliferation of *national* human rights institutions (NHRIs). International human rights institutions still dominate news headlines with their public condemnation of human wrongs and their highly visible (and often failed) attempts to address them. Yet among human rights advocates, the dominant wisdom is that the promotion and protection of human rights rely less on international efforts and more on domestic action. Whereas energies earlier on in modern international human rights system development concentrated on international and regional human rights standard setting and the establishment of international and regional mechanisms to monitor implementation of human rights norms,[1] more recently, enthusiasm lies with the creation of national-level human rights institutions. To be sure, standard setting and regional and international institution building and strengthening continue, but establishing national-level human rights mechanisms has emerged as a core part of the international human rights agenda, supported by UN technical assistance programs and bilateral donor efforts.

Here I examine the widely held belief that the power of domestic human rights bodies to influence the lived realities of people experiencing human wrongs far exceeds the practical impact of their higher profile international counterparts. Close analysis of a set of country studies both affirms this conventional wisdom on domestication of international human rights norms and challenges it. In terms of shaping local expectations and behaviors related to human rights promotion, what happens on the domestic level is essential for making human rights matter. Indeed, even the most modest national institution with a limited mandate and restricted goals can have a demonstrable effect on the human rights issues that people care about most. Conversely, the most lavishly resourced and ambitious national institution can be dismissed as irrelevant if it fails to address the human rights concern held to be most important by the populace. Ultimately, domestic human rights bodies are only as good as the local political and economic contexts permit them to be, and even those countries that are most supportive of human rights on the world stage may prove to be highly disappointing among their constituents back home.

Students of human rights often complain that human rights are taught as abstract concepts, lists of norms, and institutional diagrams. "But what do human rights organizations actually *do*?" they wonder. Practitioners of human rights, on the other hand, know a great deal about the day-to-day *doing* of human rights practice—conducting field missions, interviewing victims, lobbying policymakers, drafting grant proposals, conducting workshops—but they miss the larger picture of how human rights norms take root and become effective at the local level. (As humanitarian expert Larry Minear would caution, "Don't just do something, stand there.")[2] Through a close analysis of five country studies of five highly distinctive domestic human rights institutions, I attempt to address the needs of both students and practitioners. I provide both a window into the day-to-day operationalization of human rights for students and insight into long-term organizational design and institutional change for practitioners.

This study is both descriptive and prescriptive. For each country study I describe how the local political context helps shape what NHRIs do to promote and protect human rights.[3] I then pull the country-specific observations together to make some general observations about how NHRIs are useful for promoting international human rights at the national level and to fashion recommendations for bettering their ability to do so. The purpose of this introductory chapter is twofold. First, I provide a basic introduction to the bodies known as NHRIs, clarifying the general features of these institutions and the roles they occupy in the human rights framework and practice. Second, I outline the contours of the present study, identifying research questions and methodology and explaining the criteria for case selection.

Introduction to NHRIs

I focus on a particular type of domestic human rights institution widely heralded as the key to the realization of human rights: NHRIs. Often modest in design, pragmatic in their strategic approach, and limited in their immediate impact, NHRIs hold promise as "the practical link between international standards and their concrete application."[4]

NHRIs can take different forms, including (1) the national human rights commission model, in which the institution has multiple members and a broad mandate to monitor and promote national and international human rights within the domestic realm; (2) the ombudsman model, which consists of a single member and staff mandated to receive complaints alleging certain violations of domestic norms; (3) specialized commissions designed to tackle a particular human rights issue, such as racial discrimination; and (4) hybrid institutions, which combine various aspects of the other three models.[5] Within these structures, NHRIs can, among other things, offer advice to governments on proposed and existing legislation, monitor international treaty implementation at the domestic level, provide training and research opportunities to both governmental and nongovernmental actors, and, in some cases, assist with individual complaints.[6] Although some NHRIs have jurisdiction over both government and private conduct, most NHRIs can review only government actions. At their core, no matter how broad or narrow their mandate, NHRIs represent attempts by governments to "embed international norms in domestic structures."[7]

A distinctive aspect of NHRIs is the space in which they maneuver: an imagined space somewhere between the state and civil society. They cooperate with and contribute to the efforts of both government and civil society, yet they are to remain wholly independent of government and other actors. Given that NHRIs are government-financed and government-initiated endeavors, created by legislative decree or through the national constitution, it is extraordinary that they maintain their independent stance, and, in fact, one of the major controversies over NHRIs concerns whether they are ever able to do so. Operating in a highly charged and deeply politicized atmosphere, NHRIs not only are subject to manipulation by governmental actors but must also contend with the often conflicting agendas of the various segments of civil society.

The United Nations has supported the development of NHRIs since the 1960s, but only recently have NHRIs become a worldwide phenomenon, supported by a variety of international and regional institutions and individual states.[8] Until the 1980s, NHRIs were established mainly in Western Europe and Commonwealth countries around the world. Over the next two decades, however, they spread rapidly throughout Southern Europe, Latin America, Central and Eastern Europe, the Middle East, and Africa.[9] A main boost to their development came in 1993, when many of the governmental delegates and civil society advocates attending the United Nations Conference on Human Rights in Vienna explicitly linked NHRI building to good governance and democracy building.[10] The official document emerging from that conference, the Vienna Declaration and Programme of Action, explicitly encouraged the "establishment and strengthening" of NHRIs.[11] After the Vienna meeting, not only were dozens of NHRIs established in the democratization wave of the 1990s,[12] but NHRI establishment also became de rigueur for peace building.[13] All the peace-building strategies in El Salvador, Bosnia-Herzegovina, Northern Ireland, Sierra Leone, South Africa, Rwanda, Sudan, East Timor, Kosovo, Afghanistan, Liberia, and most recently Iraq have included measures for the establishment of some form of NHRI, and many of these organizations are still in the process of being established. Today, NHRI establishment may be mandated in peace agreements[14] or in postconflict constitutional frameworks[15] or, as in the case of East Timor,[16] as a mandate to a UN transitional administration through the UN Security Council.

The incredible popularity of NHRIs may be a sign of their ability to successfully navigate the competing demands of the state and civil society while maintaining their independence; conversely, their popularity may be an indication of states' successful co-option of their mandate. In other words, NHRIs may succeed because of or despite their effectiveness. There is no question, however, that NHRIs have exploded onto the world stage. For newly emerging democracies and countries transitioning from conflict, NHRIs have become a hallmark of democratic legitimacy.[17] As one recent South Asian study observed, "If in the 1950s, the status symbol of a developing country was a steel mill, in the 1990s, apparently, it was a human rights commission."[18] NHRIs have emerged as a force to be reckoned with.

Fitting NHRIs into the Development of Human Rights

In one sense, the field of human rights has come full circle. Human rights began as a localized phenomenon, embodied in religious and spiritual teaching, highly particularized communal practices, and ethical codes of conduct directed at recognizing and protecting the dignity of humankind.[19] Human rights gradually became internationalized through a series of international treaties, offering protections first for religious minorities and then for ethnic and national minorities. Some of the provisions from these early treaties found their way into the complex systems for minority rights protections fashioned by the League of Nations in 1919, following World War I.[20] These "minority treaties" sought to achieve the twin aims of granting legal equality to individual members of particular minority groups while preserving the groups' characteristics and traditions.[21] After these efforts failed to prevent the atrocities of World War II, the focus shifted from group rights to individual rights, and emphasis was placed on universalizing human rights guarantees through a series of new international instruments, beginning with the UN Charter and the Universal Declaration of Human Rights (UDHR).[22]

The ideological tug and pull of the cold war impaired human rights enforcement efforts, but human rights standard setting shuffled along in the 1950s and 1960s,[23] emerging as a viable political force in the 1970s and 1980s amid a proliferation of international human rights conferences, treaties, and declarations.[24] The end of the cold war fostered a sudden growth spurt in the number and capacity of governmental and nongovernmental human rights organizations interested in rights promotion in newly emerging democracies.[25] Yet even as the participation in human rights promotion broadened and deepened, involving an array of new actors and agendas, states continued to be the "primary normative units and referents"[26] for human rights promotion. With this turn, the circle was complete, as the focus of the human rights field was once again on the local.

Does this mean that human rights have returned to where it started? No, too much has changed in the intervening years. A host of domestic and international human rights systems and mechanisms for protecting human rights now exist.[27] People working on human rights concerns in governmental and nongovernmental offices have become better trained and more professional in their work processes and outputs, and, although still in need of improvement, public awareness about human rights has improved greatly.[28] The expansion in the number and variety of actors involved in human rights work can be seen as occurring in three directions: vertically, horizontally, and diagonally. The image of vertical growth refers to the way that the same human rights issue can now be addressed on at least three levels: local, national (also termed state or domestic), and international (transstate). Expansion has also occurred in a horizontal manner in that the kinds of human rights work accomplished at the same level has expanded dramatically, both in its subject matter and in its impact. Advocates operating at the level of global civil society, for example, almost without exception articulate their demands for social justice, environmental responsibility, cultural recognition, economic security, and civil rights using the moral, legal, and political language of human rights.

Closely related to the horizontal changes are developments of a diagonal nature. This diagonal movement is seen in the growth of transnational advocacy networks and the accompanying increasing ability of human rights staff working on one level to voice their concerns in new ways, with new allies working on another level (on the same or different issue). One illustration of the diagonal movement is the boomerang effect, where nonstate actors, faced with repression and blockage at home, seek out state and nonstate allies in the international arena; in some cases these nonstate actors are able to pressure their governments from above to carry out domestic political change.[29] All these changes have left a deep imprint on the understanding and operation of human rights.

Nonetheless, the sense of coming full circle on human rights is supported by a sense of renewed urgency for human rights promotion and protection at the local and national levels.[30] The notion that states bear the primary onus of human rights protection is a basic tenet of the human rights field and can be found in numerous international instruments. The Universal Declaration of Human Rights, for example, states that human rights must be protected by the rule of law,[31] a reference to the role of domestic legal systems. All international human rights agreements ask that individual states make certain concessions and/or recognize certain rights, although none of them attempt to apply international rules without reference to domestic processes. As early as 1955, with the creation of the Program of Advisory Services and Technical Cooperation in the Field of Human Rights, the United Nations began what would become a long track record of supporting states in living up to their responsibilities for domestic human rights promotion. Three noteworthy indicators of UN support for domestic human rights efforts were the UN secretary-general's 1987 decision to establish the Voluntary Fund for Technical Cooperation in the Field of Human Rights; the willingness of the UN to use the World Conference on Human Rights in Vienna in 1993 to underscore the centrality of national-level human rights efforts;[32] and the UN secretary-general's decision in 2002 to use his hallmark address on UN reform to underscore the need to improve implementation of human rights norms at the national level, especially in countries emerging from war or transitioning from authoritarian regimes to participatory democracies.[33]

Answering the call to improve the protection of human rights at the national level, human rights advocates and governments turned to the creation of NHRIs. In the 1980s, NHRIs spread rapidly throughout Southern Europe, Latin America, Central and Eastern Europe, and Africa, becoming the chosen tool for states seeking to transition from authoritarian and other nondemocratic governments to fully participatory democracies.[34] Provisions encouraging the creation of NHRIs were also included in peace treaties, and, more recently, transnational activism has fostered their development in Asia and the Middle East.[35]

In addition to being the *product* of transnational activism, NHRIs have become the *producer* of activists themselves. This phenomenon was propelled through three stages. First, the door for NHRI activism opened in 1993, when the Vienna Declaration, an authoritative document adopted by the World Conference on Human Rights, explicitly "encourage[ed] the establishment and strengthening of national [human rights] institutions."[36] Second, transgovernmental activism by NHRIs drew greater recognition as an important advocate after a special post devoted to NHRIs was created in the UN Office of the High Commissioner for Human Rights (the Special Adviser on National Institutions, Regional Arrangements, and Preventative Strategies).[37] Finally, NHRI activism spread even further and became more institutionalized after the establishment, in 1994, of the International Coordinating Committee of National Human Rights Institutions. This new umbrella organization was charged with organizing and overseeing all international and regional linkages.[38]

In 2000, the Coordinating Committee began registering members based on their compliance with the Paris Principles,[39] international standards for NHRIs.[40] The Paris Principles prescribe several criteria essential for an effective and functioning NHRI: incorporation into legislation; operation independent from government; a membership that broadly reflects the composition of the society; and cooperation with civil society.[41] Only NHRIs that were able to attest to their own compliance with the Paris Principles were eligible to apply for membership in the Coordinating Committee. Starting in 2008, existing members of the Coordinating Committee also agreed to submit to a "universal periodic review" mechanism to prove their continued full compliance with the Paris Principles. Under this system, each NHRI receives one of four grades: (1) those in full compliance are awarded an A; (2) those seeming to comply with the Paris Principles but that do not have adequate documentation are given a grade of A(R) (accommodation with reserve); (3) those falling short of full compliance are given a B and are granted observer status; and

(4) those who are noncompliant with the Paris Principles are given a grade of C and are not permitted to participate or observe.[42] Current membership status can be found on the Coordinating Committee website.[43]

Even though the mandate of the NHRIs is geared toward the national level, many NHRI activities take place at the international level. In fact, one of the main platforms for NHRI activism at the international level has been United Nations treaty-monitoring bodies. With increasing frequency, NHRIs have found that they can use their "privileged access to public authorities" to act as a "channel through which civil society can carry the provisions and concerns to officials."[44] Significantly, the decision of the UN Commission on Human Rights in 1999 to allow NHRIs to participate in relevant meetings from a special section of the floor devoted to "national institutions" was extended in 2005 by the new UN institution replacing the Commission, the United Nations Human Rights Council.[45] On the regional level, NHRIs also exert influence through regional bodies. The Asia Pacific Forum, to take one illustration of a particularly active regional body, has a strong record of responding to requests from governments in Asia for assistance in the establishment and development of national institutions.[46]

The proliferation of NHRIs and their increased visibility at both the international and national levels is in direct response to the changing field of human rights. Human rights have in a sense come full circle—from local, to international, and back to local—but they have done so within the context of enormous growth in human rights instruments and institutions. The explosion in NHRIs has created a paradox: Governments throughout the world have agreed to be criticized by institutions of their own making, based on criteria that they routinely fail to meet.[47]

Research Questions

The sudden proliferation of NHRIs has inspired a flurry of academic scholarship,[48] conference papers,[49] and reports of nongovernmental advocacy groups.[50] Book-length reports on NHRIs have been published by the leading UN expert on the topic, Bertrand Ramcharan,[51] and by a leading NHRI (the Danish Institute for Human Rights);[52] and a survey of African NHRIs has also appeared.[53] The existing literature largely concentrates on the creation of NHRIs, often advocating for the adoption of NHRIs with certain organizational structures and mandates.[54] A sizable percentage of the scholarship in this area is devoted to evaluating specific NHRIs under the Paris Principles. Although I recognize the importance of the Paris Principles (see summary in Appendix 1), I want to move beyond them and focus not only on mandate creation and independence of NHRIs but also on their day-to-day workings.

The overarching research question informing this study is, How does the local context influence the operation of NHRIs? By situating NHRIs in the particularities of local politics, I seek to present a rich and more complex understanding of the social and political experience of NHRIs and, consequently, their contribution to the advancement of human rights.[55]

One measure of the efficacy of nongovernmental organizations (NGOs) is their ability to address the issues that matter in people's everyday lives. For each country study in this book, I begin with factual information, not just to provide context for readers otherwise unfamiliar with the country (although that is important), but to help identify the political and social issues that could be addressed by the NHRI. Unpacking this question, I ask, What is the link between the local narrative and the work of the NHRI? Does the NHRI choose to work only on a limited slate of issues and to ignore others? Does it favor work on some types of issues over others (e.g., civil and political rights over economic and social rights)? To what extent does the NHRI remain relevant by addressing the issues people care about most?

The narrative of each country also helps to expose potential limitations on the work of the NHRI. The degree to which people are open to and interested in certain human rights issues, as well as their receptiveness to NHRI efforts at rights promotion, is informed by their history and by the local political context. People with a historical distrust of government, for example, may be wary of government action in any area, whereas people accustomed to government beneficence may not view rights as relevant for the betterment of their already good lives. Whether the country is in transition from war to peace and/or from one political system to another will also affect the agenda and operation of an NHRI, as will the source of the impetus for the NHRI. Thus my inquiry leads to such questions as, To what can the establishment of the NHRI be attributed? The demands of civil society within that country? The interests of the state? The interests of other states?

Case Selection

The list of examples of NHRIs under study here is atypical: Denmark, Northern Ireland, Bosnia-Herzegovina, Germany, and the Czech Republic (see Appendix 2 for each country's mandate). The first criterion for case selection was geographic and was motivated by a desire to emphasize that the local political context is important for the domestication of human rights norms in all countries, not just in the "south." Studies of the impact of local politics on the domestication of international human rights norms typically involve a European look at some faraway "other," examining Asia, Africa, and, increasingly, the Middle East.[56] But European political contexts also influence the processes through which NHRIs support the domestication of international human rights. By focusing on Europe, I address a geographic area that is largely overlooked in the literature on NHRIs and, more broadly, in work on international human rights institutions and norm diffusion.

The second criterion for case selection concentrates on the nature of the political sphere. Much of the existing literature on NHRIs focuses on the role these organizations play in countries seeking respectability and on countries desiring full entry into regional and international security and trade bodies. For well-established stable democracies, however, NHRIs also wield considerable influence over domestic expectations and help to shape both the domestic and foreign policy agenda. In addition, by addressing social and political problems at home in more mature democracies, a well-functioning NHRI can build a state's perceived legitimacy for entering into human rights disputes abroad. Thus I have tried to include both mature and transitional democracies and to look at countries where an NHRI was created in response to problems within the country and at countries where an NHRI was created primarily as a response to external factors. At the same time, I have chosen cases to reflect the fact that the creation of some NHRIs is primarily in response to political demands arising from outside state borders, whereas the existence of other NHRIs reflects domestic pressures.

The third criterion for selection was the NHRI type. In particular, I considered whether the NHRI adopts a narrow ombudsman's model, where great authority is vested in a single person in the ombudsman position, or whether a broader commission or committee model is followed, in which decision making is made by a collective. The goal was to provide as broad and inclusive a picture as possible while also acknowledging that pragmatic considerations prevent examination of all types of NHRIs in Europe.[57]

Weighing these criteria in balance, I selected the countries in this study because of the different insights they provide into the domestication of international norms and the competing pull of local politics. Denmark was chosen to lead the country studies because of the leadership role it plays in NHRI advocacy. Regarded as a model NHRI by many states, Denmark's experience with NHRIs shows how these institutions can play a key role in states regarded not only as human rights supporters but also as human rights leaders. At the same time, the Danish country study exposes some of the limitations of NHRIs in progressive countries.

Northern Ireland and Bosnia-Herzegovina were included to open discussion on the significance of NHRIs in states emerging from conflict. These two country studies differ greatly in the nature and degree of international involvement in the creation of their NHRIs. The Bosnian system was imposed entirely by outsiders, and the Northern Ireland institution was more locally conceived and thus enjoys more local legitimacy. However, both cases also illustrate the difficulties inherent in creating NHRIs in deeply divided societies and under considerable international pressure. In both countries, the general public views human rights with mistrust; in addition, the human rights advocates themselves face difficulty in transitioning their approach from one of divided struggle against an enemy to one of common struggle for human rights for all. These two country studies suggest that a successful NHRI founded in postwar times must find a way to address present and ongoing violations and adapt and change as the state matures and evolves.

The Czech Republic was identified for its ability to disclose how NHRIs matter in states experiencing relatively smoother transitions to participatory democracy. Unlike Northern Ireland and Bosnia-Herzegovina, the Czech Republic does not seek to use its NHRI as a means for addressing deep communal divisions created through a recent (or ongoing) conflict. Nor, unlike Denmark, does the Czech Republic harbor ambitions of becoming a world leader on NHRIs. The Czech Republic seeks simply to use its NHRI to improve the public trust in government and to initiate public dialogue on human rights concerns as they arise. The success of the Czech ombudsman's office in meeting these more modest goals illustrates the old adage that sometimes less is more.

Finally, Germany was selected because of its comparability to all the other cases. Like its neighbor, the Czech Republic, Germany shares a history of Soviet dominance; however, in many respects Germany is a polar opposite. Unlike the Czech Republic, only one part of Germany was under Soviet control, and eventually the two halves of the country were reunited. This difference had a profound influence on the historical development of human rights politics in both the German Democratic Republic (GDR) and the Federal

Republic of Germany (FRG). The points of convergence between Germany and Denmark relate to different aspects of history: the growth of industrial and labor safeguards and an ethos of egalitarianism and solidarity. Germany, Bosnia-Herzegovina, and Northern Ireland all share a historical relationship to conflicts and the manner in which those conflicts are reflected in everyday political and social life. Yet the conflict that has long provided the reference point for West Germans, World War II, differs significantly from the conflicts in Northern Ireland and Bosnia-Herzegovina, both in the nature and degree of human wrongs perpetrated and in the timing. Given the resulting differences in the political and economic context in Germany, it is no wonder that the German NHRI carries its own unique challenges in meeting its mandate.

To be sure, I have not included many European NHRIs of interest. However, practical considerations required narrowing the selection to a manageable number. Future work might involve additional NHRI country studies in Central and Southern Europe, in particular, the Commission Nationale Consultative des Droits de l'Homme (National Consultative Commission on Human Rights, France),[58] the Greek National Commission for Human Rights,[59] and the ombudsman's offices in Spain[60] and Portugal.[61] However, the intention of this project is not to present an overview of *all* types of NHRIs.[62] Rather, I seek to use close scrutiny of a handful of countries to better understand how they operate, paying explicit attention to whether and how the effectiveness of the NHRI in question is linked to the political context of the country.

"Snowball Interviewing"

The research methodology I used for each country study can be described as the snowball approach.[63] Snowball sampling relies on referrals from initial interview subjects to generate additional subjects. For this project, I began by collecting primary source material, such as organizational mandates and publications, and then expanded the study to interviews with current and recent NHRI staff and constituencies, including journalists, academics, members of other advocacy groups, and social justice initiatives. I then followed up on leads from these initial inquiries, both in person and by e-mail, thus expanding the scope and depth of the research.

The snowball approach has been criticized for introducing bias because the technique itself reduces the likelihood that the sample will represent a good cross-section from the population. However, this danger does not always apply. When, as in this case, a study does not seek to use interviews as a means of sampling a population, the bias inherent in snowballing is rarely troubling. This is especially true if the interviews are not being conducted for the purposes of determining factual accuracy for a given population. Indeed, throughout the text, references to interview subjects occur only where the assertions are more than contextual in their importance. The resulting text could not have been written without my having spent time in the various countries and without having the benefit of collegial exchanges in all countries under scrutiny here. Any errors that have made it into print, however, are mine alone.

Book Structure

The structure of this book is straightforward. Each of the five country studies is presented in its own chapter. Realizing that readers of this text will often have limited knowledge about the human rights context of the areas under study, the first sections of each chapter outline the relevant political, economic, and social context and introduce the reader to the immediate human rights concerns in each particular country study. The last section of each chapter examines the work of the country's specific NHRI. Although each country case illustration in this volume individually contributes to understanding the importance of local context in the domestication of international norms, the richness of the analysis comes from reading the resulting country studies against one another. In the concluding chapter I draw together the collected findings to offer specific recommendations and applications to other cases.

Chapter 2

"Opinion Doctors" and "Can Openers"

Denmark's National Human Rights Institution

RINCIPLES of solidarity and egalitarianism have long been the hallmarks of Danish identity.[1] In the public sphere, these principles are deeply embedded in social and political rules and actions emphasizing compromise, consensus, and citizen participation.[2] Denmark's democracy is known as a cooperative democracy; its economy is distinctive for its boasting of a labor force loyal to "solidarity principles"; its education system emphasizes critical thinking and nonhierarchical learning; and its civil society is a leader in championing egalitarian causes at home and abroad. Only recently has Denmark experienced its own internal critique of its emphasis on equality and solidarity principles. Critics on the right contend that strict adherence to these liberal tenets may stifle individual initiative and innovation and promote mediocrity in their stead.[3] Critics on the left allege that rigid solidarity promotes conformity at the expense of multiculturalism. Yet even as these principles and the identities and behaviors they inform are challenged and transformed, they remain of central importance for shaping domestic receptivity to international human rights norms and to molding the local operationalization of human rights.

In this chapter I focus on how the Danish Institute for Human Rights (known simply as the Danish Institute or the DIHR)[4] evolved and established its identity as a human rights institute in a context where the language of human rights is not common currency in the larger societal context of Denmark but where an egalitarian ethic historically is quite strong. I examine how the DIHR to some extent became a producer of human rights language and activism, making strategic use of international human rights norms and identifying discrimination and socioeconomic issues from a rights-based framework. I also demonstrate the extent to which the Danish model for addressing international human rights has effectively promoted domestication of human rights on the home front, even in the face of increasing pressure from the political right.

A close examination of the DIHR illustrates the importance of the local context in explaining the process through which international human rights norms are realized through the aegis of domestic institutions. Local political, economic, and social experiences and ideas influence the agenda of the DIHR and inform its ability to realize public expectations. At the same time, the DIHR's work helps shape public perceptions as to what values are important and what ways of promoting these values are effective and legitimate. For the purposes of this analysis, I pay attention to the two human rights issues receiving a great deal of attention in Denmark in recent years: (1) discrimination against racial and ethnic minorities and antiforeigner sentiment in general; and (2) economic, social, and cultural rights. These two issues provide clearer illustrations of the possibilities and limitations of the Danish NHRI model.

Political Context

Denmark's basic political framework, as set forth in its constitution,[5] establishes Denmark as a constitutional hereditary monarchy. In practice, however, the monarch's role is symbolic and representative.[6] Formally, the government is appointed by the monarch, but in practice a government is formed on the basis of negotiations among the political parties, in order to find the most acceptable (or least unacceptable) coalition. "Coalition strategies in Denmark," one analyst notes, "are complicated by the fact that the country has had mainly minority governments (often formed by more than one party) since the early 1980s."[7] Because it is extremely rare for a single party to win a majority, politicians must be unusually skillful in coalition building if they are to advance their concerns in a minority-run government. Both voters and politicians expect that a range of issues will be supported in ever-shifting coalitions.

The parliament (Folketinget) is composed of 179 seats, all of which are elected in Denmark, except for two seats set aside for Greenland and two given to the Faeroe Islands. Seats are allocated on the basis of a system of proportional representation.[8] The electoral threshold is 2 percent, compared with the 4 percent electoral threshold in other neighboring states, such as Norway and Sweden.[9] Since the establishment of parliamentary democracy in 1901, no single party has held a majority. Elections take place every four years but can be held earlier if the political situation necessitates it. Also, elections can be held when the Folketinget enters a vote of no confidence against the government.[10]

In addition to the government and parliament, political parties have played an important role in Danish politics ever since the adoption of the first constitution in 1849. Because of the great degree of homogeneity in Denmark, political parties are based on ideological affiliations and rarely on ethnic, religious, regional, or linguistic differences. Four parties have traditionally dominated Danish politics. The two main parties on the left are the Social Democrats (Socialdemokraterne; SD) and the Socialist People's Party (Socialistisk Folkeparti; SPP); the two main parties on the right are the Liberal Party of Denmark (Venstre; LP) and the Conservative People's Party (Det Konservative Folkeparti; CPP). The party system was left-right oriented (dividing politics by these polarities) until the 1973 election, when a party defined as neither right nor left but as "anti-tax," the Progress Party (Fremskridtspartiet), drew major support among the populace (15.9 percent).[11]

Intraparty factionalism has been common in Denmark.[12] A split between the fundamentalists and pragmatists within the Progress Party led in 1995 to the creation of several new political initiatives, including the following four challenges to the traditionally left-leaning government: (1) the anti-immigrant, nationalist Danish People's Party (Dansk Folkeparti);[13] (2) the June Movement (JuniBevægelsen), a cross-party initiative against the supranational traits of the European Union (EU);[14] (3) the Popular Movement Against the EU (Folkebevægelsen mod EU), an organization with individual members as well as collective members (political parties may join) working against Danish membership in the EU;[15] and (4) the right-wing Freedom 2000 (Frihed 2000), technically not a party but a group of four Progress Party ministers who objected to major changes in the Progress Party during an election period.[16] The combined efforts of these entrants to the Danish political scene combined to push the Danish political agenda further to the right.

Central issues capturing the attention of the Danish electorate include taxes, social welfare reform, the balance between public and market control, the privatization of public services, and support for or opposition to further political integration in the EU.[17] Tapping into growing public alarm over the failure of government to resolve these issues, right-wing parties and nationalists forced a historic swing to the right in Denmark's 2001 general elections.[18]

As in most elections in Denmark, no clear majority government was victorious, thus forcing the formation of a minority government. However, unlike earlier elections, the 2001 election brought the radical right into a working coalition with the mainstream right.[19]

One of the biggest winners of this historic shift was one of the groups that had broken away from the nationalist/populist Danish People's Party (DPP) in 1995. The DPP first drew public attention through its strident anti-immigrant policies. Its party platform made its intentions clear with such statements as "Denmark is not, and has never been a country intended for immigration and the Danish People's Party disagrees with the statement that Denmark will develop into a multiethnic society."[20] Building on its anti-immigration foundation, the DPP rapidly expanded its platform and constituency base by calling attention to other issues that had slipped under the radar of the larger parties, including health care reform and improvements in care for the elderly. Although small, the DPP proved capable of working to propel a populist agenda.

The new government emerging out of the 2001 historic shifts, led by Prime Minister Anders Fogh Rasmussen, introduced a number of measures favored by the right wing, including tighter immigration controls that reduce the rights of asylum seekers and a freeze on taxes that not only prohibits new taxes but also bans increases in existing taxes. In addition, under Rasmussen's oversight, budgets for overseas development aid were trimmed, expenditures for cultural activities were slashed, and more than 100 government think tanks, advisory committees, and similar bodies were axed, rationalized, or merged. Progressive groups were affected the most by these measures, with pro-immigrant and antiracist groups receiving the greatest blows to their sustainability.

Among other right-wing initiatives, in 2002 the government abolished the concept of de facto refugees, stipulating that only individuals entitled to protection under international conventions were permitted to live in Denmark.[21] Marriages between Danes and young foreigners were penalized (and, one could claim, effectively forbidden), because spouses under the age of 24 could not be brought into the country.[22] All marriages between Danes and foreigners were put to a test known as couple ties, whereby a permit to live in Denmark would be denied if the family ties were judged to be stronger in a country other than Denmark.[23] Also under the new provisions, all refugees and immigrants would receive 30 percent less in social benefits than native Danes; permanent-residence permits could be obtained by foreigners only after seven years (previously three); permits would be denied to foreigners guilty of a serious crime; and stringent tests on the Danish language and culture were imposed and were coupled with a program of incentives to gain employment and integrate into society.

Danish political analysts noticed that one aspect of recent elections[24] in Denmark stood out: Citizens were no longer being treated as participants in politics; rather, they were consumers of the political system.[25] Human rights issues were one set of issues available for "consumption" in this new political marketplace, especially when handled by the right-leaning politicians who promised to crack down on immigration and preserve Danish culture. The nature of coalition politics in Denmark provided no incentives for the parties to moderate their platforms to attract a broader range of voters. On the contrary, as one observer noted, "Voters [in Denmark] have come to expect that a minority government will form, and the ruling parties will rely on different parties to find a majority for a particular piece of legislation."[26] Knowing not only that voters would tolerate extreme views but also that they expected such views, Danish politicians were able to confidently assert more extreme positions on social issues than they would have if Danish coalition politics did not exist in its current form. One area under close scrutiny and open to more extreme positions was the Danish social welfare system.

Economic Context

Like the Danish system of cooperative democracy, Denmark's social welfare system is both a product of Danish values of solidarity and egalitarianism and a promoter of these values. As with cooperative democracy, the social welfare system has found itself in a state of transition, influenced by critiques from both the political right and the political left. Within Danish society a clear consensus exists that a developed welfare system is a nonnegotiable attribute of the Danish social model. Nonetheless, how welfare should be administered and who should have a right to what remain matters of debate.

The Danish welfare system grew out of the liberal peasant and worker movements of the late nineteenth and early twentieth centuries. Danes' attachment to their social welfare system can be explained in part by these origins. The mythology surrounding them has led to the belief that the system is created not by government but rather arises out of society itself, "by the people for the people."[27] Already in the 1890s, the basic principles were established for a system covering all citizens, with administration occurring as close to the local level as possible. From the 1890s to the 1930s, the welfare system grew, with a rather mixed result. In the 1930s, it was reformed into a so-called national insurance system. In the period after World War II, it was extended again, and in 1956 a full national pension for everyone was introduced. That meant that every Dane, regardless of income, was entitled to an old-age pension. At the same time, the social and health services were enhanced.

Since the 1960s, considerable tensions have existed between the subunits of the Danish government, as each subunit has argued over its own role in the administration of social welfare. Several legislative and administrative changes were made in the 1970s and 1980s; massive communal reforms were introduced again in 2006. In justifying the latest set of reforms, the government argued that they were necessary to safeguard the efficient administration of welfare in the future. Reformers relied heavily on the government's 2004 proposal paper, "The New Denmark: A Simple Public Sector Close to the Citizen," and they explained the structural changes as part of the government's plan to put "people first." The concept of "people before the system" had long been a mainstay of Prime Minister Rasmussen's brand of liberalism. Using words such as *closeness*, *quality*, and *efficiency*, Rasmussen promised citizens more for their money without a rise in taxes. He also vowed that his reforms would ensure less bureaucracy, a decreased need to queue at government agencies, and more manageable navigability for the individual citizen seeking public services.[28]

Although applauded by the Danish Confederation of Industries, an influential trade and business organization, as a positive and necessary modernization of the public sector,[29] these government proposals on social welfare met much criticism from the opposition and from service delivery experts and the municipalities themselves. They contended that the reforms would generate large contracts for private providers of welfare services at a tremendous price to Danish society: the further erosion of the Danish civic participation.[30] For its part, the National Association of Local Authorities in Denmark, the municipalities' interest organization, criticized the government for not having a clear picture of the true expense of the reforms and characterized the reforms as a ploy to underhandedly force through budget cuts in some municipalities.[31] In January 2006, 80 percent of the mayors of municipalities predicted that they would be forced to borrow a significant sum to pay for the restructuring.[32] The program of decentralization was launched over these objections; however, the issue of institutional reform of the welfare system remained in the public eye. Representing the culmination of lengthy negotiations between the Liberal Party, the Conservative People's

Party, the Danish People's Party, the Social Democrats, and the radical left, structural reforms centralized and restructured service delivery by mandating the merger of numerous municipalities into greater municipalities and the replacement of counties with regions.

Human Rights Context

Human Rights in Foreign Policy

Danish solidarity principles were integral to making human rights a central concern of Denmark's foreign policy. Denmark was among the first countries to connect development aid to human rights; it played a key role in the debate over human rights in China at the United Nations, and, more recently, it has been a central actor in United Nations debates on the definition of torture and its applications[33] and an active participant in the UN negotiations that led to the adoption of the United Nations Convention on the Rights of Persons with Disabilities in December 2006. In the international movement to support human rights institution building in postconflict countries and transitional democracies, Denmark is one of the undisputed leaders, and Danes have held a number of key positions in transnational NHRI networks and coalitions and have conducted some of the leading studies on the subject.[34]

The United Nations treaty-monitoring process provides specific tools to support Danish efforts for the domestication of international human rights norms. However, Denmark rarely takes the steps necessary under its domestic law to *incorporate*[35] international human rights law (and Danish law does not provide for automatic incorporation of international law).[36] Nonetheless, Danish scholars have found that "international law is part of domestic law, in the sense that international law can be used as a legal source by courts and administrative authorities, even without specific basis in national statutes."[37] Denmark must, as a matter of international law, comply with the international obligations set forth in the documents it has ratified. One of these obligations is for the state to submit, on a regular basis, reports on its own compliance under the specific treaty provisions. For the most part, Danish NGOs have illustrated "best practices" in their participation in UN treaty monitoring, research, and report writing (shadow reporting) on human rights conditions under the treaty.[38] Danish human rights NGOs often are a source of information for government reports, and, in some reporting processes, the preparers of the official state report have even offered to attach the NGO shadow report as an appendix.[39]

Experience with treaty monitoring illustrates the progressive and aspirational nature of human rights. The most recent (2006) monitoring by the Convention on the Rights of the Child (the Children's Convention) provides an excellent country study. By nearly all accounts, children fare exceptionally well in Denmark. Yet in its latest review of Denmark in 2006, the UN monitoring body for the Children's Convention, the Committee on the Rights of the Child (CRC), had not only much to praise in Denmark but also much to criticize.[40] Three of the areas singled out for scrutiny were (1) "the high level of child abuse and neglect and other forms of domestic violence"; (2) the improving yet still inadequate efforts to prevent commercial sexual exploitation of children, in particular, "the images of 'child erotica' on [the] internet and that children are encouraged and manipulated to provide sexual services"; and (3) the treatment of children with disabilities, in particular, "the fact that some of the municipalities may not have policies for children with disabilities in childcare and that the best interest of the child is not always respected."[41] In each of these three areas the CRC made specific suggestions for changing public policies and practices to better promote children's rights.

The UN treaty-monitoring system has provided several additional opportunities for human rights issues to be brought to public attention in Denmark. The members of the indigenous Thule community in Greenland have sought compensation for their displacement from their lands and the loss of traditional hunting rights on account of the construction of the military base at Thule;[42] the people of the Faeroe Islands have asserted claims to self-determination;[43] prisoners rights advocates have demanded public scrutiny of the widespread use of solitary confinement for incarcerated people following conviction;[44] advocates for asylum seekers in Denmark have expressed several concerns, including inadequate legal counsel and undue restrictions on freedom of movement and in choice of residence;[45] and advocates for prisoners rights have publicized the findings of the European Committee for the Prevention of Torture and Inhuman or Degrading Treatment or Punishment (ECPT) on the ill treatment of detained and imprisoned individuals by Danish authorities.[46]

Domestic Politics

Although human rights feature prominently in Danish foreign policy and although Denmark participates in international human rights treaty monitoring, the concept of human rights remains relatively new to Danish domestic politics, and Danes remain highly skeptical of the application of human rights within their own country. "It is almost like we are too good for human rights," one Dane explained, referring to "the notion that sophisticated people like us [the Danes] are above the fray of rights."[47] The secretary-general of the Danish Bar Association, Henrik Rothe, put it another way, explaining that "people are looking for results and they use the terminology that will make the greatest impact in Denmark, and that is not human rights terminology."[48] According to Rothe, lawyers often steer clear of framing cases in human rights terms lest they appear "political." As Rothe explained, "Some politicians have the feeling that human rights are not always legal assessments, but [instead feel that human rights] are used in a different way."[49]

The voluntary sector in Denmark does engage in advocacy on matters that might be considered human rights concerns, but they rarely use the terminology themselves. For them, "it is more comfortable to speak in terms of health care or housing [instead of human rights]."[50] They "just don't think about it that way [in human rights terms]," and it might be "too aggressive and upsetting to talk in terms of rights [referring to American hyperindividuality and inequality in sharp contrast to Danish egalitarian values]."[51] The decision to steer clear of human rights terminology appears to apply in particular to matters concerning discrimination based on race, religion, or ethnic origin. "Those are really the sensitive matters," one Danish social worker explained, referring to a desire to avoid "creating more conflicts."[52]

Danish skepticism of human rights is supported by the "junta law," a term coined in 1933 by Danish writer Aksel Sandemose to describe a kind of extreme egalitarianism that goes beyond modesty to enforced commonality. Yet in recent years, *janteloven* (living according to the ten commandments of junta) has come under scrutiny by the entire Danish political spectrum, from right to left. The nature of the evolving concept features prominently in David Nye's *Introducing Demark and the Dane*, the book distributed by the Danish Fulbright Commission to all incoming American Fulbright Scholars as *the* book explaining Danish "national mentality." Junta law has been rejected by people on the political right, who contend that it "may be suited to emergencies and times of crisis . . . but it also stifles individual initiative and self-reliance."[53] On the political left, the concept is criticized as supporting xenophobic and racist behavior, because "by definition, the Junta law cannot value ethnic diversity or underwrite the idea of a multicultural society."[54] At the same time, critics across the political spectrum have voiced a concern that junta law be modified to accommodate increased interest in new ideas, traditions, and movements in the world. Danish identity as an egalitarian people still is deeply embedded in institutions and social practices, but what it means to be an "egalitarian people" and to promote "Danish values" has changed to reflect these critiques.

Until recently, the good life in Denmark has been the product of the solidarity principle, not the result of any kind of rights-based advocacy. Under the Danish social welfare model, legislation on social and economic issues is incredibly detailed and comprehensive, but legislation on workforce matters is practically nonexistent. As Danish human rights scholar (and DIHR senior researcher) Ida Elisabeth Koch explains, "Rights which are imposed by statute in many other countries have in Denmark often been obtained by means of agreements between social partners," a tradition said to date back to 1899.[55]

Danish solidarity and egalitarianism are enforced by strong social norms that reward egalitarian behavior, support peaceful resolution of conflict, and encourage advancement of the collective over the individual. This contrasts sharply with the human rights framework, which empowers citizen rights holders to make their own particular rights claims against duty bearers (largely the Danish administrative authorities, but sometimes claims can be made against private parties).[56] Although the collective may be advanced by the human rights model, the focus remains on the individual, and, moreover, although human rights claims ideally are resolved in a peaceful manner, rights claims are often oppositional and thus conflict is anticipated.

With the junta law basis for Danish identity under attack by the shift to the right in Danish politics, an opening has been made for the human rights framework to exert greater pressure. It may be an overstatement to assert that the Danish people are transitioning from an image of "Danes as junta" to a self-image as a human rights–abiding and –promoting people. Nonetheless, it is fair to say that within the voluntary sector in Denmark interest in human rights promotion is growing. What could be viewed as an emerging human rights identity is both individualistic and collective in nature and subject to change in strategy and tactics over time.

Three trends can be identified in human rights advocacy in Denmark. First, in some cases, advocates are engaged in efforts to convince the Danish government that the benefit that human rights guarantees is in the government's interests abroad—for example, an improvement in the country's human rights profile would be a positive development for the country's reputation and influence on the world stage. Second, in other cases, advocates are offering persuasive evidence about the link between human rights–positive policies and the government's domestic interests—in promoting a strong economy, in safeguarding a high standard of living, and in promoting essential Danish values. To some extent, the disability rights movement in Denmark could be said to follow this track.[57] And third, political parties instrumentally use rights talk to showcase their advantage over other parties. For example, neglect of the elderly was front-page news for much of 2006,[58] leading the opposition party, the Social Democrats, to demand a sort of bill of rights for the elderly in Denmark.[59] All three tactics—human rights as Danish foreign policy interests, as Danish values, and as political party advantage—feature in Denmark's agonizing confrontation with racism and rising antiforeigner sentiment.

Illustration of Current Human Rights Concerns

The main human rights topic drawing the spotlight in Denmark today concerns racially motivated violence. According to the Police Intelligence Service, in 2005 there were forty-eight cases of racial discrimination or racially motivated violence reported to the authorities. Reported cases involved graffiti, vandalism, theft, and racist Internet postings and written messages. The victims were Jews and "people of an ethnic origin other than Danish" (usually meaning Muslims or Africans). One well-publicized case occurred in January 2005, when nearly 100 Muslim graves were desecrated in Venstre Kirkegaard (Cemetery) in Copenhagen. Still unknown vandals pushed over nearly fifty headstones and smashed another fifty, leaving the Christian headstones in the cemetery untouched.[60]

Despite the scattered publicity on these attacks, most of these local cases have been addressed rather quietly, with little or no apparent impact on Danes' identity as champions of egalitarianism. The same has not been true with respect to the international press. Incidents involving accusations of countrywide racism and xenophobia have attracted considerable attention in the local and international media and within other EU countries and institutions, such as the Council of Europe and the Social Democrats in Sweden.[61] The most famous such case began in September 2005, when the Danish newspaper *Jyllands-Posten* printed twelve caricatures of Mohammed, the prophet of Islam.[62] The insensitivity to people of Islamic faith, some of whom regarded the cartoons as blasphemous, caused outrage in the Muslim world, prompting angry protests and violent attacks on Danish embassies in several countries.[63]

The Danish government received further rebuke from the Muslim world when the Danish prime minister repeatedly (over a nearly four-month time period) refused to meet with twelve ambassadors from Arab or Muslim countries to hear their concerns.[64] The Danish government's staunch defense of freedom of expression was affirmed by the local court hearing the case.[65] In his decision in favor of the newspaper, the regional public prosecutor of Viborg stated that he "attache[d] importance to the fact that the article in question concerns a subject of public interest, which means that there is an extended access to make statements without these statements constituting a criminal offense."[66] He further concluded that Danish case law allows extended editorial freedom when subjects of public interest are involved. Thus the public prosecutor found no basis to conclude that the content of the article violated either Danish blasphemy laws or hate speech laws. After the ruling, the Danish government reiterated its support for freedom of religion, but the damage was done. Danes' sense of self as a people with a worldwide reputation for toleration and respect for differences was deeply shaken. Although trade relations with the Middle East were severely harmed because of the caricatures and the subsequent boycotts, Danish exports to the region normalized within two years.[67]

In Denmark, however, the issue is not resolved. In January 2008, *Jyllands-Posten* demanded that the Danish Broadcasting Corporation (DR) make editorial corrections to a radio lecture in a series held by former foreign minister Uffe Ellemann-Jensen.[68] In the lecture, Ellemann-Jensen said that *Jyllands-Posten* ordered the caricatures, whereas *Jyllands-Posten* argues that it simply asked artists to portray the prophet Mohammed "as they perceived him." The newspaper argues that the press ethics of DR, because of the latter's reluctance to correct faulty information, is a threat to the quality of public debate. DR has decided not to make the demanded corrections, partly because it sees the request as hypocritical coming from a newspaper that printed the caricatures purely to demonstrate what freedom of expression allows.[69]

The issue was on the front page again in February 2008, when Danish police arrested three individuals for plotting to kill one of the caricature artists, Kurt Westergaard. Two of the arrested men were Tunisian citizens; the third was a Danish citizen of Moroccan background.[70] At least seventeen newspapers in Denmark and one in Sweden decided, the day after the arrests, to publish Westergaard's drawing as a protest against the murder plot.[71] This led to a number of new protests and calls for boycotts of Danish goods by Muslims around the world. Danish foreign minister Per Stig Møller was hesitant to call the incidents a "second Muhammed crisis" because the protests stemmed mainly from civil society this time, not from governments.[72] The consequences were nevertheless real for Arla Foods, a major manufacturer of dairy products. One dairy operation in Bislev, a town in northern Denmark, decided to let eight to ten workers go as a result of a decrease in orders from the Middle East.[73] During the previous crisis, Arla suffered deep financial losses and was forced to lay off almost 100 workers.[74]

The Danish Institute for Human Rights

The work of Denmark's NHRI, the Danish Institute for Human Rights (DIHR), is both a product of the political and economic contexts described and a shaper of these contexts. The DIHR promotes Danish solidarity and equality principles while also stretching and, at times, challenging them to apply to domestic and international human rights claims (see Appendix 2 for mandate excerpts). Unlike many other NHRIs, the DIHR has set its sights on two levels of activity: domestic and international. To this end, it has searched to discover politically palatable ways to advance the dual goal of supporting human rights promotion and protection efforts abroad and fostering the domestication of human rights norms at home, while also retaining the many positive benefits of social solidarity and Danes' unique sense of self as an egalitarian people.

I first discuss the broad mandate and range of functions of the DIHR, spanning local *and* domestic activities, human rights *and* equality protections. I contrast this broad range of functions with the DIHR's weak powers to effectively vindicate any of these rights. This absence of enforcement mechanisms is a key constraint on the effective operation of the DIHR. I also examine how the DIHR is attempting to combine its broad mandate and more conciliatory approach to rights protections to contribute to the development of a culture of human rights in Denmark.

Evolving Structure and Mandate

The DIHR (originally called the Danish Center for Human Rights) was created by a decree of the Danish Parliament in 1987. According to the parliamentary resolution, which was supported by a 123 to 4 vote, the new institution is supported by the state but remains independent by design. The mandate for the DIHR is broad and includes research, inquiry, advice, documentation, education, and the provision of information in the field of human rights. The DIHR is a self-governing institution with a board of twelve members. Danish universities nominate six of the members, and the other six are nominated by the Center Council. The Center Council consists of representatives of about thirty NGOs (expanded later to fifty-five), political parties in parliament and ministries, and individuals having a particular knowledge of human rights. Contrary to most Danish public-sector research institutions, the DIHR's board is not to be nominated by a minister, thus enhancing the independence of the board.[75]

The activities of the DIHR include offering advice to the government on new and proposed laws; publishing an annual status report on the human rights situation in Denmark; short- and long-term fact-finding reporting on specific human rights issues of interest at home and abroad; participating in the creation of shadow reports in connection with treaty-monitoring processes; and offering numerous workshops and other public events at home and abroad.[76] Unlike most other NHRIs, the DIHR goes far beyond promotion of human rights at the national level and engages in numerous training, reporting, and research activities at the international level.[77] In particular, DIHR staff cooperate with human rights centers and humanitarian organizations in other countries as well as with the Nordic Council, the Council of Europe, the OSCE (Organization for Security and Cooperation in Europe), the European Union, and the United Nations.[78]

From its inception, the DIHR has taken a multidisciplinary approach to human rights, drawing highly credentialed and experienced staff from the areas of law, political science, economics, sociology, anthropology, and other social sciences.[79] The first fourteen years of the DIHR's existence was a time of rapid growth and enhanced legitimacy, particularly at the international level, where it was generally regarded as a leader in the field.

Political Challenges

Despite its strong start, the DIHR, like all Danish organizations demanding government support, could not escape the influence of the local political shift to the ideological right. In 2002, the DIHR found itself on a long list of organizations designated to be cut from government support. All the major organizations with strong antiracism platforms were also listed, including not only the DIHR but also the Board for Ethnic Equality (the only state-financed institution that processed individual complaints of race discrimination), the Documentation and Advisory Center on Racial Discrimination (DACORD), the Danish Center for Migration and Ethnic Studies (DAMES), and the Council of Ethnic Minorities.

Even though the closures were billed as cost-cutting measures, their ideological and political basis was undeniable. Right-leaning critics of the DIHR accused director Morten Kjaerum of being an "opinion doctor" for allegedly attempting to use his elite position to push ideas onto an otherwise unreceptive public.[80] The implication was that, if left alone, Danish society would be less sympathetic to human rights and other ideas attributed to intellectual elites.

Widespread international outrage against the planned closures embarrassed the country's center-right coalition government and was particularly ill-timed, coming at a time when Denmark was trying to burnish its image before taking over the European Union's rotating presidency.[81] Immediately, plans for resuscitating the DIHR were circulated among policymakers. The original government proposal to save the DIHR would have merged the institute with four other government institutions—the Danish Institute for International Affairs (DUPI), the Center for Development Research, the Center for Holocaust and Genocide Studies, and the Copenhagen Peace Research Institute—to form a new Danish Academy for International Affairs (DUPA, which quickly became DIIS, the Danish Institute of International Studies). Not only was "human rights" deleted from the title of the new institution but, worse yet, it was to become an official government institute under the Ministry for Foreign Affairs. This meant that Denmark, an international leader in the movement to support NHRIs operating under the tenets of the legitimizing Paris Principles, would be blocked by its own government from having an NHRI at home. The international human rights community was horrified by the implications for NHRIs worldwide. The United Nations High Commissioner for Human Rights, Mary Robinson, and other international human rights notables quickly joined in the campaign to save the Danish Center for Human Rights.[82]

In response to the groundswell of international criticism, the government eventually agreed to preserve the Danish Center for Human Rights as an independent entity under a completely new structure. Under the resulting reorganization, the Center officially became the Danish Institute for Human Rights[83] and was folded into the Danish Center for International Studies and Human Rights (i.e., the DIIS). The official name of the new umbrella organization was a mouthful, the Danish Center for International Studies and Human Rights (DCISM), and the integration of the different think tanks' staffs, libraries, and offices proved challenging. However, the NHRI emerged from the crisis rooted on firmer ground than ever before. Although the old DIHR had been established by decree, the new institution was a product of legislation. Because a decree is far more susceptible to change than legislation, the legal foundation for the new institution was arguably much stronger.

Although the DIHR was forced to advertise for a new executive director and to receive resumes from a number of candidates, it was never without an executive director and it never experienced a change in leadership. Morten Kjaerum, who was the executive director before the crisis, applied for the advertised position and was selected by a board composed of men and women who were deeply respected in a number of fields, including business, law, trade unions, and academia.[84] Despite reports to the contrary, the timing of the interviews and selection process were designed so that Kjaerum never had to leave his office. Although newspapers reported large budget cuts that gutted crucial human rights endeavors, according to DIHR staff, the budget did not suffer in any discernible manner and no projects were eliminated as the direct result of the attempted closure. The crisis did encourage the executive director and staff to think more strategically about their work and thus indirectly prompted the creation of new projects.[85]

In an effort to stem further criticism about its national activities, the DIHR underwent an internal reorganization, according to which activities would be divided among four main departments: the Research Department, the International Department, the National Department, and the Information and Education Department. "The creation of a specific department to focus on national issues was not at all an admission that the Centre was not doing national work, but it did indicate that we were being more strategic in our thinking about national work," explained Birgitte Kofod Olsen, a senior employee of the DIHR who, on January 1, 2003, would become the first director of the National Department. As part of a strategic decision, beginning in 2003, the DIHR would be represented in the press and at public events more frequently by the directors of the departments and other senior staff and not just by the executive director.[86]

Breadth of Mandate

Monitoring Equality Legislation   The mandate and operations of the new National Department at the DIHR has been shaped by the requirements of European Union antidiscrimination legislation.[87] This legislation—widely referred to simply as Article 13—requires each state "to introduce legislation to outlaw unfair discrimination on the grounds of race, sexual orientation, religion or belief, disability and age in the fields of employment and training."[88] The Danish government, in consultation with the DIHR leadership, determined that the National Department would serve as the platform for implementing Article 13 within the country.[89] Thus in 2003 the Complaints Committee for Ethnic Equal Treatment was established as part of the DIHR.[90] This small but important office was granted the authority to hear complaints of direct and indirect discrimination on grounds of race or ethnic origin in all public and private sectors in relation to social protection.[91] These included social security and health care, social advantages, education, access to and supply of goods and services that are available to the public, and membership of and involvement in an organization of workers or employers. Also as part of the EU campaign on the equal treatment directives, the DIHR launched the MIA-Prize (MIA is the Danish acronym for diversity in the workplace), which is awarded annually to enterprises that promote diversity and equal treatment both in their policies and practice.[92]

The NHRI procedures that permit individual complaints for cases involving allegations of racism have not satisfied critics who seek a more expansive individual complaint mechanism. International human rights treaty-monitoring bodies have specifically criticized Denmark for failing to provide in its NHRIs adequate procedures for monitoring individual complaints. For example, in its 2006 concluding observations on the CRC, Denmark expressed harsh criticism for such failings. Although the Children's Convention itself is silent on NHRIs, the CRC has addressed their importance in its General Comment No. 2. According to the CRC, the failure of the Danish national mechanisms to hear individual complaints of violations of children's rights renders them inadequate.[93] The CRC has recommended that the state party establish an independent body, either in the Office of the Ombudsman or the National Council for Children or as a separate organ for monitoring the implementation of the convention and, in particular, for receiving individual complaints.[94] Establishing any form of independent monitoring mechanism would go a long way toward addressing the main criticism of the DIHR, which is its relevance to actual victims of human rights violations.

Domestic and International Institution Building   The DIHR's four departments and the Complaints Committee for Ethnic Equal Treatment are complemented by a number of program areas and partner relationships that cut across the departments. The list of program areas includes civil society, NHRIs, access to justice, academic cooperation, reform of law and state institutions, and access to information. The DIHR has (or at one point has had) human rights partners in such diverse places as Afghanistan, Albania, Benin, Bosnia and Herzegovina, Burkina Faso, Cambodia, China, Croatia, Estonia, Honduras, Iraq, Malawi, Mozambique, Nepal, Niger, Rwanda, Senegal, Serbia, South Africa, Turkey, Uganda, Vietnam, and Yemen.[95]

As part of its institution building, the DIHR has conducted a number of international training programs on establishing NHRIs.[96] The DIHR has assisted in the establishment of national institutions in Bangladesh in Asia; Tanzania, Malawi, and Niger in Africa; and the newly independent states in Eastern Europe.[97] It has been well placed to play an active role in ensuring the development of democratic institutions in the newly democratizing states in the Baltic and Balkan regions.[98] It has also encouraged the establishment of NHRIs in Norway, Germany, and Nepal. In Nepal, for example, the DIHR assisted the Nepalese commission with strategic planning and with building up their capacity with regard to legislative review.[99]

Further extending its reach, the DIHR has placed Danish human rights officers in several African institutions: the South Africa Constitutional Assembly, the South African Human Rights Commission, and the Malawian Ombudsman. The human rights officer at the South African Commission supported the commission's work on economic, social, and cultural rights and contributed to the commission's role in the development of the South African National Action Plan on Human Rights. In Tanzania, the DIHR has played a role over the past four years in preparations for the establishment of an NHRI. These preparations include assistance in drafting and consulting on legislation, suggesting a framework for Danish bilateral assistance to the commission, drafting a project document, procuring international advisers to the commission, and training its newly appointed members.[100]

Training efforts have also been strong on the domestic level. Basic human rights courses as well as thematic courses are offered as part of the permanent course catalog (twelve per year). Partnering with the Children and Youth Network, the National Department of the DIHR has offered courses on children's rights and development and has created courses for NGO staff on rights-based development, including courses with the Danish Projects Counseling Services. According to National Department director Birgitte Kofod Olsen, the DIHR upgraded the citizenship curriculum throughout Denmark to encourage and improve the teaching of human rights.[101] The DIHR has already begun a two-year collaboration with schools in Norrebro, a Copenhagen neighborhood chosen because of its diverse ethnic population.

Specific Activities on Social and Economic Rights   Denmark has long been actively engaged in international standard setting and enforcement of social and economic rights.[102] Although the Danish constitution has few provisions on social and economic rights, Denmark is a party to the principal UN treaty on the topic, the International Covenant on Economic, Social, and Cultural Rights, and to the central European instrument addressing social and economic issues, the European Social Charter.[103] The Committee on Economic, Social, and Cultural Rights (CESCR), the UN committee charged with monitoring state performance under the Economic Covenant, has "note[d] with satisfaction that the Government of Denmark pays a great deal of attention to its activities for the promotion and protection of economic, social and cultural rights."[104] With regard to the promotion of human rights, the CESCR has singled out the DIHR for its integration of social and economic rights into courses for civil servants, professional human rights workshops and training seminars, human rights books and periodicals, and the provision of advice and information to the public at large.[105] The CESCR has also commended Denmark for contributing to the realization of economic, social, and cultural rights in other countries through its regular participation in multilateral development cooperation programs and for establishing a number of bilateral programs.[106]

The CESCR has praised Denmark for its advancement of women's rights in the workplace. Danish women have the highest employment frequency in the labor market in the world and the gap between women's and men's wages is among the smallest, but it is growing as unions weaken and individuals are granted more room to negotiate their own individual employment agreements.[107] Recent legislation adopted in Denmark to promote equality between men and women (in particular the enactment of the Act on Equal Payment [Act 639 of July 1992]) has also been noteworthy, according to the CESCR.[108]

The DIHR's program on diversity in the workplace provides another example of Danish society testing human rights.[109] The DIHR supports a rights-based analysis that would empower individual workers with legally enforceable rights. However, in an attempt to realize these rights, the DIHR has crafted a strategy in line with Denmark's long tradition of addressing all workplace issues, including discrimination, through cooperative problem solving and self-regulation by employers and unions. In constructing this program, the DIHR draws from the human resources trend known as diversity management to inform its own diversity strategy. Unlike a rights model, which fosters an adversarial environment, with individuals advancing claims against employers, diversity management "sees the opportunities of diversity instead of focusing solely on the problems or barriers"[110] and, in so doing, emphasizes cooperative problem solving.[111]

The DIHR's use of diversity management does not ignore human rights altogether. On the contrary, the DIHR uses a model that is intended to connect rights-based diversity management with resource-oriented diversity management "in a dynamic process in which the understanding of both opportunities and barriers is constantly developed."[112] The MIA model, Birgitte Kofod Olsen explained, depends on "human rights thriving," and its application has "led to the stressing of compliance."[113] According to Olsen, the director of the National Department at the DIHR, the MIA process creates a culture and organizational framework that "makes demands on both management and employees" and that "supports equal opportunities for all."[114] Although the model does focus on the benefits for employers of adopting a diversity approach (i.e., innovation and development), it also emphasizes that employers must comply with the Danish legislation's minimum standards for employment to reap these benefits.

In using the diversity strategy, the DIHR has taken the lead in facilitating the creation of a new Danish strategy for the implementation of the principles of nondiscrimination in the six areas governed by EU nondiscrimination provisions: age, gender, race and ethnic origin, disability, religion and belief, and sexual orientation.[115] The resulting civil society working group on nondiscrimination, which is both multi-issue (i.e., health care, housing, public welfare) and multiconstituent (i.e., individuals with disabilities, migrants, women) in approach, has attracted the kind of positive attention it needs from civil society to gain the full support of influential organizations and individuals. At the same time, the group has kept a low enough profile to avoid the kind of negative publicity in the public sphere that could cause a premature evaluation of its efforts and silence future creative cross-sectoral work in the field of human rights. Olsen credits these efforts with gaining positive political attention, leading to the creation in Denmark of a complaint body covering all grounds of discrimination (i.e., not limiting complaints to race or ethnic discrimination), and with encouraging the social minister and integration minister in their creation of new funds for further work on diversity and equal treatment.[116]

The popularity of diversity management in Demark can be explained in four ways. First, because diversity management explains difference in a non-threatening manner and espouses the business benefits of difference over homogeneity, it can provide a gentle path for introducing the largely homogeneous Danish society to different cultures. Second, the notion that the interests of the larger collective can be advanced is directly in line with the Danish values of solidarity and egalitarianism. Third, although human rights and equal opportunity policies are based on the assumption that minority groups will assimilate into the dominant culture, diversity approaches do not even attempt assimilation. This approach thus sidesteps the ongoing debate in Denmark about whether and how new Danes can be integrated into what is largely a homogeneous and closed society. Finally, one could argue that despite the drawbacks in the diversity approach, it is strategically more effective because Danish civil society has already begun to think in terms of diversity, whereas social and economic rights still tend to be viewed as alien concepts.

The drawbacks to the diversity approach, however, are not insignificant. Experience has shown that without the threat of legal penalties, "internally regulated" workplace grievance procedures and diversity training are subject to being used as symbols of compliance without any positive effect on the incidence of discrimination. In operation the diversity approach leaves substantial discretion to employers and considerable room for the co-option by other intermediaries, including management "experts," trade unions, and other constituency-based interest groups. Because employers and intermediaries have their own interests at stake, there is a real risk that the diversity approach will result in a sham or in symbolic internal processes that leave underlying patterns of bias unchanged. As one management consultant promoting diversity training explained:

> Dealing with diversity is not about civil rights or women's rights; it is not about leveling the playing field or making amends for past wrongs; it is not about eliminating racism or sexism; and it is not about doing something special for minorities and women. Rather, it is about enhancing the manager's capability to tap the potential of a diverse group of employees.[117]

Although the DIHR continues to advance the diversity model, other Danish actors working outside that body have chosen alternative approaches that rely less on enhancing benefits for employers and more on advancing human rights for employees. One of the most notable new approaches began in 2006 in Aarhus, Denmark's second largest city. Drawing from a British citizenship model, the Aarhus approach focuses on enhancing the respect of citizens for a shared set of fundamental democratic principles. The consultants behind the initiative, Allan Hjorth and Wenche Orbitz, describe the overall goal of the new integration policy in the municipality of Aarhus as "strengthening cohesion in Aarhus so that all residents no matter their ethnic or cultural background are active citizens with respect for fundamental democratic principles."[118] They stress that "ethnic minorities must enjoy the same opportunities, rights and duties as all other citizens."[119] This alternative model (the Aarhus approach) addresses discrimination more directly than the MIA model and, in so doing, balances the individual's rights with community cohesion. According to the Aarhus approach, each individual citizen must respect fundamental democratic values and comply with various precepts, such as equality, the same rights and duties for all, democratic decision making, freedom of religion, freedom of expression, respect for personal freedom, active participation in children's education, working proactively to be financially independent, and speaking or aiming to speak Danish. Aarhus has chosen to operationalize these principles by examining the manner in which it organizes its work. By taking actions to enhance citizen input in the planning of services, the Aarhus approach attempts to support citizens' sense of responsibility for justice in their local communities.[120]

Assessment

The DIHR is solidly a human rights organization at home and abroad, in words and in deeds. However, when engaged in domestic work, many individual staff members are decidedly pragmatic and strategic. They adjust their approach according to the needs and understandings of the partners and intended audiences. Thus, to attract a wider constituency for its equal treatment work, the DIHR invokes more familiar language, such as *diversity* and *nondiscrimination*, terms that track more closely with Danish egalitarian values. These alternative frameworks are not a retreat from human rights but rather, in Morten Kjaerum's words, "can openers"—that is, they help skeptical institutions and individuals open the can of human rights and sample its contents. The DIHR realizes that if it acts with a heavy hand and introduces international human rights norms too quickly, many potential partners will be scared off.[121] "The individual nature of individual human rights challenges us to think differently," Birgitte Kofod Olsen acknowledged, adding that "this is the direction Danish society is going in" and that the DIHR is in a good position to help redirect Danish society toward thinking more about human rights in international terms.

One sign that Denmark is headed in this direction can be found in popular culture. A favorite pun in television commercials involves claiming a human right to the product being sold. "You have a human right to a good kitchen," proclaims one advertisement. "You have a human right to a good steak," asserts another. In Danish, the second ad has a double meaning, because the word for "right" also means "course" (as in an entrée for a meal). Thus the advertisement is affirming both that you have a human right to a decent meal (steak) and that you should be treated well.

By encouraging the application of international human rights norms to a variety of social and economic issues, the National Department of the DIHR is simultaneously supporting the Danish values of solidarity and egalitarianism and challenging these values. For example, the work of the National Department to develop a common definition of workplace discrimination and to develop tools for furthering human rights and equal treatment in the workplace provides illustrations of the stretching of traditional Danish values outside their usual context. At the same time, the National Department's close focus on ensuring the protection of individual human rights challenges the traditional Danish focus on the communal level.

That a strong alternative to the DIHR diversity approach exists demonstrates that the DIHR does not have a complete lock on ideas and practices for human rights in Denmark. This is a positive sign. The strong research agenda of the DIHR has always aimed to promote more well informed discussion on human rights issues and to promote, not inhibit, new ideas for making human rights matter in the domestic context. Accusations that the DIHR dominates and controls public debate on human rights appear to be patently unfounded. On the contrary, even with respect to the most controversial issues facing Danish society (immigration and racism), the DIHR continues to promote constructive dialogue and to make room for new voices.

The DIHR has faced a tough battle in making the discourse of practice of human rights relevant to its local constituents. In Denmark, human rights have long been treated as a matter of foreign, not domestic, policy. Human rights are "over there," not "right here." Although this foreign policy commitment provided the impetus for the DIHR to be established in the first place and supplied the strength to shield the institute from threats of closure, the DIHR continues to struggle to make human rights locally relevant. High standards of living traditionally guaranteed to Danish citizens suggest little relevance for human rights in the day-to-day lives of Danish people. However, as the country struggles to constructively manage the recent arrival of immigrant communities, human rights may find a new salience in Danish politics. Immigrant communities have not been afforded the benefits of Danish communal membership. The hope is that certain minimum standards of living for all, by virtue of their common humanity, can be guaranteed in Denmark. By becoming a more effective voice on these issues, the DIHR can remind its constituents of its continued relevance at home, even as it continues to be engaged in human rights activities abroad.

Chapter 3

"The Hardest Job I Ever Had"

Northern Ireland's Human Rights Commission

I N MANY RESPECTS, life in Northern Ireland could not be more different from life in Denmark. Danish society is cohesive and historically stable. Northern Ireland is deeply divided and enjoys a fragile stability. The greatest obstacle to the domestication of international human rights norms in Denmark is the Danes' reliance on the values of solidarity and egalitarianism. These values exist in Northern Ireland only within each religious or cultural group (i.e., Catholics feel solidarity with Catholics and Protestants with Protestants).[1] Danes fear that abiding by international human rights will necessitate a *lowering* of standards. The people of Northern Ireland hope to reach the international human rights minimum.[2] Given the overall standard of living in a country that has been extremely stable politically and a system that focuses on egalitarianism in access to resources and meeting basic needs, people in Denmark can be said to choose to work on human rights. For people in Northern Ireland, however, human rights work is a matter of necessity.[3] Given these great differences, it is somewhat surprising that Denmark and Northern Ireland could rely on similarly structured NHRIs to achieve their respective goals.

Nearly all contemporary political developments in Northern Ireland related to human rights promotion can be traced in some manner to the Good Friday Agreement, and developments related to the field of human rights are no exception.[4] When the British and Irish governments signed the Good Friday Agreement (also known as the Belfast Agreement) in 1998, hopes were high that the document would indeed provide the framework for a fresh start in Northern Ireland.[5] Many changes have come to pass since the official end of the conflict, and certainly Northern Ireland is a much more secure place.

Nevertheless, the country has not functioned as a normal constitutional entity and has existed in an almost permanent state of emergency.[6] Although relative calm has been restored, communities remain physically segregated, and the walls between them are still high, both literally and figuratively.[7] Understanding the personal and highly politicized nature of human rights in Northern Ireland and debates over their saliency is essential for grasping the extreme nature of the challenge presented to the Northern Ireland Human Rights Commission.

Political Context

Northern Ireland has long been the site of a violent and bitter ethnopolitical conflict. The ethnopolitical loyalties are allied, though not absolutely, with the Roman Catholic and Protestant denominations, and these are the labels used to categorize the opposing views.[8] Small minority groups adhering to other religions do exist, and some people do cross political lines regardless of their religion. However, for the most part, the political lines are sharply Catholic and Protestant.

The origins of this conflict lie in the twelfth century, with the military conquest of the island of Ireland by neighboring Britain.[9] Attempts by the British administration throughout the sixteenth century to plant nonnative (mostly Scottish) Protestants on the lands of indigenous Catholics in Ireland were most successful in the northeast of the island. With the proposal of self-government for the island of Ireland at the beginning of the twentieth century (Irish home rule), the Protestant minority began an armed resistance, which led to the partitioning of Ireland in 1920. The six counties of the northeast formed the state of Northern Ireland, and the twenty-six counties to the south constituted the Irish Free State. The Northern Ireland parliament was established in Belfast in 1921; the parliament was granted extensive powers of self-government, but certain residual powers over the jurisdiction were retained by the British government at Westminster. Although the Irish Free State declared independence in 1922, the state of Northern Ireland has remained a part of the United Kingdom of Great Britain and Northern Ireland. The Protestant majority in the six counties supports the maintenance of this union. The sizable Catholic minority, however, has traditionally favored the creation of a reunified 32-county Republic of Ireland.

These competing national aspirations, combined with the failure of the Northern Ireland state to provide equally for its Protestant and Catholic citizens,[10] form the basis of the most recent phase of violent conflict (since approximately 1968).[11] In 1972, with the onset of high levels of political violence, the Northern Ireland parliament was prorogued (discontinued without dissolution), and the British government at Westminster took over direct rule of the jurisdiction. Attempts to restore the parliament during the 1980s and 1990s were unsuccessful.[12]

After thirty years of violent conflict in which more than 3,600 people were killed and more than 30,000 were injured,[13] in 1994 the largest paramilitary organization, the Irish Republican Army (IRA), declared a cease-fire.[14] Opposition paramilitary groups soon followed suit.[15] This gave all sides more space to negotiate a framework agreement setting up a governance structure for Northern Ireland.[16] Concluded on April 10, 1998, the agreement reached in the multiparty negotiations[17] (the Good Friday or Belfast Agreement) was to mark a new era in Northern Ireland politics.

Approved by Northern Ireland's main Nationalist political parties[18] and most of the Unionist parties,[19] the Good Friday Agreement provided that the constitutional status of Northern Ireland within the United Kingdom would not change without the consent of the majority of the population voting in a referendum.[20] The Irish government agreed to relinquish its territorial claim to Northern Ireland.[21] Cross-border north-south bodies between those with executive responsibilities in Northern Ireland and the Irish government would be established,[22] and a mechanism would be devised for the early release of paramilitary prisoners.[23] At the center of the Good Friday Agreement lay provision for the establishment of the 108-member single-chamber legislative Assembly for Northern Ireland, which is elected by a system of proportional representation with a power-sharing executive.[24]

Implementation of the Good Friday Agreement was fraught with complications. As a report of the United States Institute of Peace notes, "Its political institutions have been active for less than half the time since the agreement's creation."[25] The Assembly met in shadow mode for six months, from September 1998 to March 1999, because sufficient agreement could not be reached for nomination of ministers to the executive until the end of November 1999. At that point, power was formally devolved by the British government to the Assembly.[26] David Trimble, Protestant leader of the Ulster Unionist Party (UUP)[27] and joint-winner (with John Hume) of the 1998 Nobel Peace Prize, became the first minister of the Northern Ireland Assembly. The deputy leader of the Social Democratic and Labour Party (SDLP),[28] Seamus Mallon, became deputy first minister of Northern Ireland, although his party's new leader, Mark Durkan, subsequently replaced him. The Ulster Unionists, SDLP, Sinn Féin (the party generally accepted to be the IRA's political arm),[29] and the Democratic Unionist Party (DUP) each had ministers by right in the power-sharing executive.[30] Since their establishment, the Assembly and its executive have been operating on a stop-start basis, with repeated disagreements about whether the IRA was fulfilling its commitments to disarm.[31]

Former paramilitary leaders have discovered how difficult it is to abandon a reputation for violence and to mend an atmosphere of mistrust. On July 28, 2005, the IRA made a public statement ordering an end to the armed campaign and instructing its members to exchange their weapons of violence for strategies of peace. Although the British and Irish governments warmly welcomed the statement, political reaction in Northern Ireland itself demonstrated a tendency toward suspicion, engendered by years of political and social conflict. The intergroup distrust continued even after the IRA submitted its extensive decommissioning efforts to the verification of the Independent International Commission on Decommissioning. Close to a compromise solution, however, the negotiators pressed on. After three days of multiparty talks at St. Andrews in Scotland in October 2006, negotiators announced a settlement that all parties, including the DUP, would follow. In classic Northern Ireland style,[32] however, the parties never unconditionally "supported" the agreement.

The St. Andrews Agreement provided for a "Transitional Assembly" to take part in preparations for the restoration of devolved government in Northern Ireland. The Transitional Assembly was composed of those returned in the November 2003 election. It first met on November 24, 2006, when the proceedings were suspended because of a bomb threat by Loyalist[33] paramilitary leader Michael Stone.[34] Although the deadlines originally proposed by the British and Irish governments in the St. Andrews Agreement were not met,[35] in January 2007 Sinn Féin did secure the agreement of its membership to a motion to support the recently reformed police service, to take their seats on governance bodies of the Police Service of Northern Ireland (PSNI), and to devolve criminal justice and policing powers to the Northern Ireland Assembly.[36] The DUP responded by indicating its willingness to enter into a restored Assembly and power-sharing executive with Sinn Féin.[37]

The Transitional Assembly was dissolved on January 30, 2007, when campaigning for the upcoming Northern Ireland Assembly elections started.

Elections to the Assembly were held on March 7, 2007. The DUP was returned as the largest party, with thirty-six seats, and Sinn Féin as the second-largest party, with twenty-eight seats. On May 7, 2007, power was restored to the Assembly, along with the election of the first and deputy first ministers and nominations to the Northern Ireland Executive.[38] As of this writing, the Assembly continues to operate; however, there is deep disagreement between the two main parties as to the appropriate timing of the devolution of criminal justice and policing powers to the Northern Ireland Assembly. The St. Andrews Agreement provided for devolution of these powers in May 2008,[39] but the DUP describes this timetable as "wishful thinking."[40]

Economic Context

Historically, Northern Ireland has had a strong economy. Shipbuilding and the linen industry were major employers in the jurisdiction. However, the decline of shipbuilding after World War I and the collapse of the linen market internationally in the 1950s gave rise to severe economic depression. By the 1950s, Northern Ireland was the poorest economic region in the United Kingdom. Poor economic performance was greatly exacerbated by the outbreak of full-scale political violence in 1969. "The Troubles" deterred both foreign tourists and foreign direct investment from entering the jurisdiction. The peace process has clearly helped Northern Ireland's economic performance; the improved economic situation has also consolidated the peace process. With greater employment and prosperity, both the Protestant and Catholic communities are even more reluctant to see a return to violence.[41]

Northern Ireland still has the smallest economy of any of the twelve regions of the United Kingdom, about two-thirds the size of the next smallest, northeast England. However, small does not necessarily mean weak, and, in fact, many economic indicators have turned in favor of Northern Ireland compared to its neighbors. Northern Ireland has a greater GDP per capita than both northeast England and Wales.[42] Northern Ireland's GDP had the largest increase between 1990 and 1999 of all the countries in the United Kingdom, growing 1 percent per year faster than the United Kingdom during this period. In 2005 the Northern Ireland economy was estimated to have grown by 3.2 percent, almost twice as fast as the United Kingdom as a whole, and future growth is expected to be stronger than that of the rest of the United Kingdom.[43]

Unemployment in Northern Ireland fell from 16.8 percent in 1986 to

4.3 percent in the final quarter of 2007.[44] In the winter of 2008, Northern Ireland had the second lowest rate of unemployment in the United Kingdom. From March 1990 to March 2006, employee jobs increased by 30.6 percent, compared to 10.5 percent for the United Kingdom as a whole. Northern Ireland's unemployment rate was still significantly below the EU average of 8.0 percent.

Complicating the unemployment figures for Northern Ireland is the profile of the unemployed. The Northern Ireland Department of Finance and Personnel has described employment problems as geographically concentrated and "stubborn" and "long-term in nature."[45] The unemployed tend to be chronically unemployed. Almost one-third of the unemployed have been unemployed for one year or more. Traditionally, levels of unemployment have been particularly acute in the Catholic community. The 1971 census found that the unemployment rate among Catholics was more than double that for Protestants, and employment rates were lower for Catholics in both the public and the private sector. In addition, Catholics were underrepresented in the higher occupation groups.[46] Data from the 1991 census show only marginal improvements, with the unemployment rate among Catholics still more than twice as high as the unemployment rate among Protestants.[47] However, the substantial job growth in the region since 1991 has resulted in a narrowing of the gap. In 2004, the rate for Catholic unemployment stood at 6.9 percent, and the rate for Protestants reached an all-time low of 2.9 percent.[48] Catholic medium- and longer-term unemployment rates remain higher than the Protestant rates. Catholics have consistently higher economic inactivity rates.[49] Wages for employees tend to be similar, with Protestant wages slightly ahead of Catholic wages.[50] So long as a disparity exists in wages and employment rates for Catholics and Protestants, the positive impact of other economic indicators on communal tensions will not be realized.[51]

Human Rights Context

State-condoned and state-perpetrated incidents of violence have declined rapidly since the signing of the Good Friday Agreement. However, questions persist over accountability for past alleged human rights violations by the state. The issue of security force collusion in the murders perpetrated by Loyalist paramilitaries is particularly contentious. An agreed-on mechanism for the investigation and possible prosecution of such activities has proven elusive.[52] Therefore Northern Ireland's contemporary human rights context remains heavily determined by human rights concerns of the past.[53] Allegations of collusion have not entirely desisted since the signing of the Good Friday Agreement.

Rosemary Nelson, to take one prominent example, was murdered just over a year after the agreement was signed.[54] Nelson, an internationally acclaimed human rights activist and lawyer, died on March 15, 1999, after a booby-trapped bomb exploded underneath her car. Nelson was in many ways a successor to Patrick Finucane, the Belfast human rights lawyer murdered in 1989.[55] Like Finucane, Nelson represented people who had been arrested under the emergency or antiterrorism laws, including a man accused of murdering two Royal Ulster Constabulary officers. Before she was murdered, Nelson repeatedly claimed that officers of the Constabulary had harassed her, assaulted her, and threatened her life. The UN special reporter on the independence of judges and lawyers and several international human rights groups had attempted to intervene on her behalf, calling on the British government to offer protection. Not only did the government fail to protect her, but after she was killed, the government also obstructed efforts to conduct a public inquiry into allegations of security force collusion in her murder.[56]

There are also persistent concerns raised by human rights advocates over the retention of certain emergency powers by the state, now long after the suspension of major paramilitary activity.[57] Northern Ireland continues to be a violent and fearful society.[58] The physical manifestations of fear of the "other side" are ever prevalent.[59] The large concrete walls erected between communities on the interface—that is, the Catholic-Protestant fault lines—have not been torn down.[60] Paramilitary violence continues; racist, homophobic, and domestic violence have all increased since the cease-fires; public disorder has been a sustained problem over recent years; and many forms of violent crime continue to rise.[61]

A 2005 publication of the Community Relations Council[62] on sectarian violence in Northern Ireland painted a depressing picture. Sectarian violence was not only continuing but escalating in some parts of Belfast and other urban locations. Drawing from official police statistics, the Community Relations Council reported that there had been an average of five attacks a month on places of worship and that "there were 376 cases of rioting and 1,014 disturbances in interface areas of North Belfast between 1996 and 2004. Over the same period there were 3,864 cases of criminal damage and 1,327 assaults in the areas."[63] An average of 1,378 people sought rehousing every year because of sectarian, racist, or paramilitary intimidation, and, similarly, sectarian violence in the workplace drove many people to seek new employment, the Community Relations Center found in its report.

Young people fared worse than adults in the study. Among the depressing conclusions were the following:

- Young people were more likely to experience sectarian harassment and violence than adults.

- More than one in four young people had experienced sectarian verbal abuse in the previous year.

- A high percentage of young people reported feeling threatened or intimidated by murals and other visual displays, especially those of the other community.

- More than half of young people did not feel safe in areas dominated by the other community, but nearly half of young males had to travel to or through such areas at least once a week.

- A high percentage of young people favored a segregated living, schooling, and working environment.[64]

During this period, IRA-affiliated groups were held responsible for two well-publicized killings. In the first incident, IRA thugs brutally murdered Robert McCartney in what amounted to a drunken pub assault. Ironically, McCartney himself had been a longtime supporter of the Republican movement and thus was an unlikely target of IRA violence. Aside from the grisly nature of the attack (McCartney was repeatedly beaten and stabbed by a gang of approximately twenty men while bystanders looked on), the most shocking aspect of this incident was the IRA's response: Its leadership offered to execute the perpetrators as a means of providing McCartney's family a sense of justice.[65] In an audacious move, McCartney's sisters rejected the offer of vigilantism, vocally denouncing the violence in public speaking events in both Northern Ireland and the United States.[66]

McCartney's murder and the subsequent IRA execution offer bolstered claims by Unionists that the IRA continued to act above the law. Ian Paisley, leader of the DUP and vociferous foe of the IRA, seized on the incident to challenge the belief that the IRA could act as a genuine partner for peace, claiming that "the offer to shoot those responsible for the murder of Robert McCartney confirms again that terrorism is the only stock and trade of Sinn Féin/IRA."[67]

The McCartney murder also served to undermine Sinn Féin's support base in Belfast and abroad. In the days following the killing, anti-IRA graffiti appeared in the Short Strand district, a Republican stronghold and home of the McCartney family. In a striking turnabout, Sinn Féin lost its seat on the Short Strand council, a sign many interpreted as political fallout from the McCartney killing.[68] Moreover, some American supporters of Sinn Féin vowed to halt financial support of the group.[69] Under increasing local and international pressure, police charged one man with the murder.[70]

In a second example of brutal vigilantism, killers suspected of having IRA ties murdered Denis Donaldson in April 2006. Donaldson had been a leading Sinn Féin member for more than three decades, until he was outed as an informant for British intelligence in late 2005. Realizing his life was in danger, Donaldson sought refuge in rural western Ireland, living a spartan life without electricity or running water. A journalist who met with Donaldson before his murder described him as being "extremely depressed. [H]e looked like a hunted animal."[71] Shortly thereafter, Donaldson's shotgun-savaged body was discovered at his hideout. Sinn Féin leader Gerry Adams suggested that the culprits were likely Republican dissidents opposed to the ongoing peace process.[72] As of this writing, no one has been charged with the murder.

According to a major report of the Independent Monitoring Commission, the body established by the British and Irish governments in 2004 to report on paramilitary violence, in 2007 Northern Ireland experienced low levels of violence from both dissident Republican and Loyalist groups.[73] Police officers and police premises remained targets of incendiary devices from dissident Republican elements.[74] Much Loyalist activity was purely criminal and without any political objective;[75] however, the commission report recorded violence between Loyalist factions.[76] The report noted that paramilitary murders and assaults continued at a low level.[77]

Considering the pervasive sectarianism that continues to dominate Northern Ireland's sociopolitical relations today and the retention of emergency powers by the British government nearly a decade after the Good Friday Agreement became law, it is indeed a great challenge for a genuine human rights culture to take root. It is from within this environment of vigilantism and sectarian violence that the Northern Ireland Human Rights Commission (NIHRC) has evolved, realizing limited and halting success in addressing the human rights problems that matter most to Northern Ireland's communities.

The Northern Ireland Human Rights Commission

Establishment and Mandate

Created by the Good Friday Agreement,[78] the NIHRC is an independent statutory body whose role is to promote awareness of the importance of human rights in Northern Ireland, review existing law and practice, and advise government on what steps need to be taken to fully protect human rights in Northern Ireland (see Appendix 2 for mandate excerpts).[79] By permitting the NHRI to provide rights that are not already guaranteed in the European Convention on Human Rights (ECHR) (largely a civil and political rights instrument), the Good Friday Agreement paved the way for NHRI involvement in the promotion and protection of a wide range of rights, including economic, social, and cultural rights.[80]

From the outset, the NIHRC has been incredibly ambitious. Although the NIHRC is small, it distinguishes itself from other NHRIs by the breadth of the work it undertakes. The drafting of a bill of rights for Northern Ireland has consumed an inordinate amount of time for the NIHRC staff, which has held numerous public meetings and conducted several expert consultancies on the issue.[81] (As of this writing, the drafting process is still ongoing.)[82] The NIHRC has also devoted considerable energy to promoting human rights protections under existing and potential domestic laws and international treaties.[83] On the local level, the NIHRC has weighed in on a range of issues, such as government proposals on domestic violence,[84] options for improving treatment of immigration detainees,[85] prison policies on suicide prevention,[86] and the debate over the creation of a single equality bill for Northern Ireland.[87] Tasks in the international arena have included creating parallel reports, conducting follow-up studies on concluding recommendations, and advocating for additional treaties and optional protocols to existing treaties to be signed.[88]

One good illustration of this work is the NIHRC's monitoring of the concluding observations of the UN body that monitors Northern Ireland's compliance with the International Covenant on Economic, Social, and Cultural Rights. Because Northern Ireland is not recognized as an independent country, it does not have the ability to sign international human rights treaties; nor does it have the obligation to report separately to treaty-monitoring bodies. Nonetheless, international treaty bodies may consider Northern Ireland when they are reviewing the United Kingdom. With respect to social and economic rights, the Committee on Economic, Social, and Cultural Rights (CESCR) has frequently made comments on Northern Ireland. For example, in the most recent review of the United Kingdom (in 2002), the CESCR mentioned Northern Ireland in three separate sections. First, it reiterated its "concern about the persistence of considerable levels of poverty, especially in certain parts of the country, such as Northern Ireland."[89] Second, the CESCR "reiterate[d] its concern expressed in paragraph 18 of its 1997 concluding observations that the educational structure in Northern Ireland continues to be heavily segregated on the basis of religion despite the increased demand for integrated schools."[90] Third, the CESCR strongly recommended the inclusion of effective protection for economic, social, and cultural rights, consistent with the provisions of the covenant, in any bill of rights enacted for Northern Ireland.

Unlike many other NHRIs, the NIHRC works directly on individual cases involving human rights claims, identifying cases both through an on-site intake process and by working closely with other human rights attorneys. Although NIHRC staff members may provide representation before administrative bodies and courts, they often contract out this work to cooperating attorneys. This work may involve investigating complaints, assisting individuals in bringing legal proceedings, bringing proceedings in the name of the NIHRC, and intervening as a third party or amicus curiae in legal proceedings. Additional investigations and report writing complement the individual casework. Notably, the NIHRC has produced documentation of its investigations of public institutions alleged to have engaged in rights violations and has engaged in the ongoing monitoring of public institutions, such as prisons and hospitals.[91]

Finally, the NIHRC is involved in three types of outreach activities. First, through their provision of a modest library and documentation service and their provision of information through media appearances and publications, the NIHRC serves as an open resource to its immediate community. Second, the NIHRC provides human rights education services through the creation of school curriculum on human rights, training of civil society activists and police officers,[92] and other activities that seek to build the capacity of government offices and to foster dialogue through the holding of public events on particular rights topics.[93] Third, in addition to educational activities on human rights, the NIHRC educates the public on the function of NHRIs in democratic societies. By providing educational campaigns on "what is a[n] NHRI and what should be the public's expectations for a[n] NHRI,"[94] staff members hope to decrease the public's tendency to have unrealistic expectations about the NIHRC.

Political Challenges

From its inception, the NIHRC has illustrated the great difficulties associated with establishing a human rights institution in a deeply divided society.[95] "It was the toughest job I ever had," more than one commissioner remembered. The stakes were high, and the task at hand was incredibly personal. One former member of the NIHRC remembered its stormy beginning: "Here it was, we had what we wanted and we even had people we would want to work with, and then [nothing worked out the way they had anticipated]."[96]

Public expectations for the NIHRC are informed by the larger local and regional political struggles. Although the United Kingdom has begun a process of transforming its many separate "equality bodies" (demarcated on the lines of particular interest groups, e.g., race, gender, and disability) into a single human rights body, the emergence of a U.K.-wide human rights body appears unlikely to occur in the near future.[97] Nonetheless, the NIHRC is concerned about the implications of such a possible development. In particular, they worry that the new body will compromise the independence of the NIHRC and that the NIHRC will lose its status in the worldwide network of NHRIs.[98]

The initial slate of commissioners was attacked by the Protestant/Unionist community, which regarded the NIHRC as a body skewed toward Catholics/Nationalists.[99] The first round of commissioners was appointed from Northern Ireland's human rights community. Given the small size of the jurisdiction, one major indigenous human rights organization emerged over the course of the conflict: the Committee for the Administration of Justice (CAJ).[100] The CAJ was the winner of the Council of Europe's Human Rights Prize in 1998 for placing human rights at the forefront of peace negotiations. However, the CAJ was distrusted by certain Unionist politicians because of its repeated attempts to bring international attention to state-perpetrated human rights violations in the jurisdiction.[101] Controversy surrounded the initial set of appointments to the NIHRC, largely because it was thought that too many of the commissioners had been drawn from the CAJ.[102]

After several hard, contentious months, NIHRC board members soon discovered that "working against your enemies was easier than working with your friends."[103] One of the first issues that they encountered was the public perception that the NIHRC and its staff were biased, in favor of either the government or one sector of civil society.[104] One central question for the NIHRC is whether commissioners can be active members of human rights

NGOs while serving as commissioners. As noted, a number of current and former members of the NIHRC were and still are active in the CAJ or are somehow still connected with Amnesty International (AI), the international membership-driven organization that popularized human rights by involving individuals directly in letter-writing campaigns on behalf of prisoners of conscience. The proponents of these commissioners argue that attachments to these organizations are an indication of human rights experience—a desirable factor—and the fact that so many commissioners are active in the same groups is more a reflection of the "smallness of Northern Ireland and the strength of these groups and not any impermissible bias."[105] As one member of the CAJ later reflected, "They [the commissioner and staff of the NIHRC] wanted to do things right so they went overboard and practically cut off all contact with precisely the type of organizations who could help them and who they could help."[106] NIHRC commissioners from those early years now admit that they were "perhaps overly sensitive" to the "connection with CAJ."[107] Indeed, as Brian Burdekin, the UN expert on NHRIs opines, NGO membership on a human rights commission is not problematic so long as those concerned are clear about their role and responsibilities.[108]

Another obstacle to the work of the NIHRC was a lack of resources compared with other human rights commissions around the world.[109] Financial constraints were major factors leading to a series of highly publicized resignations from the body.[110] The nine-member commission was hamstrung by a large number of commissioners resigning or withdrawing: Angela Hegarty (resigned for personal reasons in January 2000), Christine Bell and Inez McCormack (resigned September 2002), Patrick Yu (resigned July 2002), Frank McGuinness and Paddy Kelly (withdrew from active service, summer 2002), Chris McGimpsey (resigned to run for Assembly, November 2003), and Paddy Kelly (resigned July 2004). Despite the attempt to juggle reappointments, at one point in time the commission had only two part-time commissioners.[111]

Fuel for Criticism: Holy Cross

The rapid turnover at the NIHRC was in part a reaction to its early, well-publicized mistakes. The Holy Cross case was by far the worst debacle. In that case, what should have been a minor case of public harassment turned into a major public indictment of the NIHRC because it demonstrated the susceptibility of individual commissioners to political pressures. In the words of commissioners who resigned over the case, Holy Cross "demonstrated that something was deeply wrong," that there was a complete "lack of independence," and that "the Commission was wounded so deeply that [no one could see] how it could recover."[112]

The Holy Cross case involved Catholic schoolgirls whose route to school took them through a Protestant neighborhood.[113] Each day, the (Protestant) residents of the neighborhood stood at the side of the road, taunting the girls as they passed, at times physically blocking their path. The UN special reporter for education, Katarina Tomaševski, reported:

> Two residentially and educationally segregated neighbourhoods, both experiencing deprivation, provide the background. Protesters blocked the passage to school, trying to exclude "the other" from "their" neighbourhood. The parents insisted on taking their daughters to school by the road claimed as theirs by "the other."[114]

Initially the police sought to deal with the problem of getting to the Catholic school by persuading the Catholic girls to take a backstreet route that minimized their chances of being attacked. The Catholic parents, however, demanded that the police guarantee the safety of their girls in taking the route of their choice to school, even if it sent them through a hostile neighborhood. In September 2001, the then-chief constable of the PSNI decided to deploy officers to clear a path for the parents and children.

In September 2001, a parent of one of the children brought a case against the PSNI for failing to protect her child while the girl walked to and from school on the route of her choosing. The NIHRC saw the case as an opportunity to demonstrate its ability to promote the human rights of *all* communities, and thus it agreed that the NHRI should fund the legal action on behalf of the Catholic schoolchildren. The decision was not unanimous, however, and the chief commissioner of the NIHRC, Brice Dickson, was particularly disgruntled. In a highly extraordinary move, Dickson, without the knowledge of the parents or the NIHRC, wrote a letter to the former chief constable informing him that support for the case was never unanimous at the NIHRC. Claiming to represent himself and three additional commissioners, Dickson declared, "I myself am strongly of the view that the policing of the protest at the Holy Cross School has not been in breach of the Human Rights Act."[115] The lawyers for the chief constable used this letter from Dickson to bolster their argument that the police acted properly in the Holy Cross case. Meanwhile, the NIHRC continued to fund the case against the police until it was dismissed by the court in June 2004.[116] Whether the outcome of the case was influenced by the letter is a matter of considerable debate.[117]

To this day, Chief Commissioner Dickson defends his actions by explaining in great detail the NIHRC's convoluted decision-making process,[118] but in its review of the matter, the Joint Committee on Human Rights (a committee appointed by the House of Lords and House of Commons) made a clear determination in their report that his actions were inappropriate.[119] Anne Smith, a scholar who has investigated the case, explains: "Independence was compromised and concomitantly the NIHRC's credibility and legitimacy have also been seriously hindered from all quarters, including the solicitors who acted for the applicant, political parties, and civil society."[120] To win back its credibility, the NIHRC needed to turn to easier cases, where more agreement on the proper courses of action existed across Catholic-Protestant lines.

Social and Economic Rights

Although the NIHRC's early track record on civil and political rights was marred by the Holy Cross case, the area of social and economic rights provided an opening for the NIHRC to establish its legitimacy. A substantial divide did exist on whether and how social and economic rights should be addressed, yet both of the main communities in Northern Ireland were in general agreement on the importance of these rights. A public opinion survey conducted by the NIHRC in July 1999, to take one illustration, found a high level of support for the inclusion of social and economic rights in a Northern Ireland bill of rights. In particular, the study found that well over 80 percent of respondents in both the Protestant and Catholic communities supported the inclusion in the bill of rights of the right to health, housing, and employment.[121]

The words of the Good Friday Agreement itself are unclear about the range of rights to be included in a bill of rights and the manner in which they should be addressed.[122] The Good Friday Agreement states:

> Northern Ireland Human Rights Commission will be invited to consult and to advise on the scope for defining, in Westminster legislation, rights supplementary to those in the European Convention on Human Rights, to reflect *the particular circumstances of Northern Ireland*, drawing as appropriate on international instruments and experience. These additional rights to reflect the principles of mutual respect for the identity and ethos of both communities and parity of esteem, and—taken together with the ECHR—to constitute a Bill of

Rights for Northern Ireland. Among the issues for consideration by the Commission will be:

- the formulation of a general obligation on government and public bodies fully to respect, on the basis of equality of treatment, the identity and ethos of both communities in Northern Ireland; and

- A clear formulation of the rights not to be discriminated against and to equality of opportunity in both the public and private sectors.[123]

The two sides of the debate on the treatment of social and economic rights center around different interpretations of the "particular circumstances" that the bill of rights is supposed to reflect. Arguing for a minimalist approach, Unionists[124] contend that any proposed bill of rights should concentrate on rights related to culture and identity and should base its wording on that found in the ECHR (which is scant on social and economic rights).[125] This position has been supported by the Confederation of British Industry, which expressed "major concern that the proposals being brought forward by the Northern Ireland Human Rights Commission go much beyond the mandate of the Belfast agreement."[126] As one critic explained:

> According to this logic, social and economic rights, including provisions for the private sector to be pro-active in its promotion of equality, have no place in a Bill. "Intercommunity tensions" and inequality are neither caused nor exacerbated by the workplace or supposed investment discrimination. The effectiveness of the MacBride principles would tell us different. But profit, not truth, is the goal of capital.[127]

Concerned that a broad spectrum of rights guaranteed in a Northern Ireland bill of rights might give rise to a disparity in rights protections between citizens in Northern Ireland and Great Britain or between those in Northern Ireland and the Republic of Ireland, both the British and Irish governments also sought to minimize the inclusion of social and economic rights.[128]

A different position was advanced by the Human Rights Consortium, an advocacy network bringing together trade unions, NGOs, and community groups representing minority and marginalized groups in Northern Ireland. Social and economic rights must be addressed by a Northern Ireland bill of rights, the consortium contended, because the "particular circumstances" of Northern Ireland "[refer] to the legacy of social and economic deprivation and inequality, that caused a war and which were exacerbated by it."[129] This position was supported by the Alliance Party, which urged that social, economic, and environmental rights be treated as "integral" to a Northern Ireland bill of rights.[130]

The more expansive interpretation of the "particular circumstances" wording has prevailed in the NIHRC's drafts for the bill of rights. In the 2004 and 2006 drafts, a general provision on social and economic rights in the bill of rights is accompanied by several specific provisions, including the following:[131]

- *Right to health care*: "Everyone is entitled to the highest attainable standard of physical and mental health and well-being; Government shall take all reasonable steps to promote good health and well-being, and to ensure adequate prevention and treatment of ill-health."

- *Right to an adequate standard of living*: "Everyone is entitled to an adequate standard of living sufficient for that person and those dependent upon him or her; Material provision for each person should be sufficient to ensure esteem for his or her health and dignity; Everyone has the right to social and civic care."

- *Right to housing*: "Everyone has the right to adequate housing; Housing should be appropriate to the material, social and mobility needs of the person."

- *Right to work*: "Everyone has the right to contribute to the economic and social life of society, including the right of access to work and the right to choose and practice a trade or profession; The State shall provide for, support and encourage the continuous development of skills, knowledge and understanding that are essential for employability and fulfillment."

- *The right to a healthy and sustainable environment*: "Everyone has the right to a healthy, safe and sustainable environment; The State has a duty to provide accurate and timely information and to communicate, consult and foster participation in planning and decision-making on matters which concern the environment."

In fashioning these social and economic rights, the NIHRC has rejected the argument that Northern Ireland cannot choose to guarantee its citizens a higher standard in health care, education, or social security than what is available in the rest of the United Kingdom. As a major consultancy document on the NIHRC explained:

There is nothing to prevent a Bill of Rights for Northern Ireland from imposing duties in respect of social and economic rights on the Northern Ireland Assembly and Executive within the resources available to them. The implementation mechanism ... would mean that directly justiciable social and economic rights, like other rights provisions, would be given effect as a matter of interpretation. Devolved legislation could be struck down where appropriate and statements of incompatibility could be issued in respect of primary legislation. Social and economic rights framed in process terms could be used to challenge all legislation, as regards whether reasonable steps to comply with the Bill had been taken in a non-discriminatory way, using processes of consultation and review.[132]

The work of the NIHRC on social and economic rights has not stopped with the drafting of the bill of rights. On the contrary, social and economic claims have figured prominently in each step of the commission's work on human rights promotion. For example, several of the eleven explanatory pamphlets published in the first months of the NIHRC covered children and young people; culture and identity; education, equality, and language; and social and economic rights;[133] one of the nine advisory working groups on different types of rights focused specifically on language, and another working group focused on economic rights. (These working groups were part of the drafting process.)[134] In addition, the NIHRC has issued several specific studies and reports on social and economic rights issues, including, in December 2000, an expansive report on the right to health, with a specific focus on the detrimental effect of housing and living conditions on the right to health, the barriers that single homeless people have encountered in accessing primary health care, and the barriers that health professionals encounter in delivering primary health care to socially excluded groups.[135]

Social and economic rights have also played a key role in activities that could be classified as human rights *protection*. A significant percentage of the more than 1,000 new legal inquiries that the NIHRC receives each year concerns social and economic rights. The vast majority of these do not proceed to a formal application for legal assistance because they are resolved, or dropped, after the provision of initial advice and (in most cases) some correspondence and informal negotiation. The NIHRC is most likely to take a case if it coincides with its strategic priorities. For 2003–2006 these priorities have been framed in terms of certain provisions of the ECHR. They are:

- Right to life (Article 2)
- Freedom from torture and inhuman or degrading treatment (Article 3)
- Right to a fair trial (Article 6)
- Right to education (Article 3 of the First Protocol)

According to the NIHRC, the most common areas of concern to individuals in Northern Ireland involve issues of family law, planning law, and employment law.[136] Over the past three years the Casework Committee has considered 150 applications and has granted assistance in 36 cases.[137]

The decision of the NIHRC to include an expansive definition of social and economic rights in the bill of rights did not resolve other controversies over the wording of the document. One particularly troublesome dilemma focused on the use of the term *minorities* or *particular communities*. Who had claims to rights? Minorities or communities? In the September 2001 draft, the word *minority* in the draft bill of rights was systematically replaced by *community*.[138] According to the NIHRC, the term *community* was to refer to "both main communities" and the use of the word *community* was meant to give the minority of the people of Northern Ireland the same rights as the majority.[139] The NIHRC sought to justify its decision to use this language with reference to oral advice it received from the OSCE high commissioner on national minorities and on a liberal commitment to recognizing each individual's rights without requiring citizens to assert either Protestant or Catholic communal identity.[140]

The communities/minorities debate called into question the liberal foundations of the Good Friday Agreement. Leading human rights lawyer Stephen Livingstone voiced the opinion of many commissioners when he asserted that the commitment to liberal individualism "places government under a duty to afford the same treatment to powerful majorities as to endangered minorities."[141] Livingstone's supporters emphasized that protecting the cultural rights of a minority susceptible to assimilation requires a different approach than that of protecting the cultural rights of the mainstream community.[142] There was also concern that the replacement of the word *minorities* with *communities* could in fact undermine the sophisticated monitoring requirement of Northern Ireland's fair employment legislation and even the consociational mechanism at the heart of the newly established Assembly.[143] In order to function, consociationalism required Assembly members to identify as either Nationalist or Unionist. An overemphasis on communities might frustrate this scheme.

The new wording also frustrated people living in Northern Ireland who did not belong to either the Catholic or Protestant communities. Patrick Yu, the sole commissioner representing these minority groups, spent weeks trying to explain the devastating impact of what he viewed as enshrining the division of Northern Ireland into two main communities.[144] "When they say 'everyone is equal,' they mean Catholics and Protestants," Commissioner Yu exclaimed, "Where is *our* equality?"[145] Although the language of the draft bill of rights would eventually change back to include mention of minorities, the problem proved to be more than the choice of wording. Concerned members of ethnic minority groups felt as though their concerns were unheard. Gaining their trust and support would prove to be an uphill battle. Even after he left the commission and resumed his post as executive director of the Northern Ireland Council for Ethnic Minorities, Yu would continue to press for changes in the draft bill of rights and participated in other NIHRC activities that would rid the bill of the use of the word *communities* and reorient it toward the rights of minorities.[146] Overall, however, the term *community* has won out over *minority* in the advocacy of the NIHRC.

Assessment

The NIHRC faces demands unique to a deeply divided society that has recently emerged from violent ethnic conflict. The NIHRC is expected to contribute to advancing respect for conflict resolution efforts and to promote the consolidation of peace in the jurisdiction. A human rights institution, operating in an independent and impartial manner, guided by international human rights standards, can serve to build legitimacy on both sides of the ethnic divide for human rights. But the price of justice may be new and renewed conflict. The NIHRC, by advancing the claims of rights holders against duty bearers, can be seen as taking sides in old conflicts and creating new sources of communal tension. Somehow, the NIHRC must straddle the responsibility of both advancing peace and promoting justice, discovering the best route for addressing the inevitable conflicts that arise as it attempts to do its job.

There is tension between the international narrative of human rights as universal and local Northern Ireland perceptions of human rights as privileging one community over another—a perception exacerbated by the motivations for establishing the NIHRC. The sophisticated human rights infrastructure that emerged from the Good Friday Agreement was the outcome of bargaining and compromise.[147] This has deeply affected the work of the NIHRC, as illustrated by the discussion of constraints on the commission. When the NIHRC attempted to address the human rights concerns at the heart of the Northern Ireland conflict, the result was deep divisions within the NIHRC and trenchant criticism from outside actors. Arguably, the NIHRC has scored its greatest success by promoting the protection of rights of groups that transcend the rigid Catholic-Protestant divide, taking on issues of concern to both communities, such as the rights of older people,[148] women,[149] youth,[150] and people with mental disabilities.[151]

Recognizing the need to pursue issues beyond conflict divisions requires good political judgment on the part of NIHRC personnel and leadership. Perceptions of human rights as owned by one particular community will persist until the NIHRC proves the relevance of human rights for all of Northern Ireland's citizens. Although the NIHRC's work on social and economic rights has not garnered universal support, divisions have not fallen along traditional ethnic cleavages. This suggests that social and economic rights offer an important opportunity for the NIHRC's role in a new political dispensation in Northern Ireland.

Members of the voluntary sector and of the NIHRC staff firmly believe in social and economic rights as issues that cut across sectoral divides and that could potentially be addressed before the civil and political rights matters that are more likely to be a source of conflagration. Certainly many social and economic issues are equally explosive as civil and political rights, and indeed, attempts to address social and economic wrongs have often set off new civil and political wrongs (e.g., the Holy Cross case). Nonetheless, the general impression in Northern Ireland is supportive of efforts to keep social and economic issues on the political burner as cutting across human rights concerns. More concerted attempts to link the NIHRC's local activities to international standards—standards that are external both to Northern Ireland and to Northern Ireland's divisions—offer an important means to convince all local constituents and the government of the value of social and economic rights.

The NIHRC, however, continues to struggle with balancing its need to engage with government and civil society while maintaining independence. Some of the difficulties are within its control. For example, the NIHRC could do more to reach out to and include community activists in its work. Community activists report feeling either used or ignored by the NIHRC.[152] Other difficulties have been beyond the immediate control of the NIHRC. For example, the NIHRC did not initially obtain the specific power of investigation,[153] including the express power to obtain documents and to subpoena witnesses. Without the power to compel government to produce documents, the commission did not have the ability to investigate claims on an independent basis. Indeed, on several occasions, the government sought to block investigations, thus compelling the NIHRC to go through the costly and time-consuming process of judicial review.[154] Other U.K. statutory organizations have this power, such as the Ombudsman, the Commission for Racial Equality, and the Equality Commission for Northern Ireland (ECNI).[155] In December 2004 the British government decided in principle that the NIHRC should be granted the right of access to places of detention, but the NIHRC reported as late as October 2006 that its investigatory powers were still restricted in practice. The British government responded in the form of a second consultation report, in which it stated that the NIHRC would be given extra investigatory powers. The recent St. Andrews Agreement contained a commitment to bring forward legislation in the subsequent parliamentary session to give these additional powers to the NIHRC. This commitment was discharged through the Justice and Security (Northern Ireland) Act of 2007,[156] which supplemented the NIHRC's powers in three important respects. The NIHRC now has powers to require the provision of information or of a document or for a person to give oral evidence, to access places of detention, and to institute judicial proceedings in the NIHRC's own right, and when doing so, to rely on the ECHR. This will mean that the NIHRC can bring test cases without the need for a victim to do so personally, thus opening the door for more creative litigation.

Human rights institutions established in the aftermath of violent conflict will, irrespective of the institution's mandate and powers, face demands to address past human rights violations. Therefore, rather than acting as a forward-looking institution set on meeting contemporary human rights demands, the NHRI can become a proxy for larger unresolved political questions that lie at the heart of the violent conflict. Rather than looking to a future in which human rights of all people are vindicated, the NHRI thus faces the danger of being rendered ineffective as a result of human rights abuses in the recent past.

Chapter 4

Counting in Threes

The Human Rights Ombudsmen in Bosnia-Herzegovina

L IKE NORTHERN IRELAND, the national human rights mechanisms established to address domestic human rights matters in Bosnia-Herzegovina (or just Bosnia) are very much a response to the civil conflict and to the highly polarized society the violence created. And like Northern Ireland, they are an attempt to make international human rights norms matter in communities that are eager to put the conflict of the past behind them and move into a more peaceful and just future. The Bosnia-Herzegovina scenario, however, is complicated by the complexity of the postwar governance plan. It is further challenged by the incredible lengths to which third-party states have gone to exercise control over the postwar Bosnian political and legal system and economy and the difficulties local leaders have had in wresting control back from their international benefactors. The extent of internationalization of Bosnia-Herzegovina in the aftermath of the conflict is staggering; although international organizations play a role in Northern Ireland, the scope of involvement does not begin to match that in Bosnia-Herzegovina. In Bosnia-Herzegovina, the international powers that brokered the peace plan for Bosnia-Herzegovina were (and in many cases remain) in full control of the initial decision making over the type of national human rights mechanisms to use, the processes they would follow, and the manner in which they would interact. The international actors even gave themselves central roles as participants in many national human rights endeavors in Bosnia-Herzegovina, deciding when and how they should turn the reins over to local actors.

When violent conflict was still raging in Bosnia-Herzegovina, international negotiators sought to end the bloodshed through the creation of a unique consociational governance structure designed to address the concerns of the three dominant ethnic groups (Serbs, Croats, and Muslims). In an effort to dissolve ethnic tensions, an ombudsman office was created at the state level along with two substate ombudsman institutions at the national level. Today, however, the most compelling issue that preoccupies human rights commissioners in Bosnia-Herzegovina is the same issue that predominates the larger political sphere: how to reverse this process and strengthen the central state institution while allowing the power of the substate entities to lessen.

The Council of Europe and the European Union have pressured the Bosnia and Herzegovina governments to agree to consolidate all three ombudsman's offices into one. The merger decision is intensely personal for the affected commissioners and staff, because the process will necessarily entail cutting positions and laying off staff. It is also incredibly political because any change will affect concentrations of power and control over the domestic human rights agenda. From a purely logistical perspective, a merger of ombudsman institutions in Bosnia-Herzegovina will be a complex balancing act. To be successful, the merger will need to preserve the best ideas and practices from the old institutions while also championing fresh ideas about how best to implement international human rights at the domestic level.

In the following examination of what could loosely be considered the Bosnian system of NHRIs, I provide insight into the difficulties with internationally driven NHRIs, especially those that may be institutionalized in the aftermath of violent conflict or political transitions.

Political Context

In the Socialist Federal Republic of Yugoslavia, Bosnia-Herzegovina was one of six federal units. Enjoying a reputation as a place where people of all ethnonational backgrounds could live freely, Bosnia-Herzegovina was one of the most ethnically and religiously diverse areas of socialist Yugoslavia.[1] Bosnia-Herzegovina's road to international recognition began in 1991, when the federal unit declared itself independent. Other units of then Yugoslavia had already begun asserting their desire for independence, and struggles for control had intensified among political factions, with leaders in Belgrade and Zagreb squaring off over who should capture the spoils in Bosnia and Herzegovina. Although many ethnic Serbs and ethnic Croats fled to Croatia or Serbia, many Bosnians of all ethnonational groups remained behind to defend their land.

The war in Bosnia officially began with the siege of Sarajevo by ethnic Serb forces, the longest siege in the history of modern warfare, lasting from April 5, 1992, to February 29, 1996.[2] The severe fighting led to 102,000 civilian deaths[3] and the uprooting of more than 1 million people from their homes.[4] Wartime abuses included torture,[5] rape,[6] and other forms of heinous mistreatment in detention as well as the widespread destruction of places of worship and cultural monuments, such as archives and libraries.[7] The war finally came to an end when internationally accepted representatives[8] of the warring parties reached agreement on a plan that divided up the country according to the battle lines and population shifts achieved through forced displacement.[9] Initialed in November 1995 in Dayton, Ohio, and signed in Paris one month later, the Dayton Agreement would become the initial blueprint for the future of Bosnia and Herzegovina.[10]

Government in Triplicate

Under the Dayton Agreement, the magic number was three, as the document repeatedly attempted to create government institutions in triplicate to accommodate the needs of the three dominant ethnic groups: Serbs, Croats, and Bosniaks (ethnic Muslims). The three structures responsible for governance in Bosnia-Herzegovina during the postwar period were (1) a central government known as the State of Bosnia-Herzegovina (or just Bosnia-Herzegovina); (2) a substate entity known as the Federation of Bosnia-Herzegovina for the predominantly Bosniak/Croat areas in the central and western parts of the country; and (3) a substate entity known as Republika Srpska, for the predominantly ethnic Serb areas bordering Serbia, which occupied the north, east, and southeast portions of Bosnia-Herzegovina in the shape of a crescent.[11]

On paper, the Dayton model appeared to champion equality. Proponents of the plan asserted that it went a long way to guarantee the representation and participation of all three major ethnic groups. They also viewed the near-identical physical dimensions of the two entities as a sign of success. The Federation of Bosnia-Herzegovina covered 51 percent of Bosnia-Herzegovina's total area, and Republika Srpska covered 49 percent. Critics of Dayton, however, pointed to the same statistics as a negative sign. They pointed out that in prewar times, although some areas were populated largely by one ethnic group or another, all the major ethnonational groups in Bosnia were spread throughout the country.[12] The new, sharp ethnic concentrations in postwar times—with ethnic Serbs gathered mainly in Republika Srpska and Croats and Bosniaks living mainly in the Federation—were the results of a brutal war in which civilians were the main targets and population displacement was a main goal.[13] Many critics of the Dayton plan objected to the artificial division on pragmatic grounds, contending that it would not work,[14] or on moral grounds, warning that it would set a bad example for the rest of the world by rewarding aggression and ethnic cleansing.[15]

The new constitution for the State of Bosnia-Herzegovina (included as Annex 4 to the Dayton Agreement) proved to be another source of great disappointment for all who had hoped that a strong Bosnian state would emerge from the peace negotiations. In an effort to come up with a text to which all parties would agree, the American negotiator in Dayton "proposed an extremely decentralized governmental structure creating hardly any effective central powers."[16] Most troublesome to the European negotiators, "the constitution did not even envision the combination of the entities' military forces."[17]

The central State of Bosnia-Herzegovina was in many ways an exaggerated example of consociationalism, as it guaranteed a share of power to each of the country's three major groups: ethnic Serbs, ethnic Croats, and ethnic Muslims (Bosniaks) in each level of government.[18] The State of Bosnia-Herzegovina was to be governed by a Parliamentary Assembly (divided into a House of Representatives and a House of Peoples), a rotating tripartite presidency (with one member from each of the constituent peoples— Bosniak, Croat, and Serb), and a Council of Ministers with nine ministries. The chair of the presidency of Bosnia-Herzegovina was to rotate among three members (Bosniak, Croat, and Serb), with each elected as the chair for an eight-month term within their four-year term as a member. Under the highly participatory structure, the three members of the presidency were to be elected directly by the people (Federation votes for the Bosniak/Croat, Republika Srpska for the Serb).[19]

The political gyrations of the central Bosnia-Herzegovina government were but a distraction from the real power center, located within the two ethnically based entities, which also followed their own form of counting in threes. The Federation of Bosnia-Herzegovina (the Bosniak-Croat entity) was to promote democratic governance through the creation of three levels of governance, each with its own mechanisms for participation. At the entity level, political affairs were to be conducted through the two-house parliament (House of Representatives and House of Peoples), a president, two vice presidents, and a government under a prime minister. At the canton level, the power to adopt cantonal laws was given to each of the ten assemblies, in each of the ten cantons. Finally, governance was to occur at the municipal level, with each municipality having its own municipal council and administrative structures.[20]

Unlike the Federation, Republika Srpska (the Serb entity) was in fact highly centralized, although on paper it also appeared to be quite complex.[21] Republika Srpska was established without cantons but with a National Assembly, a Council of Peoples, a president, two vice presidents, and a government under a prime minister. All the municipalities were have their own assemblies and administrative structures. There were three constitutional courts, one at the state level and one in each entity.

To confuse matters further, in addition to separate canton and municipal governments, the Dayton Agreement recognized "special" entities, the most notable of which is the Brčko District.[22] Created in 2000, this district was formed as an autonomous entity within Bosnia-Herzegovina, created from part of the territory of both Bosnian entities. The Brčko District is now a shared territory that belongs to both entities. This means that it officially belongs to both but is governed by neither and functions under a decentralized system of local government.[23]

One overarching assumption of the Dayton architects was that decentralization of power and devolution of power, down to the entities and further down to the cantons and municipalities, would break up ethnic alliances and encourage cross-ethnic cooperation.[24] They could not have been more wrong. "All the incentives were for the leaders of the three national groups to build three different polities and to ignore or weaken the central state."[25] With Dayton enthusiasts standing by nodding approvingly, nationalists seized the opportunity to draw, and in some cases redraw, ethnic lines of power and control.[26] Rather than countering rule by ethnicity, the Dayton Peace Accords enshrined it by creating a system in which each of the main constituent nations—Serb, Croat, and Bosniak—were to have their own electoral college, their own candidates, and their own voters. Under this scheme, three main political parties (one for each ethnonational group) have wielded significant political power at all levels of government. The Serb Democratic Party (SDS) dominates Republika Srpska, the Party of Democratic Action (SDA) is the main Bosniak nationalist party, and the Croatian Democratic Union of Bosnia and Herzegovina (HDZ) represents Croat areas. However, other parties have gained in popularity.

The Challenge of Studying Bosnian Institutions

The study of Bosnian institutions presents many challenges. First, it can be quite jarring for those accustomed to linear, rational thinking and the continual usage of clear analytical terms. Steven Austermiller, the former country director for the American Bar Association/Central European and Eurasian Law Initiative (ABA/CEELI) in Bosnia-Herzegovina, succinctly explained the confusion over political terminology.

> Under the Dayton Accords, [t]he term "State" is used in BiH [Bosnia-Herzegovina] to describe something national or federal. For instance, the "State Court," the "State Constitution," and the "State Presidency" all refer to the national BiH institutions. In contrast, the Republika Srpska and the Federation of Bosnia and Herzegovina institutions represent the constituent entities, which in U.S. parlance might be called "states."[27]

Compounding the terminology muddle is the nonlinear political chronology. Ordinarily, countries are created first and later carved into smaller substate units. In the case of Bosnia-Herzegovina, however, the Federation of Bosnia-Herzegovina (the substate dominated by Croats and Bosniaks) was created in 1994, before the Dayton Accords. Thus the constitution governing the Federation predates the constitution governing the State of Bosnia-Herzegovina. Also, it appears that an exception exists for every rule, which only further confuses the narrative. The central Bosnia-Herzegovina state has always operated as a thin shell over the two ethnically based entities, but for a period of time in the 1990s, governing power was in fact being exercised by a third entity. With the support of one of the guarantors of the Dayton Accords, Franjo Tudjman (then Croatia's president), a parastate known as Hercog-Bosna claimed the loyalty of nationalist Serbs. Hercog-Bosna, which sought unification with Croatia, ultimately failed, but for a time, as Bosnia analyst Tom Gallagher observes, "there was really a third entity which the UN was slow to grapple with."[28]

Analysis of the structure of Bosnian governance also must suspend traditional beliefs and approaches to the analysis of power in state governance. Ironically, the weakest of the three units was the structure ordinarily presumed strongest: the central government. At the same time, the strongest political force was not even an official democratic political structure: the UN Office of the High Representative (OHR). In the transition period, the security function of the state was to be performed by NATO troops, and the civilian implementation of the Dayton Agreement was to be undertaken by the OHR.[29]

The UN high representative has enjoyed significant power over Bosnia-Herzegovina, including the power "to remove from office public officials who violate legal commitments and the Dayton Peace Agreement, and to impose laws as he sees fit if Bosnia and Herzegovina's legislative bodies fail to do so."[30] The extensive powers of the high representative have been sharply criticized, both within and outside Bosnia-Herzegovina. In 2005, an authoritative report of the European Commission for Democracy Through Law (Venice Commission) concluded that the need for international bodies to exercise wide powers had existed in the early period following the conclusion of the 1995 Dayton Agreement but that the longer such an arrangement stayed in place, the more it risked becoming incompatible with Council of Europe human rights standards. Over time, the exact composition of the international forces changed, with the United Nations handing over much of its power in Bosnia-Herzegovina to the European Union (EU) and with international forces changing their colors several times. However, outside oversight and control over the Dayton architecture remained great. Exactly who would be involved in that effort is still open to question, as the slate of international actors participating in Bosnian affairs continues to shift.

The final difficulty with the study of Bosnian institutions is the outside intervener factor. International officials have flocked to Bosnia-Herzegovina, where they enjoy high salaries (10 and even 100 times as much as their local peers), low supervision from the central office, and excellent standards of living (distorting the housing market). Although some of the international officials have worked for NGOs, others were directly employed by Bosnian institutions, including several created by the Dayton Accords, such as the Constitutional Court, the Central Bank, the Ombudsman, and the Human Rights Chamber (see later discussion). Even though the Dayton Accords originally envisioned that international participation in governance would diminish over time, in many cases the practice continues. Florian Bieber, a leading Balkan scholar, explains why these individuals wield great power.

> The international judges of the Constitutional Court, the governor of the Central Bank and most other international officials are not representatives of international organizations, but merely appointed by them (the European Court of Human Rights, the Council of Europe and the IMF) respectively. As such, they become "Bosnian Actors," with the primary example of not being members of one of the three ethnic groups and thus resembling neutral arbiters and mediators within these institutions.[31]

Tracking institutional developments in Bosnia is tricky, because so much depends on the character and ability of the individual international officials holding key posts in Bosnian institutions. Although the person appointed to be high commissioner has generally been a person of great stature and ability, the same cannot be said for his staff and for the staff of the International Police Force (ITPF) and other internationally staffed organizations involved in the reconstruction. In general, states did not send their best officers on staff to work at the OHR (the "secondees"). On the contrary, the typical profile for a secondee was that of an energetic but directionless junior-level official or an experienced but weary official on the verge of retirement.[32] The reputation of international staffing at the ITPF fared even worse. Evidence points to some international staff members being involved in corrupt practices, including the illegal passing of classified information,[33] involvement in the trafficking of women (as patrons of trafficked women or as purchasers of trafficked women and their passports),[34] and the black market sale of goods.[35] Certainly many of the ITPF international staffers, and indeed most international officials in all posts, performed their jobs admirably and with good intentions. The evidence against the few engaged in criminal activity, however, proved significant enough to embitter the Bosnian populace against what they increasingly sensed was an occupation.

Economic Context

In prewar Yugoslavia, Bosnia-Herzegovina was a republic with a relatively low level of development, sharing more in common with Montenegro and Macedonia than the more prosperous republics of Slovenia, Croatia, and Serbia (especially Vojvodina). Wages in Bosnia-Herzegovina at that time were only 16.3 percent of the Yugoslav average. Nonetheless, before the most recent Balkan wars, Bosnia-Herzegovina was an egalitarian society in which nearly everyone enjoyed a good standard of living. War changed everything. Bosnia's infrastructure was destroyed, its people impoverished, and its egalitarian values demolished. Balkan expert Florian Bieber explains that during the war "opportunities arose for the rapid emergence of a new economic elite, which mostly relied on criminal activities or the grey market for large profit margin."[36] The new war economy was built on:

(a) Trade with goods plundered during the campaign of ethnic cleansing; (b) smuggling on the basis of war-time isolation of parts of Bosnia . . . ; (c) weapon trading; and the control of public services and companies.[37]

The end of the war meant the end to most of these activities, but the operational networks remained and continued to control large parts of the postwar reconstruction.[38] Although the middle class in Bosnia almost disappeared and the number of unemployed and poor grew exponentially, those at the very top of the criminal syndicates grew even richer.[39] Even the voucher system of privatization, which was intended to promote equitable distribution of resources, was hijacked by the profiteers, notes Balkan specialist Paula Pickering: "Nationalists saw to it that the voucher process was turned into 'ethnic privatization' in which wealthy individuals of the majority group with strong connections to the nationalist parties gained control of the most productive companies."[40]

In addition to the need to address the legacy and continuing impact of war profiteers, Bosnia-Herzegovina has faced the dual problem of rebuilding a war-torn country and introducing market reforms to its former centrally planned economy. Much of the production capacity has been restored, but the Bosnian economy still faces considerable difficulties. The war caused a dramatic change in the Bosnian economy. The destructive impact of the war on the economy led to a 75 percent drop in GDP,[41] caused production to plummet by 80 percent from 1992 to 1995, and caused unemployment to soar.[42] More than 2 million people—nearly half the prewar population—became refugees, either abroad or internally.[43] Since the Dayton Agreement of 1995 took effect, trade has increased in Croat areas and significant growth has begun in Muslim areas. Reconstruction programs initiated by the international community have financed the construction of infrastructure and have provided loans to the manufacturing sector.[44]

External aid in Bosnia-Herzegovina has been "colossal relative to the size of the country."[45] Between 1995 and 1999, foreign aid amounted to US$5 billion. By 2003, the inflow of international reconstruction aid had passed US$14 billion, resulting in Bosnia-Herzegovina's economy experiencing significant growth in the first postwar years. Although this aid caused growth rates to increase to 30 percent as of 2003, that rate has stabilized to around 6 percent.[46] Actual GDP growth by 2003 had reached half its prewar level.[47] Much of this growth, however, was wasted or lost as a result of corruption and mismanagement. The country was also so poor that even rapid rates of growth had little impact. In an economic report published in 2001, Bosnia-Herzegovina was ranked last—fifty-ninth of the fifty-nine countries studied—in terms of competitiveness, based on such criteria as infrastructure, government, finance, and civil institutions.[48]

Progress on structural reforms has been uneven. The banking sector has been largely privatized and modernized, and other financial sector reforms have been well advanced. Yet privatization of other state-owned companies has occurred at a slow pace, and the private sector's contribution to GDP is still lower than in most other countries in the broader region.[49] The private sector accounts for only 35 percent of the economy.[50] Early attempts at privatization have resulted in diluted ownership and weak governance. Impressive output expansion notwithstanding, the economy has yet to reach its prewar level. Poverty levels are close to 18 percent, and a further 30 percent of all citizens are in danger of falling into poverty in the event of an income shock.[51]

The poor economy frustrates the government's attempts to generate the necessary financial resources for funding even a basic system of social services and security. The situation is aggravated by the poor health conditions in Bosnia-Herzegovina and the increasing number of people becoming dependent on public support as a consequence of war. Although Bosnia-Herzegovina has made substantive progress in reconstructing and improving its health sector, the burden of disease in the country remains high. Noncommunicable diseases dominate the epidemiological profile, with 50 percent of deaths attributed to cardiovascular disorders and about 20 percent to cancer.[52] The rate of heart attacks and similar diseases (160 per 100,000) in Bosnia-Herzegovina is the highest in southeast Europe.[53] Physical injuries and posttraumatic stress disorders from the war and neonatal and maternal health problems are still a problem.[54] Road accidents, injuries (including from land mines), and suicides are at high levels and are increasing.[55]

Social ills in Bosnia-Herzegovina are more likely to be addressed by the voluntary sector than by the weak government structures. More than 1,300 NGOs have been registered in Bosnia-Herzegovina,[56] and many voluntary associations exist without formal registration as NGOs, including a diversity of religious and faith-based associations.[57] However, the proliferation of NGOs should not be automatically interpreted as a sign of a healthy democracy with a vibrant civil society component. The voluntary sector in Bosnia-Herzegovina is still very much influenced by the broader consequences of the war and the intensive international involvement, which skews the nature of projects undertaken. As one insightful study observes, "Due in part to the economic situation, the establishment of many early post-war NGOs was motivated more by a need for employment than a commitment to a particular mission."[58] Today many NGO staff are simply trying to hang on to their jobs. As the level of donor support continues to decrease on an annual basis, many organizations are having difficulties with organizational and financial sustainability.

Human Rights Context

The legacy of the 1992–1995 war in Bosnia-Herzegovina continues to define much of the country's key human rights challenges today, with war crimes accountability and the rights of former refugees and displaced people continuing to be the most pressing concerns, along with continuing reports of discrimination based on ethnic lines in all public and private spheres of activity. Although some strides have been made to improve the human rights conditions in the country, independent human rights organizations such as Human Rights Watch and the United Nations High Commission for Refugees (UNHCR) continue to view the current trends of refugee return and reintegration of displaced people critically. According to these organizations, the annual number of refugees and displaced individuals returning to their homes continues to decline. The UNHCR registered 2,946 such returns by July 31, 2006, compared to 5,059 by the same point in 2005.[59] About half of the more than 2 million people displaced during the war have registered to return to their prewar homes, with 450,000 of them returning to areas where they now constitute an ethnic minority. But the actual numbers of returns are much smaller; a 2005 field study by the Bosnian Helsinki Committee for Human Rights indicated that fewer than half of those registered as returnees actually live in their prewar places of residence.[60]

The situation for those returning to areas where they now constitute a minority remains difficult, with frequent reports of harassment and public and private sector employment discrimination. Other obstacles include insufficient funds to reconstruct destroyed properties and lack of access to social and medical benefits.[61] According to the 2006 U.S. State Department country report on human rights conditions in Bosnia, the Bosnian government's human rights record remains poor. Among the continuing human rights problems, the report documents cases of physical abuse by police officials; overcrowding and poor conditions in prisons; improper influence on the judiciary by nationalist elements, political parties, and the executive branch; pressure and harassment of the media by authorities and dominant political parties; and discrimination against women, ethnic minorities, people with disabilities, and sexual minorities.[62]

Bosnia-Herzegovina is a member of the International Covenant on Economic, Social, and Cultural Rights (ICESCR) and submits to its regular reporting process. To date, the ombudsman offices have had little involvement in the reporting process, although their decisions and special reports are a source of information. The 2005 submission of Bosnia-Herzegovina to the Committee on Economic, Social, and Cultural Rights (CESCR) was praised by the CESCR for its thorough nature and for including the input of NGOs in the drafting process.[63] Nonetheless, even as the CESCR recognized that substantial progress was being made in several areas for better rights promotion, it urged Bosnia-Herzegovina to continue to address ongoing problems with discrimination and the denial of rights; the CESCR notes that these problems continue to be detrimental to Bosnia's ability to move toward a future that is positive for all its residents.

Discrimination in employment during the 1992–1995 war as well as in the postwar period has been endemic and has affected large sectors of the Bosnia-Herzegovina workforce. Workers in all areas of Bosnia-Herzegovina and from all ethnic communities have been victims of discrimination regarding access to employment. However, such discrimination has been more widespread and systematic in certain areas under Bosnian Serb and Bosnian Croat control, where campaigns of ethnic cleansing were most aggressively carried out. The groups most affected by workplace discrimination are Roma and displaced people returning to areas in which they are a minority.[64]

The labor laws of both the Federation of Bosnia-Herzegovina and Republika Srpska incorporate antidiscrimination provisions. Both entities have also introduced provisions into their labor legislation to address the problem of the large number of workers who had been either dismissed or put on waiting lists during the war (many, if not most, on account of their ethnicity). However, these provisions have proved to be wholly inadequate and have failed to provide an effective remedy to workers affected by discriminatory dismissal or transfer to waiting lists.[65]

Three factors hinder any attempts to address discrimination and other human wrongs and to promote a more positive agenda of human rights. First, the failure to arrest many war criminals and to offer the same degree of protection to all returning refugees indicates complacency toward a climate of impunity being established and undermines faith in the state's responsibility to protect and promote human rights for all. Furthermore, selective enforcement promotes the general attitude that human rights are simply political tools that can be used selectively and instrumentally. Second, living conditions for many people remain poor, and the state appears to be unable to address their main economic concerns. The idea of human rights then appears empty, and people fall into despair. Third, human rights are still viewed skeptically, as "imposed rights," as an "alien and artificial creation," and as the agenda of outsiders.[66] Many Bosnians are well versed in human rights, and many have started their own rights initiatives; however, the first human rights projects were initiated by international organizations, and international officials are still able to use their purse strings to control which projects are funded and how they are evaluated.[67]

Ombudsman Offices

It is within this highly divisive political context—where human rights demands fall sharply within the needs of a postconflict society, in the context of a state both unwilling and at many times unable to protect and promote human rights—that the Bosnian human rights institutions evolved. Indeed, the NHRI situation in Bosnia-Herzegovina has had a complex genesis.[68] Just as the political terrain of Bosnia-Herzegovina is divided into threes, so is the NHRI. The two-plus-one structure of Bosnia-Herzegovina (two entities plus one "thin roof" of a weak central state) is mirrored in the human rights structure, with each entity and the central state having its own ombudsman office. I discuss the three human rights ombudsman offices in the order in which they were established: the Federation ombudsman, the Republic of Bosnia-Herzegovina ombudsman, and then the Republika Srpska ombudsman.

The Three Ombudsmen

The Federation Ombudsman   The Ombudsman's Office for the Federation of Bosnia and Herzegovina (the Bosniak/Croat entity) was established even before the war had ended (see Appendix 2 for mandate excerpts). In 1994, while the conflict in Bosnia was ongoing, the Bosniak and Croat governments agreed on the Constitution of the Federation of Bosnia and Herzegovina.[69] The constitution contained human rights guarantees, with an annex incorporating twenty-one human rights treaties, and created three Federation ombudsmen to uphold these rights.[70] Appointed by the Federation legislature, the ombudsmen were given the responsibility to protect human dignity, rights, and liberties contained in the Federation constitution (including the annexed treaties) and cantonal constitutions, and, "in particular, they shall act to reverse the consequences of the violations of these rights and liberties and especially of ethnic cleansing."[71] The ombudsmen were to act individually and have jurisdiction over all Federation, cantonal, and municipal institutions and "any institution or person by whom human dignity, rights, or liberties may be negated, including by accomplishing ethnic cleansing or preserving its effects."[72] They had the power to investigate, report, and initiate and intervene in court proceedings, including in the Federation Human Rights Court.[73]

International agencies played a key role in the establishment and operation of the Federation Ombudsman's Office. Before the implementation of the constitution, the first Federation ombudsmen were appointed by the Organization for Security and Cooperation in Europe (OSCE) at the end of 1994, and they commenced activities on January 20, 1995.[74] The first Human Rights Ombudsman was appointed by the chairman-in-office of the OSCE; nationals of Bosnia-Herzegovina and of neighboring states could not be appointed in these early years.[75] Because the appointees were to be selected by an international body and not by the domestic legislature or executive, they were dubbed "internal international actors."[76] In general, parties on all sides of the conflict supported the strong role played by international officials. As one advocate remarked, "We [the parties] could not trust each other . . . so the substantial role played [by international actors] was welcome."[77] Enes Hašić, the human rights commissioner in Republika Srpska, remembered fondly the days during which his commission was run by international officials, describing a time of greater fiscal resources, improved efficiency, and enhanced public acceptance.[78]

All government bodies were obliged to provide the Ombudsman's Office with preferential assistance. "The ability to compel government to comply [was] absolutely necessary, not only from the view of getting the information, but because it showed the public that the Ombudsman is separate from the government," explained Bosnia-Herzegovina human rights legal officer Boris Topić.[79] The ombudsman could demand at any time any document he or she deemed necessary for an investigation, including those classified as confidential or secret in accordance with law. Any citizen with a legitimate claim could submit a complaint to the ombudsman without any restriction. Nationality, citizenship, residence, gender, minority, ethnicity, religion, legal incapability, imprisonment for any reason, and, in general terms, a special relationship with, or dependence on, a government department could not be used to restrict the right to lodge a complaint with the ombudsman. If an official of a government body were to impede an investigation, the ombudsman could institute disciplinary proceedings against the official or bring the case before a criminal court in accordance with the Ombudsman Law. The ombudsman's powers to investigate included complaints concerning the poor functioning of the judicial system and the poor administration of an individual court case as well as violations of rights and freedoms allegedly committed by administrative authorities.

The State of Bosnia-Herzegovina   Annex 6 of the Dayton Agreement (also known as the Agreement on Human Rights) established the Human Rights Commission for the state of Bosnia-Herzegovina, which was composed of two bodies: the Ombudsman's Office (a statewide office) and the Human Rights Chamber. Annex 6 envisioned that five years after entry into force of the agreement, responsibility for the Human Rights Commission would be transferred to the institutions of Bosnia-Herzegovina.[80]

According to the Dayton Agreement, the Bosnia-Herzegovina Human Rights Ombudsman was to operate as an independent public institution with jurisdiction over civil complaints about violations of human rights guaranteed by the Bosnia-Herzegovina constitution. The ombudsman could act either on the receipt of a complaint or on his or her own initiative.[81] If the complaint was not settled informally, the ombudsman would proceed with the investigation and report its conclusion.[82] If the recipient did not comply with the ombudsman's recommendations within a specified period of time, the report was to be forwarded to the OSCE high representative and the presidency of the relevant government for further action.

The Bosnia-Herzegovina ombudsman was also granted the authority to make recommendations to a government body with a view to the adoption of new measures, including suggesting amendments to the criteria used. If the ombudsman were to find that the manner in which a rule was implemented led to inequitable results, he or she could address to the competent government authority any recommendation capable of leading to a fair solution to the situation of the affected individual, including payment of damages. The government body was obliged to inform the ombudsman in writing of the effect given to the recommendations within a period indicated by the ombudsman.[83]

Initially, the Bosnia-Herzegovina ombudsman would also refer certain cases to the Human Rights Chamber for Bosnia and Herzegovina, a specialized adjudicative body.[84] The Human Rights Ombudsman was also granted the Ombudsman's Office entitlement to intervene in any proceedings before the Chamber as a party or as an amica curiae in all other cases going to the Chamber.[85] And from 1996 to 2003, the Chamber played a crucial role in the implementation of international human rights law, offering interim protection and remedies to victims of discrimination.

The Chamber's jurisdiction was limited to "applications concerning such human rights violations directly from any Party to Annex 6, or from any person, non-governmental organization or group of individuals claiming to be the victim of a violation by any Party or acting on behalf of alleged victims who are deceased or missing."[86] The Chamber also had jurisdiction over matters that fell within the responsibility of one of the parties to Annex 6 and that occurred or continued after the entry into force of the Dayton Agreement.[87] Priority was given to exceptionally grave or systematic violations as well as to complaints founded on alleged discrimination on prohibited grounds.

The professionalism of the Chamber quickly won the respect of lawyers and government officials. "For once we had an institution that actually could act with authority on human rights," said Dino Abazović, director of the Center for Human Rights at the University of Sarajevo.[88] Although Abazović remained critical of many aspects of the Chamber's performance, he still viewed it as a significant improvement. "Unlike the Ombudsman's offices, the Chamber's decisions had real authority . . . they [the respondent Parties] just couldn't ignore them," said Srđan Dizdarević, president of the Helsinki Committee for Human Rights in Bosnia.[89] Decisions of the Chamber were forwarded to the international organizations charged with monitoring their implementation, the OHR and the OSCE.

Aggrieved citizens soon learned that the major difference between filing a claim with the Ombudsman's Office and the Chamber was that the ombudsman's procedure would be lengthy and the resulting decision would be advisory and that the Chamber would act more quickly and produce a binding decision. It made more sense for citizens to bypass the Ombudsman's Office and file their claim directly with the Chamber, and this is exactly what they did. "The Human Rights Commission thus found itself operating as two separate institutions, not as one single national human rights institution," explains Miroslav Zivanovic, the head librarian at the Human Rights Center, University of Sarajevo.[90] In 2000, the OHR legalized this "*de facto* division" by imposing a law that transformed the former Ombudsman's Office into a national institution at the state level.[91] Hence the official birth of the state Ombudsman's Office was a cesarean; it was pulled out of the practice of the Federation-level Ombudsman's Office.[92]

The decision of international agencies to create an ombudsman's office at the state level proved far less controversial than their decision to permit the mandate for the Chamber to expire. "It was one of the only things that were working. Why would you want to dismantle it?" exclaimed Boris Topic, a legal officer at the Institution of the Human Rights Ombudsman of Bosnia and Herzegovina.[93] "This [the Chamber] was the only thing that has a positive public image," said Topić's colleague, Sladana Marić, adding "Taking it away sent a bad signal on human rights [i.e., that human rights could be easily manipulated.]"[94] "Maybe it was just incompetence," suggested Ahmed Zilic, a member of the Advisor Committee for the Council of Europe. "I try not to read into it [the decision to dissolve the Chamber] any nefarious motives, but how else can you explain getting rid of one of the best things we had here [in Bosnia] on human rights?"[95] Echoing this sentiment, the Centre for Human Right's Miroslav Zivanovic wrote, "The question remains to what extent the Chamber's successful performance motivated the extremely strong coalition of the international community and BiH politicians that was working on abolishing it."[96]

A significant problem existed with the termination of the work of the Chamber: Somehow someone had to consider the hundreds of applications already received before dissolution. The solution reached by agreement of the parties was to set up an entirely new institution—the Human Rights Commission within the Constitutional Court of Bosnia and Herzegovina—to render decisions on applications received by December 31, 2003. The new body was to be physically located in the Constitutional Court, but it was "not part of the business of the [Constitutional Court]." As Nedim Ademović, the Constitutional Court registrar stated, the new body was "really the Chamber in new clothing."[97] Signs that the new organization was a continuation of the old included the fact that it "applies the same legislation as the Human Rights Chamber and its decisions are final and binding and the respondents are obliged to implement them fully."[98]

Republika Srpska   The third human rights commission to be established was the Republika Srpska Ombudsman, a relative latecomer. The impetus for creating this entity came almost wholly from outside Bosnia-Herzegovina. To provide some symmetry on citizen access to human rights institutions, the Venice

Commission (an advisory body to the Council of Europe that focuses on constitutional law)[99] together with the OHR and the OSCE, took up the task of preparing the Draft Organic Law on the Ombudsman of Republika Srpska. The final agreement was adopted by the Republika Srpska National Assembly and was published on February 9, 2000.[100] The Republika Srpska ombudsman's office is composed of three people—one Bosniak, one Croat, and one Serb. A head office was established in Banja Luka, with four additional field offices throughout Republika Srpska.

Substantively, the Republika Srpska ombudsman's office was given the same mandate as the already existing Federation office. Not surprisingly then, the agendas of the offices do not differ significantly. Both the Republika Srpska and Federation ombudsmen hear an enormous number of complaints each year, the vast majority of which are without merit or improperly filed (e.g., the complaints should have been filed with another administrative or judicial body). The ombudsman offices also prepare special reports on specific human rights issues and conduct "terrain visits" that "[aim] to make the Ombudsman institution more close to the citizens . . . [and to] review [the] state of respect for human rights on [the] . . . terrain."[101] The scope of activities and the general tone of the two entity officers differ substantially, mirroring the political developments in each entity.

By the time the Republika Srpska Ombudsman office opened its doors, the Federation office had already cultivated a reputation as a forceful and independent rights advocate. In scrambling to keep up with its more experienced peer institution, the Republika Srpska ombudsman's office was far more deferential to the authorities. Its willingness to take the lead from international experts and institutions led to accusations of lack of independence in the establishment of its mandate, and its close, cooperative relationship with its own government led to accusations of lack of independence in the operation of its mandate. This distinction between the two offices was maintained over time. Even after years of operation, the Republika Srpska ombudsman's office prided itself on being "soft" and "conciliatory" in tone, ready and willing to work with any and all international organizations that were offering support. In contrast, the Federation staff, while valuing international interest, described their own behavior as "louder" and "more confrontational."[102] The different relationships to international agencies affected not only the tone of the offices but also the focus of their work. The Republika Srpska ombudsman's office was more open and inclined to make agenda decisions based on the input of outsiders, for example, devoting a great deal of resources to the rights of children after Save the Children Norway and Save the Children UK expressed interest in funding work on such matters.[103] The Federation office's focus, in contrast, might have begun with the same donor orientation, but as the office matured, so did its confidence with more internally driven decisions, for example, refusing to abandon an already existing, well-respected program on human rights promotion just because donor priorities had shifted.

Social and Economic Rights

All aspects of Bosnia-Herzegovina human rights infrastructure have been heavily influenced by international organizations, and the treatment of social and economic rights is no exception. Social and economic rights have been a rhetorical focus for the many international organizations at work in Bosnia-Herzegovina, and many of their democratization and development projects are framed in rights-based terms. However, internationally sponsored social and economic rights programs are chimerical. Even as the goal of promoting equitable development and enhancing public welfare is touted by international agencies as desirable and essential, the lack of effective enforcement is also tacitly accepted. International organizations are viewed as providing resources for Bosnia-Herzegovina in line with larger political designs (and, some would say, out of charitable impulses), not because of some sense of legal responsibility or theory of estoppel (i.e., once an assistance has begun, it creates justifiable expectations of its continuance to a certain stage of realization, and thus reliance on continuance warrants legal protection).

With respect to legal enforcement of social and economic claims, the human rights institutions in Bosnia-Herzegovina seem to have done better than their international benefactors. There are repeated references to social and economic rights in the constitutive documents of Bosnia-Herzegovina, including the Bosnia-Herzegovina constitution and the Dayton Agreement and all international instruments referenced therein. However, ultimately the Bosnia-Herzegovina institutions also fall short because they, like their international counterparts, accept "inability to pay" as a defense to many social and economic rights violations.

The rhetorical embrace of social and economic rights by international organizations can be found in their public pronouncements about their goals in Bosnia-Herzegovina. The OSCE Mission to Bosnia-Herzegovina, for example, asserts that its "mission focus[es] its efforts on creating conditions for everyone to enjoy his/her economic, social, and cultural rights as well as his/her civil and political rights."[104] The OSCE explains that its mission's Economic and Social Rights Program is designed to

- Bring a human rights perspective to economic and social development in Bosnia and Herzegovina;

- Assist public authorities in identifying and addressing human rights concerns so that while they carry out their mandate, they do so in a way that is human-rights compliant and which aims at the progressive realization of the international standards;

- Identify structural focus issues which if addressed by the authorities will lead to the progressive realization of these rights for all persons, and in particular for those who are most vulnerable;

- Enhance the work of other international agencies and external donors involved in economic and social development.[105]

Similarly, a human rights–based approach to assessment and development planning in Bosnia-Herzegovina—known as the Rights-Based Municipal Assessment and Planning Project (RMAP)—has been implemented through a joint initiative by the UN Office of the High Commissioner for Human Rights and the UN Development Program (UNDP) in Bosnia-Herzegovina.[106] Another good example of well-publicized plans to embrace social and economic rights is provided by the work of UNICEF, which has begun applying a human rights analysis to its work in Bosnia-Herzegovina and elsewhere on social and economic issues affecting children.[107]

Despite these and many other public pronouncements of rights-based approaches to social and economic issues, international organizations involved in Bosnia-Herzegovina continue to disagree on whether social and economic rights are legally enforceable. Unsurprisingly then, their plans for Bosnia-Herzegovina (and elsewhere) do not include a clear statement on justiciability of social and economic rights. This has caused some confusion in Bosnia-Herzegovina, where even leading human rights advocates recognize "inability to pay" arguments as defenses to unrealized social and economic rights. The Human Rights Center's Miroslav Zivanovic illustrates this kind of thinking well when he writes in a leading text on the status of human rights in Bosnia-Herzegovina:

> The state of Bosnia and Herzegovina and its entities and other levels of authority are unable to ensure the respect of economic, social and cultural rights of

citizens due to the extremely unstable and insecure social and political environment, deficient economic order, inefficient legal protection system, undeveloped
economy and the material and cultural poverty of the country. To make matters
worse, even the existing resources are manipulated with and abused, at the expense of BiH citizens.[108]

All of Zivanovic's points are well taken, but the failure to locate some
kind of legal responsibility for social and economic rights—of local or international actors or of both—supports a culture of legal double-talk in Bosnia-
Herzegovina. Bosnia-Herzegovina is a signatory to nearly all international
documents pertaining to social and economic rights (except for the European Social Charter). Social and economic rights are trumpeted in organizational mandates and in constitutive documents, and the ombudsman's
offices entertain a host of social and economic questions. Yet they still are
not treated as positive constitutional rights to claim a benefit or access to a
service from public authorities. The United Nations Social and Economic
Council (ECOSOC) has specifically recognized that economic arguments
are frequently used to rebuff concerns about civil and political rights violations. However, ECOSOC has found that "problems in Bosnia and Herzegovina cannot be simplistically explained in economic and financial terms."[109]
ECOSOC has warned:

> It would not be an exaggeration to state that the deprivation of economic and
> social rights is a mere continuation of policies of ethnic cleansing. In areas
> where security is not at stake any more, such deprivation constitutes an obvious
> obstruction to sustainable return. . . . The economic situation must not prevent
> the international and local communities from protecting economic and social
> rights and from combating all forms of discrimination.[110]

The three ombudsman's offices have already devoted substantial energy to
social and economic rights through individual casework, the undertaking of
investigations, the writing of special reports, and educational activities and
other promotional endeavors. The main differences between the offices appear
to be the degree to which the ombudsmen are truly independent actors, as
opposed to political appointees representing a particular party line. The offices have markedly different tones (adversarial versus conciliatory) and styles
of operation with respect to the government (confrontational versus noncon-
frontational). Also, the impact of Bosnification (turning power over from international actors to local actors), which led to 40–60 percent salary cuts, has

been absorbed quite differently by each office. The state ombudsman's office was the most sharply affected by staff quitting for more lucrative employment elsewhere, leaving it with only a skeleton staff. All three offices fear the impending merger of offices, which they view as threatening their successes. Regarding promotion and protection of economic and social rights, however, they report similar endeavors.

Republika Srpska Ombudsman Office   In the first two years of operation, with regards to economic, social, and cultural rights, the Republika Srpska ombudsman's office, a mainly ethnic Serb subentity, worked almost exclusively on property rights and, specifically, on repossession and compensation issues related to properties lost, abandoned, or destroyed during the war.[111] Other crucial early cases involved the right to choose one's place of residence and the right to not be ill-treated by authorities. In the past two years, the office has undertaken a broader array of issues, with economic issues such as access to health care and public assistance receiving more attention. In 2005, one-third of all complaints received were related to the judiciary (e.g., judicial delay). The other main areas causing complaints (in descending order) were employment-related issues, property rights, pension and disability insurance, property repossession, public communal services, and social and health protection.[112]

The Federation Ombudsman Office   The Federation Ombudsman's Office (entity level) is charged with a different set of responsibilities with respect to economic, social, and cultural rights.[113] The office handles individual complaints on a range of issues and investigates red flags that ombudsman staff discover in their regular inspections of state-run institutions. For example, individual complaints against a state-run mental health facility might be initiated after the ombudsman's visit to the facility uncovers several examples of mistreatment of patients. In addition, the office has made specific recommendations on social and economic issues in their special reports aimed at removing the source of large-scale violations. The most recent annual report is scathing in its rebuke of the Bosnia-Herzegovina government for failing to create the appropriate democratic institutions and enact the necessary legislation that is a "guarantee and precondition for human rights respect."[114]

The Republic Ombudsman's Office   The Republic Ombudsman's Office (state level) could be described as a more specialized unit.[115] Sample economic rights issues taken up by the office include the right to work, the right to pensions and other forms of public welfare, and access to health care. The most recent report of the office notes, however, that it still suffers from a lack of visibility. "The citizens have not been fully informed or are not aware of the Institution's function and competence."[116] Staff in the Republic Ombudsman's Office expressed a concern that its work and capacities need to be better understood and appreciated by the public.[117]

Assessment

As with the other case studies in this book, the Bosnia-Herzegovina example clearly highlights how the mandate, practices, platform, and enforceability of the NHRI is deeply informed by the local context and the social and political dynamics of the realities on the ground. In the Bosnian context, the tensions between the internationalization of the NGO and governance sectors continue to inform and influence the work and parameters of the three Bosnian institutions, and the deep-seated entrenchment of social and economic disparities, especially with regard to refugees and internally displaced individuals, continue to dominate much of the work of all three offices.

The slow-changing, complex world of Bosnian politics[118] has forced its human rights institutions to continually adapt to remain intact and relevant. Through Bosnification, power is being devolved from international to local entities and steps are being taken to enhance the power of the federal government. Under the watchful eye of both the international community, which has made a large investment in peace making in the region, and Balkan nationalists, who stand ready for renewed conflict, this evolution irrefutably comes with a unique set of challenges.

The first and most onerous challenge relates to the restructuring of the three NHRIs as one central state entity. Bosnian commissioners, ombudsmen, legal officers, and advocates all agree that merging the three separate systems while retaining the strengths of the most successful bodies is a difficult task. As with other Bosnian structures, the entity ombudsman's offices and all other entity-level human rights bodies are generally stronger than the parallel structures at the state level. Thus, if the decision as to which office to keep open and which staff to retain were merely one of seniority, the Bosnia-Herzegovina office would be the first to be closed and the staff there would be the first to be reassigned to other posts. However, under the strong influence of international organizations, Bosnian leaders have agreed that the central entity should be preserved and the state entities jettisoned. Explaining this decision and gaining acceptance for its consequences will test the diplomatic skills of Bosnian human rights leadership.

The second challenge facing Bosnian NHRIs concerns the need to achieve local "buy in" to NHRI mandates and programs that had been imposed by outsiders as part of peace plans. Bosnians have had little say in the creation of their own NHRIs, and the notion of human rights institutions is still closely tied to wartime and to ideas brought by international actors (who were often well intentioned but misguided). For human rights to have some coherence and impact in peacetime, all the people of Bosnia-Herzegovina must have more input into the understanding and application of these norms. So long as human rights are delivered to the people of the Balkans in a heavy-handed, top-down manner, achieving local buy-in will be difficult, if not impossible.

The third challenge involves the phenomenon of Bosnification, which is the transfer of institutional control from international organizations to local ones. Few critics dispute that Bosnification has had a profound effect on all human rights institutions, leading to a downgrading of their importance and impact, a lessening of their independence, and a weakening of their credibility among the general public. Bosnification led to a 50 percent pay cut for employees of the institutions and a drastic reduction in benefits. This in turn led many staff members, including the most well trained human rights lawyers, to seek employment elsewhere. After Bosnification led the state ombudsman's office to the complete politicization of the appointment process, attorneys fled the office in droves: within months, a staff of sixteen lawyers was reduced to only three. Bosnification must be handled more effectively or the NHRIs will collapse.

The great dependency of Bosnia-Herzegovina on its international benefactors has left its politicians leery of biting the hand that feeds them. Bosnification faced a tremendous blow to its credibility in January 2002, when, without any concrete incriminating evidence, Bosnian authorities handed over six Bosnian citizens of Algerian origin to the United States, which promptly transferred them to a prison camp in Guantanamo.[119] To make matters worse, the Bosnian authorities attempted to appease the United States even after the Human Rights Chamber had ordered a temporary moratorium on the extradition and even though the Federation Supreme Court had ruled that the six men should be released for lack of evidence after the United States refused to produce what it claimed was incriminating telephone recordings.

Twelve years after the Dayton Agreement, the puzzle that is Bosnia-Herzegovina is still falling into place. The level of international involvement is highly significant, with the presence of international peacekeeping forces and an overall European presence continuing to assist in building a multiethnic, democratic Bosnia. Some notable progress has been made, especially relating to the return of refugees and internally displaced people into the region since the signing of the Dayton Agreement, but the region has yet to return to a state of normalcy. The country's governance is still divided into three awkward parts, and representation is still chiseled into three identity groupings, fashioned to suit the expediency of the international community more than the needs of local residents. Among the institutions impaired by this hasty arrangement are those related to human rights promotion and protection. The significant contributions that Bosnian NHRIs have made to peace and justice in the region should not be overlooked. However, their full potential will not be realized until they are given the opportunity to work as a unified and truly national institution, with decision-making authority over both their mandate and its implementation.

Chapter 5

When Less Is More

*Considering the Ombudsman System
in the Czech Republic*

T HE GOAL of the Czech government in establishing an NHRI was far more modest than that of any other country included thus far in this study. Unlike Bosnia-Herzegovina and Northern Ireland, the Czech Republic did not seek systematic and large-scale international assistance in addressing ongoing communal conflicts or recent civil wars. And although the Czech Republic sought to be viewed as a human rights supportive country and to take part in major global human rights debates, unlike Germany and Denmark, it harbored no ambition of using its role in NHRI networks to propel itself to a leadership role in global human rights politics. In turning to the establishment of an NHRI, the Czech Republic was responding to a problem historically central to its own specific political psychology: a deep public mistrust of government and a legacy of forced participation in state-controlled collectives. Unlike the other countries studied here, Czech domestic human rights efforts are part of a larger overall transition from a society in which the citizens viewed the state as an untrustworthy opponent to be resisted and as an obstacle to independent organizations, to a partner in progress in a newly transformed Europe, with a vibrant and open civil society.

To create and nurture a more supportive citizen-government relationship, the Czech Republic chose the ombudsman model. This model ordinarily is considered the most limited form of NHRI, because its jurisdiction is often limited to public administration. In the Czech case, however, this model has been stretched to permit a broad range of inquiry into human wrongs. The degree to which the ombudsman model successfully addresses the needs of the Czech Republic requires an understanding of Czech history, which has nearly always taken a velvet and modest approach over more extreme measures, and of the development of the current Czech political system, which continues to prefer velvet to iron.

Political Context

Czech politics have long been marked by patterns of domination and resistance. The political lineage of the Czech Republic traces its roots to Czechoslovakia, a country carved out of the remains of the Austrian-Hungarian Empire. While World War I was still raging in Europe, Czech and Slovak leaders, under the leadership of the scholar Thomas Masaryk and with the encouragement of U.S. president Woodrow Wilson, met in Pittsburgh, Pennsylvania, to iron out plans for a new unified state. At that time, it suited world powers to unite Czechs and Slovaks under a single state, along with large German, Polish, Hungarian, and Ruthenian (Ukrainian) minority populations, the inclusion of which later provided several of its neighbors with claims to parts of its territory. As soon as the war ended, Masaryk returned to Prague as the country's first president. Integrating minorities into the new democracy and satisfying the demands of the different nationalities served to enhance citizen distrust of politics. As one scholar notes:

> The Czechs, constituting only half of the country's population, received the greatest benefits, dominated political and economic life, and refused to relinquish control. Czech domination of political life caused constant friction not only with the German, Polish, Hungarian and Ruthenian (Ukrainian) minorities, but also with the Slovaks, supposedly the other half of an equal partnership that was running the state. The Slovaks chafed at the bureaucratic and political domination by the Czechs.[1]

The unresolved internal ethnonational divisions left a negative legacy of "poisonous distrust."[2]

The global depression of the 1930s hit Czechoslovakia hard; yet, compared with other Eastern European states, it was thriving.[3] But the country's economic success proved also to be its downfall, because world leaders viewed the relatively rich little country as a promising token to be sacrificed when necessary to mollify aggressive nations. At three of the most pivotal moments in European history, world leaders had little difficulty giving away Czech territory to regimes intent on breaking and destroying Czech character.

First, in a desperate attempt to save their own countries from war with Hitler, world powers acquiesced to Germany's takeover of Czechoslovakia in

1938. Meeting in Munich without the Czech leaders present, British prime minister Neville Chamberlain and French prime minister Edouard Daladier agreed with Hitler and Mussolini on details for Czechoslovakia's "peaceful" dismemberment. Under the Munich Pact, Czech lands became incorporated into the Third Reich, and Slovakia served as an "independent" puppet state.[4] Czechoslovakia was given away for a second time after World War II, this time to the Soviets. In 1948, world leaders sat by and watched as Communists seized power in a reunified Czechoslovakia. Twenty years later, after the period of openness in Czechoslovakia known as the Prague Spring,[5] this pattern was repeated for the third time; in August 1968, world leaders stood by and watched while an estimated half-million Soviet bloc troops poured into Czechoslovakia, beginning what would be a nearly twenty-year occupation and ending the brief period of reform.[6]

In each case of domination, Czechs responded with nonviolent resistance. Characterized by self-deprecating humor, irony, and an unquestionable ability to defy authority, Czech nonviolence was captured in the play *The Good Soldier Schweik*. Written in the 1920s by Jaroslav Hasek, this classic play featured a Czech soldier named Schweik who played the fool in order to defy authority. Reading war manuals literally with hilarious results, getting lost on the way to the front, and misdirecting ammunitions through bumbling incompetence, Schweik was a source of inspiration for Czechs who prided themselves on appearing to submit to their fate while actually actively resisting privately. Czechs also are staunch realists. As regional specialist Carol Skalnik Leff observes, "The Czech is no hero who sacrifices nobly for a cause, but rather a canny realist more accomplished in political and diplomatic judo than swordplay."[7] This image, Leff notes, was reinforced by the Czechs' seemingly "sensible and pragmatic" behavior in Munich in 1938 and during the Soviet invasion of 1968.[8]

Under Communist rule the ability of people to organize themselves independently from the state was strictly prohibited. Nonetheless, people were encouraged to be organized in state-approved and state-controlled organizations. Participation in the state-controlled trade unions, for example, was a badge of honor and was interpreted as a sign of loyalty to the state.[9] Application forms for high school and university studies asked explicitly for evidence of the parents' proper organizational affiliation. At the same time, the attempted participation in independent organizations was treated as an indication of disloyalty and, in some cases, of criminal antistate behavior. Under this system of state-mandated and state-controlled participation, the space for formulating demands from below was exceedingly narrow, and open political debate was virtually nonexistent.

The state's tight grip on society began to crack in the 1980s, when groups of independent young people associated with the officially sanctioned youth organization, the Socialist Union of Youth, brazenly began to make demands on the state. Underground cultural activities, including some of the region's most creative rock 'n' roll stars, also played a key role in inspiring dissent.[10] Although courted by the West, the group of active Czech dissidents was actually "rather small and existed mostly in isolation from the public, particularly when compared to Hungary and Poland."[11] Debates over civil society were prominent among this group. Drawing inspiration from Václav Havel (a novelist who was then a dissident and later president), this fledgling movement discussed the importance of building an independent, vibrant "civil society" where people could "live in truth."[12] As Czech political scholars Petr Kopecký and Edward Barnfield observed, over time "the notion of civil society became an articulated political theory of opposition to totalitarianism. It was envisioned as a strategy of opposition against the communist regime; but it was also presented as a programme for a post-communist society."[13]

Czech civil society enthusiasts benefited substantially from the cold war thaw encouraged by Soviet leader Mikhail Gorbachev, who envisaged a new era to be marked by glasnost, or political, economic, and social openness. In 1989, the Czech and Slovak protest movements, loosely led by the Czech Civic Forum (many of whose members were involved in the Charter 77 movement[14] and the Slovak Public Against Violence), swelled to many thousands.[15] The climate of protest culminated in the November 1989 birth of the Velvet Revolution, a series of peaceful demonstrations that engendered the collapse of the Communist regime (and, eventually, the division of the country into the Czech Republic and Slovakia).[16]

Expectations ran high as Czechs tested their newfound freedom.[17] When a new election law that removed the barrier to establishing new political parties was quickly enacted, Czech political life exploded in a frenzied effort to acquire political power through the creation of political parties. "Old parties were renewed, new parties were formed, and associations and unions of the most distinct nature, whose objectives and functions were often intertwined, confused and mistaken, took the name of a party."[18] By June 1990, an incredible sixty-six political parties had registered with the Ministry of the Interior and an additional twenty-seven parties were still waiting processing. Sixteen political parties were on the ballot for the June 2000 elections. In an attempt to prevent extreme political fragmentation, a 5 percent electoral threshold was created for a party's entrance into the federal parliament. This threshold requirement served to winnow the political parties active in the new federal parliament down to four, with the conservative, cosmopolitan, civic, and market-oriented Civic Democratic Party (Občanská demokratická strana; ODS) emerging victorious.[19]

Other influential parties include the Czech Social Democratic Party (Česká strana sociálně demokratická; ČSSD), the Czech Republic's oldest political party. After World War II, the ČSSD was taken over by the Communist Party. The ČSSD would not reemerge as a viable, independent party for half a century, when it declared its rebirth in the early days of the Velvet Revolution. The newly reconstituted party initially struggled to gain a foothold in the inchoate political scene; in the 1990 elections it failed to garner enough votes to win a single parliamentary seat. However, in a mere six years the ČSSD had regained a following and had become a political force, receiving 26.4 percent of the votes in the 1996 election. This upward trend continued, and in 2002 the party collaborated with the Christian Democrats and the Union of Freedom to form a majority coalition government.[20]

Further illustrating the diversity of Czech parties, the Green Party (Strana zelených) was founded in the Czech Republic in February 1990. For a long time, however, it struggled to obtain significant influence in Czech politics. According to the 2006 European Greens Charter, of which the Czech Greens are a signatory, "The European Greens proudly stand for the sustainable development of humanity on planet Earth, a mode of development respectful of human rights and built upon the values of environmental responsibility, freedom, justice, diversity and non-violence."[21] As of 2006, the party held a single seat in the Senate, the upper house of the Parliament of the Czech Republic, and six seats in the lower house.

Although Czechs received high marks internationally for a largely successful transition to a participatory democracy, they were far from satisfied. Much of the disappointment stems from the consistent weakness that marks the nature of Czech civil society. Czech scholar Vladimír Dvoráková explains: "The main problem seems to be its structure [less connected with concrete problems of everyday life], the low level of participation of the citizenry, and the low ability to transfer demands into politics."[22] The absence of legal rules regarding financing of nonprofit organizations left them underfunded and open to criticism.[23] Political parties have fared even worse in the public eye. A series of well-publicized political scandals has only deepened public skepticism.[24] According to political commentator Jiri Pehe, "Most people believe Czech politics is a dirty business, that corruption is widespread among all politicians. . . . If one politician is caught people tend to think it is perhaps good that one corruption scandal was uncovered but on the other hand we know that other politicians have their hands dirty as well."[25]

Economic Context

Following its 1993 velvet divorce from what became Slovakia, the Czech economy began its transition to a free market system.[26] The Czech economy is characterized by a strong manufacturing sector, a skilled workforce, and a growing service sector. Privatization and deregulation have turned the country into an affluent, economically competitive market economy, and the Czech Republic has become a member of the World Trade Organization (WTO) and the European Union (EU). Private companies now account for approximately 80 percent of GDP, and most industrial infrastructure has been deregulated and opened to competition.[27]

Following a period of comparatively weak growth, the Czech economy improved markedly in 2005, with investment surging against the backdrop of a supportive monetary policy, EU accession, and strong corporate profitability.[28] Today, as a full member of the EU, the Czech Republic is experiencing strong capital inflows and steady economic growth.[29] In 2004, inflation was about 2.8 percent,[30] mainly because of increases in value-added tax rates and higher fuel costs, and hovered at 2 percent for 2005.[31] Continuing reports of corruption are troubling to investors,[32] however, and the old industries, such as steel and energy, which were propped up by the state in the planned economy, are still resistant to change.[33] The Czech Republic also "still faces serious challenges in increasing transparency in capital market transactions, transforming the housing sector, reforming the pension and health care systems, and solving serious environmental problems."[34]

The Czech Republic became a member of the EU on May 1, 2004. The process of accession has been generally viewed as having a positive impact on reform in the Czech Republic. The EU's reports on the Czech economy provided an important external critique of Czech reforms by exposing deficiencies in the Czech privatization process. The EU's active leverage not only shaped the business environment but also left a deep imprint on the political environment. As political scientist Milda Anna Vachudova found in her study of the EU enlargement process:

> The EU's active leverage also helped organize and strengthen the opposition to the ruling parties. The parties of the center-left and the center-right performed poorly as watchdogs because of their crippling fragmentation in the 1990s. However, . . . EU membership became a focal point for cooperation among the Czech Republic's fragmented centrist parties and among various civic groups and initiatives.[35]

Not only were civil society organizations and political parties affected by the EU accession process, but so was the government. In the past, the Czech government claimed to be "'West' of the West Europeans,"[36] and it "retained a provincial confidence in Czech superiority."[37] The EU accession process challenged all forms of Euroskepticism and pushed the country's leaders to make rapid reforms to bring the Czech Republic into compliance with international standards.

Human Rights Context

Human Rights and Foreign Policy

From the 1960s until its demise in 1989, the unified Soviet satellite state of Czechoslovakia consistently supported the emerging body of positivist international human rights protections.[38] Although Czechoslovakia's actual behavior was certainly not always in line with international human rights treaties, the country's formal agreement with these international scriptures gave human rights activists in Czechoslovakia an opening for urging compliance. After the Czech Republic broke from Slovakia in January 1993, it signaled its continued dedication to human rights principles by declaring that the new nation would be bound by its previous accession to UN conventions. Thus in February 1993 the Czech Republic simultaneously ratified the bulk of existing international instruments.

Over the course of the next ten years, the Czech Republic proceeded to agree to several additional important international human rights instruments, including the Optional Protocol to the Convention on the Rights of the Child on the Involvement of Children in Armed Conflicts (October 2000) and the Hague Convention on the Protection of Children and Cooperation in Respect of Inter-Country Adoption (January 2000).[39] The Czech Republic has also ratified several treaties in the Council of Europe, and, significantly for the rights of refugees and the rights of foreign nationals, it acceded to the European Agreement on Transfer of Responsibility for Refugees.

The Czech Republic's human rights record on treaties is mixed, however. The country has the distinction of being the only country in the present study—and, indeed, the only member of the EU—that has failed to ratify the Rome Statute, which established the International Criminal Court. Beyond treaty negotiation, ratification, and enforcement, the broad mandate of the Human Rights Department refers to its general responsibility for "the application of international and regional standards in human rights, mainly in creating national norms."[40] To carry out this responsibility, the Ministry of Foreign Affairs is charged with collaborating with national institutions to draw up national reports on implementation of the commitments arising from international and regional human rights.[41]

Human Rights as a Domestic Concern

One of the prime motivators for the Velvet Revolution in the 1980s was human rights, and many of the most vociferous supporters of human rights quickly became part of the new government, taking their beliefs in human rights with them. The constitution of the new country made clear the supremacy of the international human rights treaties to domestic legislation[42] and clarified Czechoslovakia's understanding of and commitment to human rights through the comprehensive Bill of Rights and Fundamental Freedoms (now part of the Czech constitution).[43] At the same time, several institutions and mechanisms were created that could address human rights issues. A judicial system was established, which provided for a full judicial review of administrative acts; a Constitutional Court was created with the ability to hear individual complaints;[44] and a Human Rights Department was created at the Ministry of Foreign Affairs. On the parliamentary side, human rights supportive developments included the Senate's establishment of the Committee on Education, Science, Culture, Human Rights, and Petitions, which included human rights in its mandate, and the development of the Parliamentary Institute, which was tasked with providing research on a range of issues, including human rights concerns.

The initial investment in human rights in the Czech Republic proved to be a double-edged sword, however. On the one hand, it institutionalized the new government's commitment to human rights and significantly enhanced the country's international reputation in the field of human rights. However, the rapid institutionalization of human rights also served to stifle many governmental and nongovernmental human rights actors who thought that the issue of human rights had been solved and thus that it was time for them to devote their energies elsewhere. The resulting deadening of interest in human rights led one group of Czech scholars to wonder:

> Perhaps it is always the case that when the demand for human rights becomes a significant instrument of political struggle, establishing those rights ceases to be the goal after a political victory: If the totalitarian system has been defeated in the name of human rights then one assumes [that] the rights have been attained.[45]

Instead of using the creation of a new human rights infrastructure as a means for accelerating their demands for the realization of human rights, supporters of human rights tended to view the new mechanisms as the end of human rights activism. Similarly, Czech political leaders tended to view human rights as "taken care of" or "over."[46] As Czech scholar Andrea Baršová observes in her comprehensive analysis of nonjudicial human rights protection measures in the Czech Republic:

> For most conservatives and liberals, who formed governments from 1992 until 1998 (and replaced as a leading political force the broad pro-reform grouping, the Civic Forum), the human rights mission was accomplished. This, of course is not to say that the Government would deny that any human rights abuses might occur. Yet, the prevailing opinion was that the standard state machinery should deal with any human rights issues: the legislature, the judiciary or the executive—whatever was appropriate for the individual cases.[47]

This lukewarm response to human rights concerns has also been attributed in part to the "automatization" of Czech civil society—that is, its fragmentation and overspecialization. According to Hana Havelková, "In the Czech Republic there is a wide-spread belief that all society needs to do to form a functioning democratic society is to create the basic institutions of the legal state, build a standard party system and add a bill of rights to the constitution."[48] By accepting a simplistic democratic formula as sufficient evidence of having arrived as a participatory democracy, the Czech Republic could consider human rights abuses as settled and turn its attention to what it perceived as more important matters, such as the encouragement of foreign investment. After the Velvet Revolution had reached its initial goals, Václav Havel himself dismissed the need for the creation of the Czech Helsinki Committee, because "democracy" had taken hold in the new republic, vitiating the need for issue-specific human rights institutions.[49] Thus national human rights mechanisms were created *despite* this lack of support from key politicians. By creating the Commissioner for Human Rights, the Czech government identified a single individual in government responsible for human rights promotion and protection. Petr Uhl, a journalist and widely respected former dissident, was the first person to hold this title. Among other tasks, the commissioner was charged with monitoring state compliance with international human rights treaties, submitting government reports on compliance with human rights treaties to treaty-monitoring bodies, and preparing annual and periodic reports on human rights for the government.[50] As a high-ranking government official, the commissioner was charged with working in the interests of the government and had limited power to act independently. One glaring example of this fundamental lack of independence is that the commissioner's annual human rights reports were not to be made public until after government review and revision.[51]

In addition to the commissioner, the Human Rights Council was created as a permanent consultative body of the government, composed of representatives of the executive, at the deputy minister level, and representatives of the civil sector.[52] Among other tasks, the Council was given the responsibility of increasing public awareness of human rights, monitoring the compliance of state legislation with international human rights standards, and providing information to international human rights treaty-monitoring bodies.[53] Although the Council may request information and opinions from ministries and other bodies of the state administration, the Council was not designed with specific power to investigate individual complaints, nor was it designed to be responsive to and inclusive of concerns of civil society.[54]

Human Rights Record

Although the Czech record on human rights has been admirable in recent years, several serious problems remain.[55] The single issue garnering the most public attention is the failure to accord full rights and protections to the republic's 250,000 Roma residents.[56] In April 2007, the United Nations Committee on the Elimination of Racial Discrimination criticized the Czech Republic for its treatment of Romanies.[57] Among other matters, the relocation of Czech Romanies against their will and their segregation, in housing and schooling especially, has been a difficult issue for the Czech government to address. Aversion toward Roma people is deeply rooted in a society that has historically used

Roma as convenient scapegoats, blaming them for all social, political, and economic problems that negatively affect their everyday life.[58]

Racism in the public sphere in the Czech Republic has been institutionalized through the relatively open political party structure. The recently formed National Party runs an Internet radio station that broadcasts music by neo-Nazi groups. Among other pet issues, the National Party has taken it upon itself to push government for the abolition of alleged "advantages for Roma" and has called for the rewriting of the history of the Holocaust that would eliminate (or, in the very least, greatly reduce) the persecution of Roma prisoners.[59] In January 2006, the National Party held a demonstration at the site of a former World War II concentration camp that housed a great number of Roma prisoners. Speaker after speaker at the demonstration reportedly aired views that the "real victims" of World War II were ethnic Czechs and that Roma were responsible for their own deaths. These inflammatory statements did not go entirely unnoticed by the government. In 2005 the Czech legislature was credited with passing a series of tough hate crime laws. This legislation included bans on hate groups and public hate speech and outlawed Holocaust denial.[60] Despite these measures, the National Party still retained its registration as a political party.

A 2007 report of the Commissioner for Human Rights of the Council of Europe found that Roma face discrimination in nearly every aspect of their daily life.[61] According to the report, Roma face disproportionately high levels of poverty, unemployment, interethnic violence, xenophobic acts of violence by skinheads,[62] and illiteracy. Roma are often segregated in special schools for children with disabilities, denied residency permits, and refused jobs, solely because of their race or ethnicity.[63] In the years since the Velvet Revolution in 1989, there has been only one significant Romani political party, campaigning specifically for the minority's interests.

Hate-related attacks are all too common, and Roma are frequently targeted by skinhead groups. In 2006 an estimated 7,000 skinheads were active in the country, although some observers believe these numbers do not reflect the true nature of the problem.[64] A 1996 report by Human Rights Watch warned:

> Local police often display an open sympathy for "skinheads," allowing them to hold unauthorized marches and threaten non-ethnic Czechs. Police are often slow to respond to Romani calls for help and hesitant to make arrests, even after a violent attack. In some cases, police themselves have used excessive force against Roma, sometimes causing death. Despite improvements, the judicial system still does not always punish the perpetrators of racially motivated violence

to the fullest extent of the law. When cases do go to court, the attack is often viewed as a "personal fight" rather than a premeditated act of violence against an individual on account of his race, ethnicity, or color. Sentences are often light, which sends the message that such attacks are not considered serious.[65]

Compounding these problems is the Czech Republic's citizenship law, which came into effect after the split of Czechoslovakia in January 1993. Although the law does not specifically refer to Roma, its requirements on proof of residence, ancestry, and absence of criminality have a disproportionate impact on Roma.[66] In addition, many Roma who met all the requirements of the law were arbitrarily denied citizenship by local officials. As a result, many Roma living in the Czech Republic do not have Czech citizenship, even though they are longtime or lifelong residents of the republic.

Although not as high on the list of priorities as combating race and ethnic discrimination, women's rights issues have also garnered considerable attention in the Czech Republic.[67] The constitution of the Czech Republic states that it will promote gender equality. Following this framework, a number of laws prohibiting gender discrimination have emerged from the constitution (e.g., the labor law, which prohibits any discrimination based on gender).[68] Nonetheless, women's position in the labor force is also troubling. One EU gender equality watchdog group reported that the problems regarding women's participation in the labor market were even worse than imagined.

> The difference between female and male unemployment rates has been growing since the beginning of the nineties and the situation hasn't improved since 1997. The biggest difference between the sexes is in the 24–35 age groups, when women either have small children to care for or employers apparently assume that they will have children at this stage of their lives. If we take into account the fact that in the Czech Republic women can stay at home for four years and continue to receive parental benefit from the state (approximately 83 Euro per month) then we can understand why they are unlikely to register as unemployed as they would lose their right to receive this benefit. It can be assumed that the true level of women's unemployment in this age group is much higher than officially recorded.[69]

According to Open Society director Monika Landmanova, Czech advocacy groups have undertaken a new campaign to address discrimination against women in both the workforce and political life.[70] One of the greatest roadblocks, however, is the lack of proper legal authority to address discrimination issues. "There is no single, truly authoritative office that can be effective on gender discrimination," reports Gwendolyn Albert, director of the human rights group LIGA (Lidských Práv), noting that the Office of the Defender does not have the mandate to work on gender issues.[71] In 1998, the Unit for Equality of Men and Women was established within the Department for EU Integration and International Relations at the Ministry of Labor and Social Affairs (MSLA). The Unit, consisting of three female employees, prepares the yearly Czech National Action Plan ("Priorities") and also reports on its implementation. Other bodies with authority on gender issues include the Czech Committee on the Elimination of All Forms of Discrimination Against Women (CEDAW) under the Governmental Council for Human Rights (established in 1999), the Governmental Council for Equal Opportunities of Women and Men (2001), and the Permanent Parliamentary Commission on the Family and Equal Opportunities (2002). None of these bodies, however, has the power to resolve complaints of discrimination.[72]

The Office of the Public Defender of Rights

Several political developments created an environment and indeed the opportunity for a human rights institution with a limited mandate to be established in the Czech Republic. The first development, as has been noted earlier, was the Velvet Revolution, which brought the discussion of human rights onto the national agenda. The second development was the Czech Republic's entry into the European Union and the recognition of the need to incorporate international human rights norms, which were seen to be superior to the existing domestic framework. The subsequent legislation in the Czech constitution and the establishment of a judicial system focused on rights created another degree of opportunity and momentum for rights-based advocacy and practice at the national level.

Established by law in 1999[73] and opening its doors in 2000, the Office of the Public Defender of Rights is a product of Czech civil society (see Appendix 2 for mandate excerpts). Spearheaded by the Czech Helsinki Committee, the campaign called for the establishment of a more comprehensive human rights institution. The resulting more modest mandate of an ombudsman office fell short of the campaign goals but did endow the public defender's office with the authority to hear complaints about public administration. Although the staff of the office rarely utter the words *human rights*, their work addresses what many Czechs have long perceived as an overarching human rights concern:

unfair and corrupt public administration, ranging from such matters as undue court delays to improper taxation. The Czech government was well aware of public mistrust of state authority, based "on both objective and subjective negative experience with the way state administration officials execute the authority of state."[74]

In its first annual report, the Office of the Public Defender recognized that its role as a public advocate was to reaffirm citizen's trust in government.

> With a certain level of simplification it might be said that the disadvantageous situation of the citizens in their dealings with the system of state administration results to a large extent from the very nature of such relations. Citizens are sensitive to situations in which, actually or supposedly, they might feel neglected, overlooked or humbled, since citizens often do not know where, how and in what way their rights and interests can be exerted.[75]

The Defender's jurisdiction covers generally the public administration, including army, police, prison service, detention and imprisonment facilities, and other public institutions where they act in their administrative capacity.[76] The Defender's primary function is to protect the rights of individuals who are victims of unjust and improper treatment by state organs and agencies. Accordingly, the Defender acts as an impartial mediator between an aggrieved individual and the administrative agency concerned. By paying attention to the grievances of citizens and by educating citizens about their rights, the Defender is to address their feelings of neglect. "We know that there are so many people who come to us with cases that have no place here [in the Defender's office]," remarked one staff lawyer. "But that is part of our function . . . to give people the sense that they can complain to the state and that we will listen."[77]

Another goal of the Defender is to provide a significantly less complicated, complex, and costly way to settle disputes than that provided by courts, including administrative courts, which were often equally time-consuming and inefficient.[78] In considering cases, the Defender is not bound by the advocacy model in which one party loses under the law and another party wins. The Defender is instead able to take into account equitable, extralegal concerns, fashioning a solution that can appeal to both sides. As the office noted in its first year of operation:

> Unlike court-type institutions serving to rectify cases in which failure to comply with legal standards is uncovered, the Public Defender of Rights can ensure remedy even in cases when the action of a relevant office or an institution com-

plies with the law but might be in other ways incorrect, inadequate or unjust or even in cases when the relevant institution fails to act.[79]

Because opinions of the Defender are rarely legally enforceable, they have to rely on the moral authority of the office for their de facto enforcement. Whenever the Defender uncovers maladministration, he can request that the relevant office or institution remedy the situation, but the impact of the Defender's investigations is limited by several restrictions. The Defender is not entitled to substitute for the activities of bodies of state administration, nor is he entitled to alter or replace their decisions. Moreover, the Defender is explicitly forbidden from interfering with the decision-making power of courts or other adjudicative bodies, a restriction that appears just only if courts and other adjudicative bodies are functioning fairly.[80]

The Importance of Staffing   The staff of the Defender's office and Czech rights advocates are in basic agreement that the success of the ombudsman system in the Czech Republic is due in large part to the high moral standing and extremely positive reputations of the defender of rights, Otakar Motejl, and the deputy defender, Anna Sabatova. Neither had ties with the previous Communist regime. On the contrary, Ms. Sabatova is a well-known dissident and signatory of Charter 77, and Mr. Motejl served as an active defense counsel for dissidents before totalitarian courts. Later, he became the respected president of the Supreme Court and the minister of justice. After their election the Defender's office was deluged with complaints (in January 2001, more than 650 per month compared with 390 eight months later), illustrating the deep confidence of the public as well as the apparent need for the office.

Beginning with nine employees (one lawyer) in temporary quarters at Masaryk University (Brno) in December 2000, within six months the office boasted nearly forty-seven employees (seventeen lawyers), and by September 2001 that number had ballooned to seventy-four employees (thirty-three lawyers). In 2008, more than ninety people were on staff at the Defender's office. Agreements for external cooperation with lecturers in some legal disciplines (constitutional law, administrative law, law of social security, environmental law, and land law) at some faculties of law in Brno and Prague have also enhanced the expertise and capacity of the office considerably.

Taking up their posts in a nicely renovated and beautifully equipped former Communist office building[81] at the edge of Brno's downtown, the legal staff in the Defender's office is drawn heavily from recent law school graduates, a hiring strategy proposed by the deputy defender. The hope was that the younger employees would be "less set in bad work habits," "easier to train," "more energetic," and even "more up-to-date with the relevant law."[82] Another innovation was to place the young lawyers in areas of their interests and allow them to develop subject matter expertise (e.g., on pensions or on administration of courts). Instead of specializing in "intake," a job most staff members disliked, staffers would take turns rotating into that position, thus minimizing staff burnout and improving morale. "Usually during the day there are at least three in-take officers," one staff member explained, pointing out the well-organized corridor where citizens can walk in with their complaints (and/or their advocates, but usually the allegedly aggrieved citizen alone). "It really can be a stressful and overwhelming job," he explained, noting that although one staff member preferred to work on a permanent basis with the public in the intake office (and thus did fill one of the intake desks), the rest of the staff was grateful for the rotation. Another morale booster for the office was the amenities of the building, such as a tidy modern café, auditorium, and media room, which made it a nicer place to work.[83] These and other staffing innovations appear to have worked. Staff morale is reportedly high, turnover low, and professionalism good and ever improving.

The Work of the Defender   The law that created the Defender's office authorized it to address complaints about the conduct of a wide range of state actors, including ministries and administrative offices, the Czech National Bank (when acting as an office of state administration), the Council for Radio and Television Broadcasting, the police of the Czech Republic (with the exception of investigations within criminal proceedings), the army of the Czech Republic and the Castle Guards, the Prison Service of the Czech Republic, and public health insurance institutions.[84] The conduct of municipalities related to the activities of state administration also fall within the Defender's mandate, as do judicial bodies that conduct state administration (mainly issues of procedural delays, inactivity of the court, and inappropriate conduct of judges).

The workload of the Defender has steadily expanded since the creation of the office. In 2005 the Office of the Public Defender of Rights received 4,939 complaints, an increase of 524 over the 4,415 complaints registered in 2004. In an improvement over earlier years, 57 percent were determined to make it past the initial screening stage for complaints.[85] The Defender's office ascribes the increase in the number of well-founded complaints to higher public awareness of the purpose of the institution. In addition to the formal complaint process, thousands of calls come in each year to the Defender's telephone hotline.

The Defender's office has placed a great emphasis on using the media to improve public awareness of its functions. The staff has been charged with running monthly press conferences on topical issues. These efforts were helped along by Czech TV's decision to run *A Case for the Ombudsman*, a thirteen-part series that offered a new and accessible way of acquainting the public with the Defender's work. Modeled after popular real-crime shows, the new series used concrete cases to introduce the public to the human dimensions of complaints and the fates of those addressing the Defender. According to Czech TV's ratings, the series was watched by an average 360,000 viewers and was labeled the best watched series from the Brno Television Studio.

The Defender has also used his significant legal power to act without petition and has opened investigations on his own initiative in thirty-eight cases. These generally involved cases in which the Defender learned of a problem he deemed necessary to investigate from different sources or as secondary information while investigating common complaints. The most notorious of these investigations, concerning forced sterilization of Roma women, is discussed later.

Social and Economic Rights

The caseload of the Defender's office has a strong focus on social and economic rights issues, although the cases are seldom framed in human rights terms. The greatest number of admissible complaints received in 2005 related to social security, and complaints in this field represent the greatest increase compared to 2004, along with health care and the prison system. The number of land law complaints was substantial but had declined over previous years. In addition to the large number of individual cases, a great number of on-the-spot inquiries carried out by the Defender in 2005 touched on social and economic issues in some manner.[86] For example, they concerned the protection of the environment as well as the protection of the rights of children and adolescents and in the prison system.

An issue that the Defender is under pressure from the European countries to address concerns the social and economic discrimination against the Roma population in the Czech Republic. Advocates for the Roma population contend that Czech authorities have failed to adequately promote Roma rights in the workplace and to protect Roma from the ever increasing danger of racist attacks. When attacks do occur, Roma are often denied equal treatment before the law, a direct violation of both Czech and international law.

The failure of the Czech government to address Romani rights came to the fore in 2004, when the European Roma Rights Center (ERRC)[87] accused the government of continuing the forced sterilization policies of the former Communist regime. Eighty-seven women (approximately ten of whom were non-Roma) complained about forced sterilizations to the Office of the Public Defender of Rights. In November 2005 the district court in Ostrava ordered the Ostrava hospital to apologize to Helena Ferencikova, a Romani woman sterilized in 2001 following the birth of her second child. Ferencikova appealed the decision to seek monetary damages, and the Defender passed these on to the Ministry of Health to investigate.[88] Simultaneously with monitoring and subsequent assessment of the Ministry's progress in the inquiry, the Defender performed his own investigation.

As a result of the investigation, in December 2005 the Defender published a report on the sterilization issue that recommended restitution to the victims. The Defender found that the allegations were well founded and that in a number of cases women had been sterilized without their informed consent. Upon examination of the facts, the Defender found a pattern and practice of doctors asking for an immediate decision on sterilization under stressful conditions (under which informed consent was not possible). The Defender recommended to the Chamber of Deputies to amend the draft Act on Public Healthcare to include the following sentence in Section 49: "A reasonable period of time must elapse between providing information in accordance with section 48 and expressing consent in accordance with the previous sentence; this period must not be shorter than 7 days." The Defender further proposed that Section 48 be amended by including the following sentence: "Before performing sterilization for health reasons or for other than health reasons, the doctor has a duty to inform the patient of the nature of the intervention, its permanent consequences and potential risks as well as the available alternatives to sterilization." The Defender also urged the Chamber of Deputies to consider the adoption of reparation provisions for women who underwent sexual sterilization between 1973 and 1990, under the conditions specified by the Defender.[89]

The Defender's work on the sterilization issue generated considerable publicity both for Roma rights and for the work of the Office of the Public Defender. After the Defender issued its report on the issue, the UN Committee on the Elimination of Racial Discrimination (CERD) and CEDAW published their own strong statements against the sterilization of Roma women, specifically calling for implementation of the recommendations of the Czech Defender.[90] To follow up on CEDAW's recommendations, Czech NGOs, such as the ERRC, Gender Studies,[91] and the League of Human Rights,[92] submitted their own independent assessments of CEDAW's work in this area.

Assessment

The Czech Republic provides another effective example of how the local narrative both determines and drives the mandate, protocol, and corresponding activities of an NHRI. The ombudsman model chosen by the Czech Republic is so limited in its mandate that some may not even recognize it as a human rights institution. After all, the term *human rights* is neither a clearly stated part of its mandate nor apparently a contemplated goal of its operations. Nonetheless, looks can be deceiving. The Office of the Public Defender of Rights does respond to long-standing and deep-rooted concerns over governmental accountability to the public and to the consistent public disengagement, indifference, and distrust fostered by governmental bureaucracy since the separation of Czechoslovakia. But this is not all. The record of the Defender suggests that so long as the public views it as relevant and legitimate, it will enjoy room to interpret its mandate broadly, drawing in human rights concerns of great interest to its constituency.

That the Office of the Public Defender of Rights rarely uses human rights terminology does not negate the fact that its actions are promoting and protecting some important aspects of human rights. For example, the Defender's challenge to the practice of sterilization of Roma women in public hospitals, where they are said to be subjected to sterilization without informed consent, may steer clear of human rights terminology and instead argue the matter in the terms most recognizable to the field of public administration. Whether the argument in these cases is framed in the lingo of maladministration or human rights, the core concern is the same: a desire to defend human dignity and bodily integrity and to address discrimination—all basic human rights. In the Czech context, framing human rights issues as public administration concerns has emerged as an innovative and strategic way for the NHRI to address human rights accountability in an environment not outwardly supportive of confrontational human rights language.

The failure to adopt a clear human rights framework for contemporary social and political problems might be expected in a society like the Czech Republic, where "human rights" appear to be concepts of the past.[93] As one young lawyer explained, "Rights were something my parents wanted, but now we [mostly] have them, so with this achieved . . . [we can] move on to something else."[94] With constitutional and legislative guarantees for rights "in the bag,"[95] the protection and promotion of rights appears to be something done to or for some other country. To be sure, given its history of tensions between various ethnic groups (Czech vs. Slovak, Czech/Slovak vs. German, etc.), if there is one human rights area that has captured the attention of Czechs, it is nondiscrimination against minorities. Yet today, with the Czech Republic and Slovakia amicably divorced and Germany peacefully united, Czech citizens do not feel a sense of urgency to do something to address communal tensions and to eliminate discriminatory practices. Even as workplace discrimination against minorities and women continues to be prevalent and reports of violence against Romani and migrant workers occur with greater frequency, the attention of the Czech citizenry has turned away from human rights. "Everyone is busy here," says human rights advocate Gwendolyn Albert with a wave of her arm, pointing to the well-dressed people chatting on cell phones as they race past blocks upon blocks of high-end stores. "They have no time anymore for organizing about anything."[96]

Czech apathy toward human rights should not be overgeneralized, however. Human rights organizations still exist in the Czech Republic; law school classes on rights have become more prevalent; and Czech civil society organizations are increasingly active in international human rights advocacy.[97] Some advocates today have even called for the Defender's mandate to be enlarged so that it makes explicit reference to human rights.[98] Like many other rights-granting democracies, however, the Czech Republic does not face a public groundswell in support of improved human rights standards at home. And, like other places with well-trained researchers and advocates, the staffs of rights advocacy groups in the Czech Republic are as likely to view their human rights endeavors as work as their predecessors viewed it as a passion. "We're all pretty passionate about rights," said one young lawyer who had intently studied the lives and careers of American civil rights heroes. "But these days we also need enough money [to live] . . . [the bottom line is] a job is a job."[99]

Operating in this challenging environment, the Office of the Public Defender of Rights has served its purpose of providing citizens with the sense that they have the right to make claims against the state and that even in the most difficult cases their voices will be heard. Simultaneously it has created space for civil society to negotiate more effectively with the state on issues of accountability and responsibility in human rights. In so doing, the Defender has adopted such creative and innovative strategies as the use of young, enthusiastic employees who work on less desirable tasks (e.g., the complaint intake window), a focus on the media to ensure transparency and accountability of the Office of the Public Defender of Rights, and the adoption of educational campaigns to counter the culture of distrust and misinformation. The pace and strategy with which the Defender has begun to tackle the issue of social and economic rights also has intensified, especially under the pressure of the European Union.

The challenges facing the Office of the Public Defender are many. Yet the little space it has been able to negotiate with its limited mandate has begun to usher in a new approach to human rights in the country. The Defender has played a critical role in infusing human rights with the language of law and the jurisdiction of the state in responding to the demands of the Czech people. In the end, it has created a buffer through which state administration officials who execute the authority of state can be made more accountable. Ideally, the mandate of the Defender would be revised to directly address human rights. However, even if the mandate sees little change, the Defender's office will continue to be an important institution for rights promotion in the Czech Republic.

Chapter 6

Straddling Checkpoint Charlie

The German Human Rights Institute

G ERMANY SHARES similarities with every other country included in this book, notwithstanding substantial points of divergence. Like its neighbor the Czech Republic, Germany shares a history of Soviet bloc dominance. However, only a portion of Germany was under Soviet control, and eventually the two halves of the country were reunited. In that process, the East would "bid farewell to existence," to use the words of the Conference on Security and Cooperation in Europe (CSCE), and be absorbed into the West.[1] In contrast to Germany, *all* of Czechoslovakia was under Soviet bloc control, and eventually the two separate parts of Czechoslovakia would create their own separate identities and split apart. To the extent that regrets and nostalgic thinking would influence contemporary politics in the former Czechoslovakia, they would do so within the province of two separate states, each of which had its own incentives to manage conflict and transform "backward thinking" into more productive "forward thinking."[2] To the extent that regrets and nostalgic thinking would influence contemporary politics in the former East and West Germany, it would do so within the context of new and reemerging political struggles within a single state and the disparate experiences of the former East and West.

The points of convergence between Germany and Denmark relate to the growth of industrial and labor safeguards. Like Denmark, Germany is a highly industrialized participatory democracy with a history of social welfare protections and a strong interest in garnering international recognition as a leader in human rights. A persistent social undercurrent for many in Germany, as for many in Denmark, is an idealized attachment to notions of equality and solidarity. However, the ways in which these concepts have become understood and internalized in Germany are uniquely informed by the different histories and contemporary realities of the former East and West Germany.

The connection between Germany, Bosnia-Herzegovina, and Northern Ireland points to their historical relationships to atrocities committed by the state in past conflicts and the manner in which this history is reflected in everyday political and social life. In all these countries, almost any major issue or event can be understood by reference to historical accounts of human wrongs. For contemporary observers, Germany has at least two conflict reference points in this regard—World War II and the cold war—and both of these points can be used in political argumentation, including assertions related to human rights. Similarly, debates on human rights in Bosnia-Herzegovina and Northern Ireland are informed not only by the most recent conflicts within those areas but also by a legacy of citizenry struggling to survive massive human rights abuses. Which particular narratives matter most in history-conscious places such as Germany, Bosnia-Herzegovina, and Northern Ireland change to suit immediate political goals.

In its own unique way, then, making human rights matter in Germany has been a project informed by the local context.[3]

Economic Context

The summer of 1990 was a heady time for Germans, especially for the residents of the former East Germany. They watched as their legislature voted to dissolve itself and join West Germany, and they applauded as the wall between East Germany (German Democratic Republic [GDR]) and West Germany (Federal Republic of Germany [FRG]) was literally torn down.[4] A new era was beginning: a time rich in freedoms—of movement, assembly, and speech and, not inconsequentially, to buy a fabulous array of consumer goods provided by a free market economy. For the workers and companies of East Germany, the declared end of central planning "conveyed a feeling of unlimited possibilities, of joy in action, and in the regained meaning of life, awakening utopian visions for the near future."[5] The optimistic citizens of Germany—East and West—were blindsided by the social and economic costs of unification: "the reality of raised taxes, rising inflation, slowed economic growth and a government preoccupied by matters in the east."[6]

The unification process was devastating for the East German economy.[7] To speed the former East Germany's transition to a market economy, shock measures were introduced to blend the two economies together. The conversion rate of parity between the two currencies propped up East German industry for only a moment, as the overpricing of East German goods led them to be largely unmarketable anywhere. As East German industry collapsed, unemployment skyrocketed. The subsequent drain on the welfare systems was enormous.[8]

Although the economic costs of unification were substantial, the impact was exponentially greater when coupled with the social costs. As the Organization for Security and Cooperation in Europe (OSCE) observed:

> East Germany brought almost nothing from its system into the new union, accepting instead virtually every aspect of West Germany's constitutional and legal framework. Suddenly, easterners found themselves relegated uneasily to the sidelines as westerners came to occupy leadership positions in public administration, universities, and other civic institutions, as well as making rapid inroads into the Eastern German market.[9]

Between 1991 and 1998 alone, DM1.37 billion was transferred to the former East Germany for social security, state aids, investment, and infrastructure programs. Payment for these large expenditures substantially depended on input from the former West Germany. In 1991, Germany created a special tax (*Solidaritätszuschlag*) on income and a specific corporate income tax to finance the costs of the unification. Originally set at 3.5 percent, the rate of the taxation rose to 5.5 percent by May 2007. Although the federal government successfully raises more than €10 billion through this measure, it is deeply resented, especially in the former West Germany.[10]

The economic difficulties and social marginalization led in turn to bitterness with the present and nostalgia for the past.[11] Pejoratives began to creep into German discourse, with easterners becoming *Jammerossi* (whiners) and westerners turning into *Besserwessi* (know-it-alls). Many citizens of the former East Germany felt a loss of a sense of community as well as a loss of jobs and social support. These sentiments persist, despite improvements in Germany's economy. Even dramatic improvements in the employment rate have not helped to stem nostalgia for the old days and a desire to overturn reforms—the very reforms that government officials credit with creating such a healthy economy.[12]

A major challenge faced by the newly unified German state was to combine aspects of West and East German social welfare ideals to form a nexus of social welfare protection capable of satisfying the needs of the "new" German citizenry. West German law included a tacit acknowledgment of a *general* right to social welfare and a few specific provisions identifying concrete social welfare protections. As a result, in West Germany it was the judicial system that played a key role in developing the scope of social welfare guarantees, through the courts' interpretation of other constitutional guarantees.[13] The situation was much different in the former East Germany, where the explicit constitutional guarantee to a variety of social welfare benefits became the (albeit imperfectly) realized symbol of the Communist ideal, and its provisions were consistently executed.

Germany's social welfare and health programs have also had to contend with the structural challenges of unification.[14] West Germany's approach to social insurance, health insurance, unemployment insurance (which did not exist in the former East Germany), accident insurance, and social aid and assistance has been applied to East Germany. This has meant that the complex and heterogeneous organizational and financial arrangements present in the former West Germany to deliver health and social services have had to be built up in the former East Germany, in many cases entirely from scratch. By the mid-1990s total annual spending by the state, employers, and private households on health care, pensions, and other aspects of what Germans call the social safety net amounted to roughly DM1 trillion and accounted for about one-third of the country's gross national product.[15]

By international standards, the German welfare system is comprehensive and generous.[16] However, not everyone benefits equally. In the mid-1990s, the so-called safety net was deficient for the lower-income strata and the unemployed.[17] It was also inadequate for people needing what Germans term social aid, that is, assistance in times of hardship. In 1994, for example, 4.6 million people needed social aid, a 100 percent increase since the 1980s. Germans who had been citizens of the former East Germany, which became part of the Federal Republic of Germany in 1990, tend to be overrepresented in each of these groups.[18]

Human Rights Context

Human Rights in German Foreign Policy

The unification of Germany has fundamentally changed the international and domestic parameters of German foreign policy relating to human rights in three crucial respects.[19] First, it has become more multilateral in orientation;

second, it has ended its reluctance to use military force;[20] and, third, it has become increasingly willing to invoke human rights or humanitarian grounds to justify its actions.[21]

Following unification Germany adopted a policy that aimed at fully integrating the newly enlarged Federal Republic into the primary instruments of international cooperation: the United Nations (UN), the European Union (EU), the North Atlantic Treaty Organization (NATO), and the OSCE. German involvement in multilateral affairs has been explained as part of its "policy of responsibility."[22] Along with a preference for multilateralism, this new foreign policy platform sought to establish a higher international profile in economics, human rights, and environmental issues.[23] The unified German state is a party to every major international and European treaty on human rights[24] and is proactively engaged in UN and European human rights bodies. In contemporary times, Germany has been an active participant in the field of international justice. Germany was a leading proponent of the International Criminal Court (ICC) and a supporter of the International Criminal Tribunal for the Former Yugoslavia; German judges have sat on both of these tribunals.

One post–cold war belief motivating this approach was the notion that economics had superseded military power in political influence. Germany viewed the support of a strong market economy coupled with support for human rights and democratic governance in Eastern Europe and in the Soviet Union's successor states as a wise investment in German economic prosperity and security. German checkbook diplomacy proved to be a significant factor in the immediate crises of the post–cold war era, from the Gulf War to the humanitarian relief mission in the Horn of Africa.[25] In 1990 Germany established criteria for developmental assistance based on a recipient country's respect for human rights; commitment to democracy and participation, due process and legal certainty, a market-friendly economy, and sustainable development; and responsibility in arms development and procurement.[26] In 2006, these criteria were updated to include the peaceful resolution of conflict, sustainable development, and respect for and protection of all human rights, including women's rights, democracy, and legal security.[27]

German politicians advanced a number of reasons for the expanded public commitment to human rights as a component of German foreign policy, varying from pragmatic, political concerns to ethical considerations. In October 1997, for example, German foreign minister Klaus Kinkel promised that

Germany would take a more assertive role on all human rights issues—civil, political, economic, and social alike.

> It is not enough to prosecute and punish human rights violations that have already been committed. We need to pursue a preventive human rights policy in order to ensure that human rights violations do not occur in the first place. The means for doing this are dialogue and cooperation, but also monitoring, public criticism and coercive measures.[28]

The turning point for the role of human rights in German foreign policy came in 1999 with the German involvement in the NATO war in Kosovo. Not only did Germany support the air strikes, but, in a profound change in the orientation of German foreign policy,[29] it did so on human rights terms. To rally support for the military action, German proponents of the NATO military action relied heavily on images of atrocities, with implicit and at times explicit references to the concentration camps of World War II.[30]

Germany's arrival as an international power broker on human rights was confirmed by its 2006 election to a seat on the new United Nations Human Rights Council (the replacement of the Human Rights Committee). Foreign Minister Frank-Walter Steinmeier pointed to the election results, with 154 of 191 members of the General Assembly in favor of Germany, proving the "recognition for Germany's clear and reliable stance on international human rights policy."[31] Germany's first representative to the Council, Güenther Nooke (the commissioner for human rights policy and humanitarian aid at the Federal Foreign Office) similarly opined that the number of votes for Germany, the highest in the group of Western European states, demonstrated the high level of expectations placed on Germany in the field of human rights.

Human Rights as a Domestic Concern

German law explicitly recognizes and seeks to protect human rights.[32] The first nineteen articles of the constitution—known as the Basic Law—delineate basic rights that apply to all German citizens, including equality before the law; freedom of speech, assembly, the news media, and worship; freedom from discrimination based on race, gender, religion, or political beliefs; and the right to conscientious objection to compulsory military service.[33]

The constitutional provisions are supported by a strong underlying belief in equality. For residents (or former residents) of the former East Germany, particularly the generation in their 50s and 60s, these concepts can be traced to the East German official policy of equality.[34] East Germany attempted to win over the hearts and minds of workers by promoting the idea, if not the reality, of a flat pay scale (with workers paid well in comparison with professionals) and of state-mandated equal treatment of men and women. The concept of equality promoted in the former West Germany, in contrast, was one of equal opportunity; that the professional class in Germany is one of the least permeable in all of Europe has had little impact on the continued widespread circulation of this equality myth.

The equality myth runs in sharp contrast to the reality of everyday life for many Germans.[35] Year after year, the U.S. Department of State country report on human rights in Germany has painted a disappointing picture. The 2006 report saw an increase in the ill-treatment of prisoners and detainees by police; limits on freedom of speech, press, assembly, and association aimed at neo-Nazi groups; government and societal discrimination against minority religious groups; violence against women; instances of honor killings and forced marriages; human trafficking; and harassment of foreigners and racial minorities.[36] A growing number of right-wing crimes against other minorities, such as people with disabilities and lesbians and gay men, were also reported. The report concluded that

> Germany is currently confronted with a political and social crisis that has profound consequences for German citizens, as well as for the foreigners who seek refuge within its borders. . . . Rioting skinheads throwing Molotov cocktails at refugee shelters, onlookers applauding and cheering, slogans such as "foreigners out" and "Germany for Germans," inevitably recall images of Nazi terror during the Third Reich. Physical injury, fear and humiliation have become a daily experience for foreigners in unified Germany.[37]

The European Union Agency for Fundamental Rights noted that there was a marked upward trend in racially and ethnically motivated crimes in both Germany and France between 2001 and 2006. Incidents increased more than 12 percent during that time, causing some German officials to question whether or not to ban certain far-right political groups.[38] In 2003, the Constitutional Court rejected such a plan and would probably do so again, amid concerns that banning such groups would simply send them underground where they would be harder to track. Although most racially linked violence is perpetrated by Germans against foreigners, an attack on a German man by a youth of Turkish origin and another of Greek origin has touched off a spark in Hesse, where violence and crime by foreigners has become a major campaign issue, even though these crimes are far more rare than the frequent right-wing attacks.[39]

Violent attacks committed by neo-Nazis, skinheads, and other right-wing groups are reported in Germany's newspapers on an almost routine basis. Two subcultures are said to be responsible for much of this violence: skinheads and neo-Nazis. Skinheads, generally identifiable by their outward appearance and conduct, promote xenophobic, nationalist, and anti-Semitic attitudes. Their violent acts, which are directed against foreigners, homeless people, and political opponents, are generally regarded as spontaneous. In contrast, neo-Nazi attacks are more likely to be highly planned and even "ordered" from "commanders." Neo-Nazis in Germany are organized in *Kameradschaften* (groups of comrades) and are characterized by their rigid structures, hierarchies, and ability to act. Their ideology combines aggressive support for the national socialist system with open racism, xenophobia, and anti-Semitism.

Contributing to the long-standing prejudices against foreign-born residents are the tightly restrictive German citizenship rules. Traditionally, German citizenship has been based on the citizenship of one's parents, with few exceptions.[40] As a result, children born in Germany to families that have lived there for three generations historically have not been awarded German citizenship if neither parent has German citizenship. German citizenship law has been overhauled in recent years to permit children born in Germany to foreign parents to acquire German nationality automatically when certain requirements are met.[41] The child can acquire German nationality on the basis of *jus soli* (the principle of birthright citizenship) if one parent has had his or her ordinary and lawful residence in Germany for eight years and has the right of unlimited residence (*Aufenthaltsberechtigung*) or has had an unlimited residence permit (*Aufenthaltserlaubnis*) for three years. The law of naturalization for adults was also liberalized. The period of residence in Germany required for adult foreign nationals to be entitled to naturalization was reduced from fifteen years to eight years. A new element was added to the requirements, however, making sufficient knowledge of the German language and commitment to the Basic Law requirements for naturalization. In addition, new measures were created to guard against multiple nationality.[42] Still daunted by the cumbersome process, few of the 7 million foreigners living in Germany have applied for citizenship, even under the reformed law.[43]

Between 1955 and 1973, when the postwar *Wirtschaftswunder* (economic miracle) led to a demand of labor that could not be satisfied with Germans alone, the federal government signed a number of agreements with predominantly southern European countries to recruit workers. Under this plan, the workers would never become immigrants but would always remain temporary guest workers (*Gastarbeiter*). The temporary nature of their stay soon became permanent. Families of guest workers are often in the second or third generation. Although some of them have never even been outside Germany, Germans classify them all as *Ausländer* (foreigners, literally people from "out of the country") as opposed to *Inländer* Germans.[44] They are "attracted by a relatively liberal asylum law anchored in the constitution, existing family bonds, and the promise of a free and both economically and physically secure life."[45] However, few of these new arrivals ever become citizens. The only exceptions are the migrants of German descent who arrived from former Soviet bloc countries in the 1990s. Unlike all other groups, this population was able to take advantage of the definition of a German citizen as a descendant of a German (*jus sanguinis*).

The strict rules on migration were loosened only slightly in February 2000, when Chancellor Gerhard Schröder announced a green card scheme for computing specialists, followed by a thorough overhaul of citizenship rules. This modest move did "mark a significant departure from years of denial that immigration is welcome let alone necessary in the light of a declining birth rate and other economic considerations."[46] Yet the issuance of green cards did little to address public hostility toward foreigners. With the citizenship law excluding immigrants from political participation and broader societal integration, the likelihood of change is slim.[47]

Development of Human Rights Advocacy

Germany has a long history of independent citizen advocacy campaigns, including internationally and domestically active human rights organizations.[48] A time line of German human rights organizations reveals the steady progressive development of such advocacy in West Germany and a more circuitous path in East Germany.

The first German human rights organization, the German Liga für Menschenrechte (League for Human Rights), emerged out of the pre–World War I peace movement and was affiliated with the French Fédération Internationale des Droits de l'Homme. In the 1920s and early 1930s, the League identified itself as democratic, secular, pacifist, antiracist, and internationalist (it supported joining the League of Nations). The prominence of Jewish intellectuals in the League and the League's refusal to expel them exposed it to attack by the nationalist right and the Nazi Party. League members during the Nazi era had two public choices: flee or be arrested.

After World War II, the surviving members of the League who chose to return to Germany tried to resurrect their organization. In the ensuing struggle over who had the authority and legitimacy to resurrect the organization, one central debate concerned the priority of human rights abuses *against* Germans versus human rights abuses committed *by* Germans. Another debate for activists during this time period was the extent to which the focus should be on promoting anti-Nazi and pro–human rights ideas or on more pragmatic and immediate concerns, such as delivering food and other forms of charity to survivors of atrocities.[49]

In 1945 some of the original members of the League formed a new organization to resume the League's work: the International League for Human Rights (Internationale Liga für Menschenrechte). The involvement of the new organization in international affairs distinguished it from its predecessor, as did the political atmosphere in which it was to operate. After World War II, the world was much more conducive to thinking in human rights terms and, indeed, the then-new Universal Declaration of Human Rights and the United Nations Charter affirmed the commitment of all states to human rights. The manner in which the League impartially applied the emerging human rights framework gave it considerable moral authority, both inside and outside the country. As scholar Lora Wildenthal observed, "The League never engaged in apologies for Nazism, nationalism, militarism, or anti-Semitism, and that set it apart from many West German political organizations and parties."[50]

Branches of the League sprung up around Germany throughout the 1950s, often without support of the central organization, and thus in many respects they operated as independent entities. The second and third human rights organizations of West Germany were not founded until the 1960s: the Humanist Union (Humanistische Union) and the West German section of Amnesty International. Building on the momentum of 1960s protest movements,[51] a fourth German human rights organization, the Society for Threatened Peoples (Gesellschaft für bedrohte Völker), was founded in 1968.

East Germany's experience with human rights advocacy differs considerably not only from West Germany but also from many other east-central

European countries. The embrace of human rights as a political concept came belatedly to East Germany. Three factors related to the unique nature of politics in a divided country are particularly useful for explaining why this is so.

First, human rights were deemed to be oppositional to socialism, and not everyone was willing to relinquish socialist ideals. "The fact that for much longer than other countries, GDR oppositionists embraced socialism as a political ideal," political historian Christiane Olivo explains, created a unique situation in East Germany, where "ideas of a 'third way' or 'socialism with a human face' were heard even after the fall of the Berlin wall."[52] The intransigence of many East German intellectuals on "bourgeois rights" granted in Western democracies and denied at home has been called "the most important ideological factor delaying the emergence in East Germany of a truly oppositional movement for 'bourgeois' civil rights."[53]

Second, a contributing factor to the inability of human rights ideas to garner much support in East Germany relates to the country's uncommon relationship with the West. East Germany was a special case in the Soviet bloc because it had an option that no other state had: "an exit option," whereupon those adopting viewpoints contrary to the state, such as human rights, could more readily find a way to exit. The potential for every East German citizen to emigrate as an individual to West Germany, especially in the 1980s, provided a sort of safety valve that made activism both less attractive and more difficult. "The possibility of deporting critics to West Germany as well as the FRG's policy of buying freedom for political prisoners in the GDR effectively encouraged a political selection process among citizens."[54] The result was a more complacent status quo. It is perhaps only a slight exaggeration to claim that "those who stayed were those who still believed in the possibility of reforming socialism."[55]

Third, the concept and operation of civil society in East Germany differed considerably from the West German variant. For West Germany, the term *civil society* referred to the collection of institutions and social organizations that operated independent of the state.[56] According to this definition, civil society was working so long as it was promoting public scrutiny of government actions; a sign of healthy civil society was the degree to which it promoted popular participation. In contrast, in East Germany, civil society referred to "a more personal (than institutional) freedom apart from the all-encompassing state."[57] Measuring success according to this conception of civil society was far more difficult, because the main source of resistance was hidden away in the "sphere of private life," where small groups of friends and family could engage in an "uncontrollable sea of private conversations." Unlike the liberal democratic version of civil society, this personal version—known within Eastern and Central Europe as "antipolitics"[58]—did not seek to "conquer institutions," nor did it seek to promote open participation. Rather, as Kerry Kathleen Riley has convincingly demonstrated in her work on "everyday subversion" in East Germany, "antipolitics seeks to extend the bounds of private existence."[59]

Melding together two radically different understandings of civil society would prove difficult. Of course, not all activity of East German civil society occurred in the private realm. Opposition to the East German regime was spearheaded by public citizen movements, such as New Forum, Democracy Now, and the Initiative for Peace and Human Rights. In 1989, the most popular of these initiatives, New Forum, claimed a membership of 200,000[60]—a far cry from the intimate circles of antipolitics. However, by the spring of 1990, membership had plummeted to 15,000, and by 1994 it had fallen below the 1,500 mark.[61] Incorporating East German citizens' movements into the country's already consolidated liberal democracy could have widened and strengthened citizen participation in politics, but this would have required compromise and accommodation. "The West German political establishment," however, "rejected the idea of supplementing its established liberal democracy with an alternative participatory ideal."[62] Instead the West German political establishment was content with absorbing East Germany into its already existing system.

Human Rights Advocacy in Germany Today

Classifying groups as human rights organizations in Germany is complicated by the fact that many groups address social justice and environmental issues without using the term *human rights*.[63] Also at issue is whether groups with missions that are essentially charitable in nature or are service-delivery-driven warrant the appellation of human rights. An inclusive estimate of German organizations focusing on human rights, which would allow groups to self-identify, would set the number in the hundreds, with Amnesty International as the leading human rights organization and environmental issues a leading subject for advocates.

Germany, long a standard-bearer in environmental conservation,[64] has held considerable sway over EU policies regarding such issues as industrial pollution and global warming.[65] Germany has successfully used its sizable import power to influence EU environmental practices, and in the 1990s its threats to close its market to EU car manufacturers that failed to meet its rigorous national standards proved persuasive, forcing car producers into compliance. According to the Earth Island Institute, "German leadership in the EU has given a distinct green tinge to the block's policies. Germany's insistence on high levels of environmental protection has spread throughout EU member states."[66] The experiences of successful advocacy and policy making on environmental issues[67] created a solid foundation for the creation of an NHRI that would, like German environmental institutions, be engaged on both the national and international levels.

The German Institute for Human Rights

Mandate and Structure

In Germany, unlike most of the countries in this study, the central impetus for an NHRI came from civil society, not from any particular political party or governmental body.[68] Human Rights Forum (Forum Menschenrechte), a network of human rights groups, first introduced the idea in 1991, when NHRIs were still novel in Europe. In those early days, reluctance to embrace NHRIs stemmed from the belief that they would duplicate and draw attention away from efforts to apply and develop the already strong guarantees in the German Basic Law.

Support for an NHRI gathered momentum two years later when the solidarity benefits of participation in an international movement for human rights was demonstrated at the World Conference on Human Rights in Vienna. The vibrant NGO faction[69] in Vienna, which included a strong contingent of German human rights advocates, succeeded in convincing their governments to reaffirm the interconnectedness of human rights,[70] to create the position of the United Nations high commissioner for human rights,[71] and to recommend that each state establish or strengthen an NHRI in its country.[72] When, in the groundswell of enthusiasm for the Vienna Declaration, German politicians and human rights activists signaled their approval for the establishment of an NHRI, the idea appeared to be quickly materializing. Yet it would take another ten years to be realized.

By the time a German NHRI did finally emerge, it was with political support across the ideological spectrum and with unanimity in parliament. In December 2000, the German parliament passed a decision calling for the establishment of the German Institute for Human Rights (Deutsches Institut für Menschenrechte) (see Appendix 2 for mandate excerpts).[73] The Institute was to be registered as a nonprofit association, a private legal entity, and would be regulated by its founding statutes of March 8, 2001.[74] Three federal ministries were to contribute to the financial basis of the Institute: the Ministry of Justice, the Ministry of Foreign Affairs, and the Ministry for Economic Development and Cooperation.[75]

The Institute was to be governed by a management board of two people, the director and vice-director, appointed for a four-year period. The management board would be appointed and advised by a general council (Kuratorium) consisting of sixteen people. Twelve of these would have voting rights and represent NGOs, academia, media, parliamentarians, and public authorities.[76] To strengthen the Institute's political independence, neither the three human rights experts from the federal ministries funding the Institute (Justice, Foreign Affairs, and Development and Cooperation) nor the representative of the Bundesrat (parliamentary chamber representing the federal states) on the Institute's sixteen-member board of trustees (Kuratorium) would have voting rights.

In many respects, the creation of an NHRI through parliamentary decision rather than through legislation was less desirable. As one critic of the origins of the Institute noted, "The parliamentary decision does not provide a legal foundation for the activities, funding or appointment of key personnel (director and Kuratorium members)."[77] Nonetheless, given the strong multiparty support for the Institute, German human rights advocates were not troubled by the lack of specific establishment legislation for the Institute.

The Institute's constitutive statute identified the following six areas of activity:[78]

- *Information and documentation*: Provide a specialist reference library, including a collection of basic texts, treaties, judicial rulings, resolutions of international human rights organizations, and parliamentary decisions on human rights issues.

- *Research*: Undertake or commission studies that will provide a basis for developing strategies to prevent and avoid situations that would violate human rights as well as deal with such situations when they do arise.

- *Policy advising*: Offer advice to policymakers and society at large on human rights issues and recommend strategies for action.

- *Human rights education in Germany*: Develop curricula and materials for human rights education in particularly relevant areas (e.g., for police and prison authorities as well as staff of psychiatric institutions);

write proposals for school curricula; train civilian conflict management personnel on various aspects and issues relating to human rights; and organize events, seminars, and symposia on human rights issues.

- *International cooperation*: Collaborate with similar institutions abroad and monitor developments relating to EU, Council of Europe, OSCE, and UN human rights mechanisms.

- *Promotion of dialogue and cooperation in Germany*: Act as a catalyst and, through its public relations and communication activities, enhance the human rights work done by nongovernmental organizations.

Limitations   Although the mandate of the Institute appears to be broad, its operation is in fact somewhat limited by the decision made at its founding to deny it the power to hear individual complaints. The constitutive documents of the Institute do not address the power to hear individual complaints, nor does the Institute have a formal competence to screen legislation for compatibility with human rights norms. Thus, when individual cases are brought to the Institute's attention, the Institute can assist only by referring the matter to the relevant competent bodies. The decision was also made at the outset to deny the Institute formal power to analyze existing and proposed legislation regarding consistency with international human rights norms. Critics contend that monitoring of state behavior is essential to the work of NHRIs and to their ongoing independence from the state.

Many of the troublesome oversights with the Institute were outlined in the authoritative study conducted by Rikke Frank Jorgensen in 2004. A staff member of the Danish Institute for Human Rights, Jorgensen participated in an office exchange that allowed her to switch places with a German Institute staff member for a two-month stint. Her written report on the German Institute identified several deficits with its mandate.

> First of all, the parliamentary decision does not provide a legal foundation for the activities, funding or appointment of key personnel (director and *Kuratorium* members). Secondly, the mandate outlined in the decision is limited in scope and with no explicit reference to international human rights law or Paris Principles.
>
> Areas such as monitoring state compliance with human right standards or to inquire into alleged human rights violations and handle complaints are not mentioned in the decision.[79]

On the positive side, Jorgensen noted, in the statutes there was a clear reference to the Paris Principles, and thus a decision of the General Assembly could
invoke the principles in offering a more expansive interpretation of the mandate. Also, because the decision and statutes do not explicitly forbid systematic
state monitoring, Jorgensen suggested that states could choose to do so if they
wished.[80] Although the Institute is rightly concerned about becoming over-
extended and losing its sense of direction, the addition of systematic monitoring
to the Institute's portfolio would go a long way to answering critics who suggest
that the Institute should pay more attention to human rights issues *at home*.
This concern was vividly expressed in public debates over staffing issues.

Early Challenges   Like the other countries described in this book, the expectations for the new Institute were exceedingly high from the outset. As soon as
it opened its doors, the Institute was pushed to make a name for itself. Deputy
director Frauke Seidensticker, formerly with Amnesty International, assumed her
position in October 2001. At that point, she operated the Institute on a shoe-
string, supported by an academic adviser and administrative staff on short-term
contracts, but not in cooperation with a director, as was the original plan of the
founding board.[81] The hiring of the five initial staff members took more than a
year. Finally, by early 2003, five staff positions were filled, including a human
rights lawyer, an expert on human rights education, a librarian, and administrative staff.[82]

The hiring of an executive director, however, proved to be a more elusive
task. Expectations from the board of trustees were high, and the civil society
groups that had pushed for the Institute wanted immediate results. The person to be installed as the executive director, Percy MacLean, did not survive
his probationary period. The 2002 annual report for the Institute explains the
tenure of this former administrative law judge in a single paragraph.

> On May 15, 2002 the governing board appointed Percy MacLean, formerly pre-
> siding judge at the administrative court in Berlin, as director of the Institute. He
> assumed office in August 2002 and resigned on January 17, 2003. The director's
> position will be led by Heiner Bielefeldt from August 1st 2003. In the meantime,
> Barbara Unmüssig, one of the two vice presidents of the governing board, is act-
> ing director on a voluntary basis.[83]

Following a written agreement between the board of trustees and the former
director, the board of trustees decided not to comment on the separation. In an

apparent breach of this agreement, MacLean turned to the press for support for what he claims was improper conduct. Specifically, he complained to the press that he had been fired because of his attempts to reorient the Institute's work to focus more on economic, social, and cultural rights and on other "controversial" issues, such as German racism and anti-immigrant policies.[84] In his published account of his resignation,[85] MacLean also alleged that the conditions under which he was forced to give up his post were procedurally flawed.[86]

Press reports on the change in personnel at the Institute were divided to some degree along ideological lines.[87] For most media outlets, there was no story. The change in human resources at the Institute warranted at most a short notice or no mention at all. The publications and Web outlets that ran substantive articles were in general negative. Headlines lamented MacLean's departure: "Great Hopes Give Way to Disappointment" (*Stuttgarter Nachrichten*); "When Someone Raises Too Much Dust" (*Stuttgarter Zeitung*); "Too Much Commitment Was His Doom" (*Kölner Stadtanzeiger*); "The Consequences of Sweeping Your Own Door-Step" (*Berliner Zeitung*); "Percy MacLean Criticized Human Rights Abuses in Germany" (*Frankfurter Rundschau*).[88]

In an interview with *FAZ* (*Frankfurter Allgemeine Zeitung*) weekly,[89] MacLean denied ever suggesting that the Institute had *no* projects planned for promoting and protecting human rights in Germany. He explained, "There were certain disagreements on how detailed we should look into certain issues, not a dispute over whether domestic issues should be dealt with at all."[90] *FAZ* reported MacLean as also stating that the board considered it "politically too explosive" to check whether the country actually complies with international human rights obligations.[91]

MacLean's account was backed by some of the human rights and other civil society advocates who were already skeptical of the Institute's independence and critical of the scope of its mandate. For example, the same *FAZ* article that quoted MacLean also included an excerpt from an interview with Günter Burkhardt, the managing director of Pro Asyl (a national working group for refugees). Burkhardt is quoted as saying that MacLean's resignation was a "severe setback that plunges the Institute into crisis." MacLean addressed the central human rights issues in Germany, such as deportation custody of one and a half years. Burkhardt opined that MacLean's abrupt departure drew into question the credibility of the federal government, because "one can only stand up for human rights abroad credibly if one does so in one's own country."[92] The critical stories contended that MacLean was pushed out because he sought to place more emphasis on the monitoring of human rights in Germany, whereas his opponents at the Institute favored a greater emphasis on international human rights promotion.

The controversy over MacLean's firing illustrates an important challenge for the Institute: the need to demonstrate its relevance at home. That MacLean even raised the issue of the Institute neglecting domestic human rights issues in favor of international human rights concerns suggests that the argument had at least some currency. The Institute reacted with genuine shock over these allegations because it believed that it had already solidly demonstrated its desire to work domestically. After all, it chose to physically locate itself close to Checkpoint Charlie, on a street where the two Germanys were separated by a wall before November 1989. The 2002 annual report for the Institute explained this decision: "Choosing this historic site strongly signals the Institute's desire to play a role in both the prevention of human rights violations in Germany and the raising awareness of human rights issues. . . . The Institute wishes to contribute to the implementation and promotion [of human rights] both at the national and regional/international level."[93] The MacLean incident served to remind the Institute that establishing domestic relevance is an ongoing task that must be continually proven through its work.[94]

The Work of the Institute   The Institute's activities have been both reactive and proactive.[95] On the one hand, the Institute attempts to play a role in contemporary human rights debates by responding to them as they arise. For example, when the "head scarves debate" arose, not only in Germany but also throughout Europe, the Institute spoke out against the prohibition of the Islamic head scarves for teachers in public schools and participated in parliamentary hearings on that issue.[96] And in the public debate on forced marriages—triggered by an incident of honor killing in early 2005—the Institute participated actively in a working group devoted to overcoming discrimination against migrant women in Germany.[97] Also in response to public debates on human trafficking, in 2006 the Institute organized a series of lectures devoted to "contemporary forms of slavery."[98]

At the same time, the Institute attempts to advance human rights in Germany through the provision of information and educational activities on topics of long-term concern, thus shaping the human rights field not only as a respondent to human rights problems but also as a strategic participant.[99] Like many think tanks, the Institute sponsors talks on areas of contemporary concern. What makes the Institute's approach uniquely valuable, however, is its record of engaging with a wide range of governmental and nongovernmental participants for policy-oriented discussions that are sustained in follow-up meetings. For example, one subject of concern to the Institute is human rights promotion through international justice mechanisms, in particular the ICC. In 2003, in cooperation with Amnesty International and the German United Nations Association, the Institute hosted a conference[100] on the German criminal law designed to bring the country into compliance with the ICC, the *Völkerstrafgesetzbuch*.[101] The Institute continued to cooperate with an ongoing ICC working group that included the Federal Foreign Office, and in April 2005 an expert talk at the Institute addressed the practical experience Germany has gained so far with its International Criminal Code and its implications for foreign policy and development cooperation policy.[102]

Germany's relationship to European human rights mechanisms has also been a priority for the Institute, and the Institute has used a deliberately strategic approach in this area as well.[103] The Institute participated in the debate on the development of a coherent and effective human rights architecture that includes both the European Union (currently with twenty-seven member states) and the Council of Europe (forty-six member states). The Institute supports and follows Germany-related reports of this committee, the European Commission Against Racism and Intolerance (ECRI), and the human rights commissioners of the Council of Europe and the European Union.

In 2005 the Institute drew up a statement concerning the European Commission's plans to establish an EU agency for fundamental rights, particularly addressing the German debate on the subject. That same year, the Institute participated in a public hearing on this issue in Paris. In January 2006 the Institute hosted a high-level international workshop on the reform of the European Court of Human Rights (based in Strasbourg). The Institute also comments occasionally on the foreign human rights policy of the European Union (e.g., their human rights dialogues with countries such as Iran or China). Most recently, the Institute published a survey of the EU's peace operations from a human rights perspective.[104]

For more than two years, the Institute has actively campaigned for German signature and ratification of the Optional Protocol to the UN Convention Against Torture and Other Forms of Cruel, Inhumane, and Degrading Treatment or Punishment. In so doing, the Institute held a number of strategically timed conferences and meetings on the subject.[105] For example, a temporary deadlock in the negotiations between the federal government and the states concerning Germany's signing of the Optional Protocol and its ratification prompted the Institute to hold a conference, titled "Germany and the Optional Protocol to the UN Convention Against Torture and Cruel, Inhuman, or Degrading Treatment or Punishment," on December 14, 2005.[106] The focus of the meeting—which included fifty participants representing states, federal ministries, parliament, civil society, professional organizations, and academia—was less on *whether* Germany should accept the Optional Protocol and more on *how* it should set up efficient national monitoring mechanisms.

Among other issues, the Institute has published papers on the strict limits of preventive detention, arguing that even the need for taking counterterrorism measures cannot justify preventive detention based on mere risk prognoses.[107] The Institute has also actively participated in political discussions on counterterrorism legislation. It developed criteria for an independent and thorough evaluation of such legislation that implies restrictions on civil liberties in order to check periodically whether the principle of proportionality is actually met. Workshops with members of the federal parliament were organized to discuss the topic of an appropriate evaluation in depth.

The Institute has garnered praise for its creation of useful human rights manuals, including how-to manuals on the complaint and/or monitoring mechanisms. It has a full set of printed materials connected to the main international human rights treaties and a computerized "knowledge tool" on the European Convention. Another widely used resource is the Institute's German translation of the Council of Europe's human rights training program (known as KOMPASS). In addition, the Institute is a prolific publisher of studies, policy papers, and reports on human rights and offers seminars and workshops on human rights education for a range of professional groups, such as police officers, teachers, social workers, and lawyers.[108] These well-regarded reports, which have been professionally produced with astonishing speed, are available on the Institute's web page.[109]

Social and Economic Rights

Although there is no specific provision in the Basic Law addressing social and economic rights, several provisions of the constitution can be read as inferring Germany's commitments in this area.[110] In particular, Article 20 states that "the Federal Republic of Germany is a democratic and social federal state."[111] The word *social* has been commonly interpreted to mean that the state has the responsibility to provide for the basic social welfare of its citizens. The Basic Law, however, does not enumerate specific social duties of the state, and the exact nature of social and economic rights continues to be disputed.[112] However, a seminal ruling of the federal Constitutional Court stated that "constitutional rights are not just defensive rights of the individual against the state, but embody an objective order of values, which applies to all areas of the law . . . and which provides guidelines and impulses for the legislature, administration and judiciary."[113]

In line with these constitutional developments, the Institute's work has long placed an emphasis on economic, social, and cultural rights.[114] Significant publications in this area include Jacob Schneider's study on the justiciability of economic, social, and cultural rights (*Die Justiziabilität wirtschaftlicher, sozialer und kultureller Rechte*), Marita Körner's study on the international human right to work (*Das internationale Menschenrecht auf Arbeit*), and, importantly, a study by Valentin Aichele and Jacob Schneider on the social rights of the elderly (*Soziale Menschenrechte älterer Personen in Pflege*). Perhaps the strongest sign of an institutional commitment to economic rights is the creation of a programmatic staff position with a specific mandate to work on economic and social rights.

The Institute has also played an expert role in debates over German antidiscrimination legislation. Since 2004 the Institute has held background talks with the press and the proponents of antidiscrimination legislation.[115] Significantly, in 2005, the Institute took part in the federal parliament's (Bundestag) expert hearing on the antidiscrimination draft law. In anchoring its statements to "the daily reality of discrimination in Germany" and international human rights law and practice, the Institute has—in its own words—attempted to rise above "an emotional and partly polemical public debate."[116] Many projects of the Institute have a strong antidiscrimination aspect.[117] Other recent projects have included the publication of a handbook in September 2005 on individual communications, which incorporates the principles of Article 14 of the International Convention on the Elimination of All Forms of Racial Discrimination (ICERD), and the production of a revised work by David Nii Addy titled "Racist Discrimination: International Obligations and National Challenges for Human Rights Work in Germany." Also, the Institute has undertaken a range of projects related to the Convention on the Elimination of All Forms of Discrimination Against Women—encouraging shadow reports to the CEDAW by civil society, studying concluding observations, or discussing economic and social rights of women at public conferences.[118]

Assessment

From its inception, the German Institute for Human Rights has sought to advance the human rights concerns of all Germans, without a bright line distinction between East and West. The Institute could take such a neutral position because, unlike some German civil society organizations, it is not captured by any political party, nor does it bear the imprint of either "former East" or "former West." This frees the Institute to work on the areas of concern highlighted here, especially all forms of the denial of equality (e.g., based on race, gender, and citizenship status), the failure of authorities to respond adequately to racist and xenophobic violence, and the human rights implications of economic injustice. However, being effective in addressing these issues as an impartial organization of a unified Germany may at times require open recognition of historical and ongoing differences between the former East Germany and the former West Germany. German citizens may be unified by law, but they often do not share the same prioritization of concerns, nor do they suffer the same consequences should a grievance go unaddressed.

Whether and how the cold war era of division continues to affect Germany remains greatly disputed: There is no single "German opinion" on the matter, nor is there one unified position of the "former East" and "former West." Yet few would disagree that the division casts a shadow over day-to-day life and politics in Germany today and that the field of human rights provides no exception. For example, despite considerable efforts to successfully integrate West Germany and East Germany, significant disparities continue to exist, not only in cultural terms but also in economic terms: Unemployment rates continue to be much higher in the east, and there is still large-scale emigration to the west and a resulting depopulation of vast areas. To its credit, the Institute took steps to acknowledge and address these and other differences between East and West Germany, responding to salary differentials between East and West Germany and other social and economic issues.[119]

The Institute continually reminds itself and its constituency—the German people and government—of the dark history that gave rise to the creation of the modern human rights regime. A statement adopted by the Institute's Board of Trustees in 2004 reads:

> In its preamble, the United Nations' Universal Declaration of Human Rights of 1948 speaks of "barbarous acts which have outraged the conscience of mankind." Above all, this is a reference to the crimes of the Nazi regime. The German

Institute for Human Rights views the efforts to keep the memory alive of the immoral and unjust regimes of the past as an important source of today's human rights work. It is in this sense that it feels a strong connection with organizations that honour the victims of the Nazi terror regime but also with those who keep alive the memory of the victims of East Germany's communist dictatorship.[120]

Given the imperative of history in Germany, human rights advocacy will always be in some sense backward looking. Yet turning the largely successful German Institute into a tremendously successful organization also requires forward-looking steps.

First, the Institute should continue to demonstrate to the German citizenry its ongoing relevance. The more a citizenry deems its NHRI to be engaged in issues of local concern, the more likely it is to view the NHRI as legitimate and to cooperate with it. Demonstrating the earmarks of a legitimate institution can be difficult under all circumstances. It is a particularly difficult task in Germany, where substantial taboos exist against airing ongoing points of tension between East and West. The Institute should continue its efforts to open discussions on these difficult issues.

Second, the Institute should address the issue of inclusion by hiring more high-ranking staff from the former East Germany. Ideally, the Institute would draw from the experiences and talents of both East and West German human rights activists in structuring its projects, especially its meetings and reports. However, the staff composition is heavily tilted toward the former West Germany, especially at the high levels.

Third, a study should be undertaken to assess the feasibility of adding a new complaint mechanism to the Institute. Like the Czech Republic, Germany could benefit greatly from the creation of such a department. The executive director of the Institute, Heiner Bielefeldt, has expressed concern that the addition of a complaint mechanism to the Institute is neither practical nor desirable. An individual complaint procedure could not simply be folded into the existing Institute, said Bielefeldt. "It could be done, but it would require a new, different institution."[121] The new, different institution would tend to a need that is currently unaddressed—that is, the need to improve respect for the rule of law and to enhance citizen's belief that administrative units and government agents cannot continuously violate the law with impunity. Even as it is pragmatic about its role in society and circumspect about the dangers of overreaching its capacity, the Institute can improve its impact with the addition of a complaints procedure.

Chapter 7

Conclusion

THE COUNTRY STUDIES in this volume illustrate some of the ways that local context influences the creation and operationalization of national-level human rights institutions. NHRIs are designed to bridge the disconnect between abstract and seemingly unobtainable human rights standards at the international level and practical national-level action. Advocacy is channeled through NHRIs, encouraging human rights supporters to concentrate on the domestic level, where human wrongs are perpetrated, survived, and, in ideal cases, overcome. By translating normative commitments into specific programs, NHRIs support and strengthen domestic human rights constituencies and influence the international reputations of states on the basis of their human rights practices. Transnational NHRI networks then further these goals by establishing acceptable standards and patterns of behavior for NHRIs that help to socialize states into the NHRI fold.

The commitment of states to NHRIs in this manner might be expected to lead to norm and policy diffusion, whereby countries facing similar problems and attempting to address them with NHRI assistance would adopt the same human rights norms and policies. The country studies in this volume, however, paint a much more complex picture. Although the countries considered here do offer ample evidence of the accomplishments of NHRIs and suggest an important role for their human rights promotion and protection activities in the future, a closer look at the specific NHRIs discloses their imperfections and exposes the uneven nature of domestication of international human rights norms. The link made by NHRIs between international norms and local action does not necessarily lead to the diffusion of international norms into local political and social processes. The local context generates too many additional variables that act as a filter, preventing a symmetric and human-rights-informed norm diffusion process. As one observer explains, "International norms and institutional designs do not diffuse linearly; they are filtered, contested, reinterpreted and appropriated, even misused domestically for quite local political processes."[1] The temporal dimension of NHRIs is an important factor in this process. To extend the analogy of local political and economic context as a filter, the exact shape of the filter (i.e., whether it is funnel-like or flat-bottomed) changes over time, influencing the demands placed on particular NHRIs, creating both constraints and opportunities for furthering the protection and promotion of human rights institutions.

The purpose of this conclusion is twofold: first, to state in clear terms the challenges ahead in each of the case studies and invite a comparison of the differences and similarities between and among cases; and, second, to draw out the contextual factors that warrant additional consideration by future researchers, advocates, and policymakers. To this end, I begin by distilling the conclusions of the narratives down to their core and presenting specific recommendations. I then unpack the most salient points of comparison of general applicability to other cases.

Reviewing the Narratives

Bosnia-Herzegovina

The Bosnian example demonstrates the considerable challenges of a complex NHRI system created wholly by outsiders, initially in the context of armed conflict and, later, evolving under periods of postconflict transition. That Bosnia-Herzegovina should have an interest in establishing its own NHRI should come as no surprise, given the prominent role of human rights in the Balkans. Unaddressed human rights violations were both a cause and a consequence of the conflict there, and international peace brokers inserted human rights into the peace process and made them central to civil reconstruction efforts. In the short term the promotion of human rights in Bosnia-Herzegovina has depended on intensive international involvement in the establishment of human rights mechanisms and, in many cases, their day-to-day operations. Wedding Bosnia-Herzegovina to human rights promotion and protection over the long run, however, will require a transfer of control from international organizations to local ones, a process known colloquially as Bosnification. In the case of the human rights ombudsman offices in Bosnia-Herzegovina, reform will also require the consolidation of the three NHRIs into one central office with control over the entire country.

Even if Bosnia-Herzegovina successfully surmounts these organizational hurdles, a Bosnian NHRI faces an extremely skeptical citizenry for whom government action in the name of human rights is instinctively viewed with distrust. If any institution can make a difference in influencing public opinion in Bosnia-Herzegovina, it will be a local entity and not another foreign imposition. To be successful, then, a unified Bosnian NHRI must find a way to address human rights violations of both past and present and to work more closely with the local voluntary sector to address harms that are deterring progress on democratic reforms.

Germany

The Bosnian example of institutions imposed by an outside group of international military allies is familiar in the twentieth century. The German example, however, represents a rather unique twist on this pattern. Rather than creating new institutions for the newly reunited Germany, the political institutions of one unit, West Germany, were imposed on the other unit, and little from the second unit was preserved in the new state. As a result, East German accomplishments were not reflected in the new institutions, and they remain untested as novel developments of the new united Germany. Unlike Bosnia-Herzegovina, the impetus for a German NHRI came from within Germany. However, the problems identified by German human rights advocates are as much internal as external, and solutions are both forward and backward looking, addressing not only contemporary questions of antiforeigner sentiment and racism but also grievances from both World War II and the time of division, carrying into the present day. The German Institute for Human Rights has proven itself capable of responding to the challenge of operating in a newly reunited country, but it has not acknowledged and addressed the lingering problems that still remain from reunification and the new social ills arising in the wake of unification.

The speed at which the German Institute established itself as an international human rights leader is remarkable. Nonetheless, its reputation at home has lagged. The problem is not one of a *bad* reputation but rather of *no* reputation: Despite its strong publications and open public meetings, the Institute has not garnered the kind of attention it needs to be a consistently visible player in domestic politics and remains a largely marginal actor. A strong argument can be made that the Institute would enhance its reputation at home by involving itself more in the issues that matter most to its local constituency, with special attention devoted to racial discrimination and economic and social rights. Although the Institute has addressed these issues in its reports and meetings, it could engage more fully with members of the voluntary sector who are also addressing these issues. Germany may also wish to reconsider its reluctance to establish a comprehensive human rights complaint mechanism. NHRI complaint mechanisms provide aggrieved individuals with an opportunity to be heard and, in so doing, build trust for the rule of law and for government institutions. Germany's stature at home and abroad will only be enhanced by the development of a comprehensive complaint mechanism.

Northern Ireland

Although proposed and certainly supported by outside actors, the Northern Ireland Human Rights Commission (NIHRC), was very much the result of local efforts, and, not surprisingly, the main roadblocks to success are of a local nature. In its day-to-day operations, including its participation in international treaty creation and monitoring, its complaint procedures, and its public education campaign, the NIHRC has proven quite capable. However, the NIHRC that activists worked hard to establish has been beset by internal dissension. Its challenge lies in its identification of and ability to address larger, difficult cases. Thus, for example, the decision to address head-on the matter of community harassment of public school children proved to be unwise because the NIHRC itself was not yet unified in its opinion and the issue was so controversial and divisive that success would be highly unlikely. To make its mark on society, the NIHRC will be called on to take a position on emotional issues, but it cannot do so until it has achieved institutional maturity and unity.

Northern Ireland has a vibrant voluntary sector, covering a wide range of neighborhood associations, faith-based and secular charities, labor organizations, constituency-driven advocacy groups (e.g., women, the elderly, people with disabilities), and issue-oriented organizations.[2] An important part of an NHRI's mandate is cultivating its relationship with the voluntary sector. NHRIs can serve the voluntary sector through providing relevant training, library resources, access to documentation, and other support tailored to specific joint projects suggested by and initiated outside the NHRI. From a purely instrumental perspective, NHRIs need input and ideas from the voluntary sector. NHRI legitimacy depends on voluntary sector ownership of issues taken up by the NHRI and the manner in which they are addressed. The case study of Northern Ireland underscores that NHRI cultivation of the voluntary sector should be considered an imperative for the development of the NHRI and for its continued and expanded success.

Czech Republic

The establishment of a human rights ombudsman (the Public Defender of Rights) in the Czech Republic was an accomplishment of Czech civil society and was supported by the proponents of the Velvet Revolution. Almost immediately after the Defender began his work, however, civil society lost interest and politicians turned to more pressing matters. Their human rights goals appeared to be settled by their country's transition of government from an authoritarian regime to a participatory democracy. The challenge faced by human rights supporters in the Czech Republic thus rests on discovering meaningful ways to remind both the citizenry and the government of the continued importance of vigilant human rights promotion and protection locally.

By addressing cases of maladministration, the Defender's office has played a role in restoring people's trust in government institutions. It has shown how even the most modest ombudsman's office can expand its reach significantly by broadening its mandate to include the regular inspections of state-run institutions, such as prisons, hospitals, and orphanages, and by including in its work special reports on systemic abuses. Similarly, the Defender's office might wish to formally expand its mandate so that it aligns more fully with the Paris Principles, operating independently from government and addressing a full range of human rights issues.

Denmark

Like the Czech Office of the Public Defender of Rights, the Danish Institute for Human Rights (DIHR) was generated internally, and, to a greater extent than the Czech Republic, it has flourished in a society that prides itself on its positive human rights climate. However, the DIHR enjoys a longer record of success. There is no reason to doubt that the DIHR will continue to be a driving force behind the campaign for NHRI establishment and strengthening internationally. At home, however, the DIHR will continue to be tested for its relevance. Political leaders and organizations on the left of the political spectrum will continue to demand that the Institute take on the issues of antiforeigner sentiment, xenophobia, and racism more directly. Politicians on the right of the political spectrum will continue to demand that the DIHR demonstrate that it truly represents Danish opinion and thereby shield itself from the label "opinion doctor."[3]

The attempts by the right wing to shut down the DIHR should stand as a warning for other NHRIs, insofar as government transition, even in stable participatory democracies, can create new threats to human rights institutions. When NHRIs intervene in the "internal affairs" of their own country—one of their prime tasks as national human rights bodies—there is always a danger that they will generate opposition. In particular, the governmental *and* nongovernmental actors who have a vested interest in the status quo are likely to feel threatened. Successful human rights advocacy on one's own home ground is possible, the Danish case study teaches us, only when the mandate and position of its commissioners and staff are secure and are not called into question whenever the organization takes an unpopular position, invoking criticism. Denmark, like the Czech Republic, would do well to continue to engage effectively with the voluntary sector and media in demonstrating its continuing relevance and reaffirming its local legitimacy.

Unpacking Context

These case studies expose the variables that are most salient in determining *how* local context matters and in suggesting whether and to what extent an NHRI can successfully fulfill its mandate to the satisfaction of human rights advocates, political leaders, and their constituents. The most important variables fall into two categories: (1) those related to the nature of demands placed on NHRIs and (2) those concerning meaningful stakeholder participation (see Table 7.1 for the variability of local context and Table 7.2 for the tasks performed by the five NHRIs studied here).

Nature of Demands

The specific demands placed on NHRIs can be linked to three stages of their development. Identification of the stage at which an NHRI has been established or reestablished (i.e., substantially reformed) sheds light on the sources and purpose of the demands. Whether originating inside or outside the state, with beneficent or self-serving goals, the nature of the demand for NHRIs helps to explain their reception within the local context.

In the early stage of NHRI development, pressures for the creation of these institutions were linked to democratization processes, and international support for their creation was largely limited to encouraging the creation of

Table 7.1 Comparison of local context for NHRIs

	Human Rights Ombudsman for Bosnia-Herzegovina	Czech Republic Public Defender of Rights	Danish Institute for Human Rights	German Institute for Human Rights	Northern Ireland Human Rights Commission
Product of external pressure	Yes	Somewhat	No	No	Yes
Product of internal pressure	No	Yes	Somewhat	Yes	Somewhat
Recent violent conflict	Yes	No	No	No	Yes
Recent government transition	Yes	Yes	No	No	No
Compliant with Paris Principles	Yes	No	Yes	Yes	Yes
Country signatory to International Criminal Court	Yes	No	Yes	Yes	Yes
Human rights top domestic concern	Yes	No	No	No	Yes
Human rights top foreign policy concern	No	No	Yes	Increasingly yes	Not much
Strong history of human rights organizing	No	No	No	Yes	Yes
Boasts well-developed voluntary sector	Increasingly	Decreasingly	Yes	Yes	Yes

note: This table includes only one out of the three mechanisms in Bosnia-Herzegovina, that is, the state institution; the two entities are omitted.

democratic forms of governance. As the Office of the High Commissioner for Human Rights (OHCHR) notes:

> The emergence or re-emergence of democratic rule in many countries has focused attention on the importance of democratic institutions in safeguarding the legal and political foundations upon which human rights are based. It has therefore become increasingly apparent that the effective enjoyment of human

Table 7.2 Tasks performed by NHRIs

	Hearing individual complaints	Exercising right to compel evidence	Investigating systematic violations	Inspecting state institutions	Monitoring treaties	Giving legal advice to government	Writing reports	Sponsoring academic research	Providing education	Providing professional training	Participating in international NHRI network
Bosnia-Herzegovina	Yes	Limited	Limited	Yes	No	Rarely heard	Increasing ability	No	Limited	No	Not very active
Czech Republic	Yes (but not necessarily human rights)	Yes	Growing ability	Yes	No	Rarely heard	Yes	No	Selective (e.g., of media)	No	Not very active
Denmark	Limited to race	Rarely	Not on regular basis	Possibility exists	Yes, but selective	Yes	Yes	Concentration in this area	Yes	Yes	Very active
Germany	No	Rarely	No	Not on regular basis	Possibility exists	Yes	Yes	Yes	Concentration in this area	Yes	Very active
Northern Ireland	Yes	Rarely	Limited	Yes	Yes	Yes	Yes	Yes	Very limited	Yes	Very active

rights calls for the establishment of national infrastructures for their protection and promotion.[4]

NHRIs are expected to play a role in democratization by identifying and promoting the *substance* of international human rights and by improving on the *process* of good governance through greater transparency and accountability. By opening new spaces for citizen participation, then, NHRIs shine a light on the operations of public administration and reestablish faith in government institutions. When these goals coincide with local goals, enthusiastic embrace of NHRIs at the local level can be anticipated.

NHRI development was energized by the United Nations World Conference on Human Rights in 1993 and given further impetus by the appointment, in 1995, of a UN special adviser on NHRIs.[5] During this second period of NHRI development, the United Nations and other transnational institutions and individual member states accelerated their direct engagement in creating and strengthening these institutions through technical assistance programs.[6] Expectations for these outsider-imposed institutions (illustrated here most dramatically by Bosnia-Herzegovina) have a temporal component: The outside influence is expected to be limited in time, and control over the NHRI is expected to be transferred to local actors over time.

The temporal component proved important for the local reception of NHRIs because it enhanced the willingness of local actors to embrace a new institution. Like card sharks at a casino who double their bets after they have already lost their houses, many states were convinced to accept NHRIs because they had little to lose; they were emerging from conflict and/or transitioning rapidly to democratic governance and were already under tremendous pressure to modify their domestic institutions in line with international human rights standards.

The third stage of NHRI development emerged after the terrorist attacks in the United States on September 11, 2001, and the subsequent U.S.-announced war on terror. During this third stage, the range of actors involved and the nature of the motives for NHRI promotion are decidedly more dynamic and complex. Although UN involvement has remained important, a broader array of individual states and regional and international transnational institutions are demanding (and, in many cases, financially supporting) NHRI creation as one of several steps that states must take to signal their alliance with democratic nations.[7] Pressured by the United States and its allies in the war on terror, many states eagerly established wholly new NHRIs or improved and expanded the activities of existing NHRIs. Insofar as NHRI establishment is part of an outside agenda and is funded largely by international donors, concerns arise as to the depth of the democratic process by which the new NHRIs are established. As Janet Lord argues, the time line created by the United Nations to establish an NHRI in Iraq was driven by UN pressure to secure a success in Iraq and was neither participatory nor in compliance with the UN's own standards on the establishment of NHRIs.[8]

State promotion of the establishment of NHRIs has become increasingly disingenuous as this third stage has progressed. Some governments with long records of breaching fundamental human rights have cynically agreed to NHRI establishment, hoping that the mere existence of the NHRI could serve as a badge of human rights observance in the wake of abiding human rights violations. Human Rights Watch has reported on examples of this kind of NHRI instrumentalism in Africa;[9] from the present case study, Bosnia-Herzegovina and Northern Ireland provide their own version of states embracing NHRIs as a stage in shedding their image (and their history) as human rights abusers. Some of the biggest supporters of NHRI establishment view them as necessary mechanisms, not for themselves but for other states. The U.S. position on NHRIs provides a good illustration of a state committed to the spread of NHRIs in other states but opposed to NHRIs on its home soil (and, indeed, opposed to human rights treaty ratification and implementation on home soil).[10] In this stage of exceptionalism and exemptionism,[11] in which NHRIs are viewed as appropriate for only certain countries and the U.S. opts out of NHRI and human rights treaty participation, local actors are likely to be highly skeptical of NHRIs promoted by third parties.

Meaningful Stakeholder Participation

The creation of NHRIs may be the product of international involvement far more than domestic initiative, as NHRI scholar Sonia Cardenas has persuasively argued,[12] but the health of an NHRI depends almost entirely on the domestic reception awaiting it. Best practice standards on NHRI development also stress the vital necessity of meaningful and sustained stakeholder participation in the establishment process.[13] Stakeholders include all those who have an investment in the creation and operation of NHRIs. Stakeholder participation is a process by which stakeholders "play an active role in decision-making and in the consequent activities which affect them."[14] A number of factors influence stakeholder participation in NHRIs, but two of the most important are access to avenues of participation and local human rights literacy.

An NHRI thrives better in an atmosphere marked by awareness of the importance and desirability of human rights. Although the presence of an active voluntary sector may be helpful for the domestification of human rights norms, this is not always the case. The presence of voluntary organizations may just as likely prove to be a roadblock where human rights are alien concepts to local voluntary organizations and where the grassroots is already organized around an alternative framework to that suggested by human rights. In these cases, NHRI supporters need to emphasize the ways that the human rights framework complements rather than competes with the alternative framework. Only by appearing nonthreatening and inclusive can an NHRI attract sufficient stakeholder participation. Stakeholder participation in NHRIs helps to ensure that the organizations are responsive to community interests and values while remaining open and inclusive.

The task of preparing a locality for an NHRI by encouraging human rights literacy is extraordinarily difficult where a citizenry has a long history of mistrusting state institutions and where "people had become accustomed to having their political thinking done by others."[15] Active local involvement in NHRIs, from the earliest stages in which the institution is planned to the day-to-day operations, helps to build an informed citizenry, promotes communal trust, and, in so doing, reduces the potential for future conflicts over the NHRI. For many states, NHRIs can play an important "legitimizing role," in that they "signal the stamp of democratic legitimacy."[16] But in doing so, they may create new sources of conflict. NHRIs are more successful when they find a way to address human rights abuses while courting stakeholders to take an increasingly active role in the creation and operation of NHRIs.

The case studies in this volume suggest that the involvement of stakeholders is also particularly important in deeply divided societies, where expectations for NHRIs run high and the personal stakes are great. Yet it is precisely in these difficult cases that NHRIs can do the most good. As peace agreement expert Christine Bell observes, "Human rights institutions aim not merely to police the division between law and politics found in the polity, as in the classic liberal-democratic state, but also to create the polity by mediating communal divisions."[17] Empowered by human rights, which turns all citizenry into rights holders and the state into a duty bearer, the polity created and watched over by an NHRI is more resilient to new conflicts and better equipped to address past violations and present communal tensions peacefully.

Several scholars have commented on the overly legalistic approach taken when building NHRIs and the overemphasis on establishing quasijudicial complaint procedures to the exclusion of other strategies considered vital in postconflict settings, such as creating structures that build a culture of human rights.[18] Strategies that have been given short shrift include the integration of human rights education into primary, secondary, and university curricula and into informal education; strengthening human rights organizational capacities; and deepening human rights capacity among the judiciary and foreign ministries tasked with applying and monitoring human rights implementation, respectively. Further empirical research on NHRIs would do well to consider also the broad educational mandate of NHRIs. Even without an explicit educational agenda, every NHRI, by providing a space for civil discourse on human rights norms and by introducing actions consonant with the protection and promotion of human dignity, contributes to the construction of a human rights culture.

Scholarship on NHRIs can advance theoretical understandings of human rights practice, explaining, for example, how power relations between NHRIs and other domestic structures work to constrain or empower NHRIs within domestic politics and assessing power differentials among new NHRIs within regional and international structures. In making such observations, scholars should be mindful of the local context. As the present study attests, the operation of NHRIs can be evaluated only in reference to the local.[19] Raj Kumar puts it plainly when he says, after having closely studied numerous NHRIs, that these institutions "are [at best] functioning well only when the legal, constitutional and the governance framework respects the rule of law, promotes good governance and pursues sound development policies and at worst one more institution that legitimizes the functions of the state and does not intervene even when blatant violations of civil and political rights and economic and social rights occur."[20]

Given the importance of local context, the establishment of NHRIs can never, by itself, be a human rights panacea. However, these institutions can and indeed do play important roles in making human rights matter.

Reference Matter

Appendix 1

*Principles Relating to the Status of National Institutions
(The Paris Principles), Adopted by General Assembly Resolution
48/134 of 20 December 1993*

Competence and responsibilities

1. A national institution shall be vested with competence to promote and protect human rights.

2. A national institution shall be given as broad a mandate as possible, which shall be clearly set forth in a constitutional or legislative text, specifying its composition and its sphere of competence.

3. A national institution shall, inter alia, have the following responsibilities:

    (a) To submit to the Government, Parliament and any other competent body, on an advisory basis either at the request of the authorities concerned or through the exercise of its power to hear a matter without higher referral, opinions, recommendations, proposals and reports on any matters concerning the promotion and protection of human rights; the national institution may decide to publicize them; these opinions, recommendations, proposals and reports, as well as any prerogative of the national institution, shall relate to the following areas:

        (i) Any legislative or administrative provisions, as well as provisions relating to judicial organizations, intended to preserve and extend the protection of human rights; in that connection, the national institution shall examine the legislation and administrative provisions in force, as well as bills and proposals, and shall make such recommendations as it deems appropriate in order to ensure that these provisions conform to the fundamental principles of human rights; it shall, if necessary, recommend the adoption of new legislation, the amendment of legislation in force and the adoption or amendment of administrative measures;

(ii) Any situation of violation of human rights which it decides to take up;

(iii) The preparation of reports on the national situation with regard to human rights in general, and on more specific matters;

(iv) Drawing the attention of the Government to situations in any part of the country where human rights are violated and making proposals to it for initiatives to put an end to such situations and, where necessary, expressing an opinion on the positions and reactions of the Government;

(b) To promote and ensure the harmonization of national legislation, regulations and practices with the international human rights instruments to which the State is a party, and their effective implementation;

(c) To encourage ratification of the above-mentioned instruments or accession to those instruments, and to ensure their implementation;

(d) To contribute to the reports which States are required to submit to United Nations bodies and committees, and to regional institutions, pursuant to their treaty obligations and, where necessary, to express an opinion on the subject, with due respect for their independence;

(e) To cooperate with the United Nations and any other organization in the United Nations system, the regional institutions and the national institutions of other countries that are competent in the areas of the protection and promotion of human rights;

(f) To assist in the formulation of programmes for the teaching of, and research into, human rights and to take part in their execution in schools, universities and professional circles;

(g) To publicize human rights and efforts to combat all forms of discrimination, in particular racial discrimination, by increasing public awareness, especially through information and education and by making use of all press organs.

Composition and guarantees of independence and pluralism

1. The composition of the national institution and the appointment of its members, whether by means of an election or otherwise, shall be established in accordance with a procedure which affords all necessary guarantees to ensure the pluralist representation of the social forces (of civilian society) involved in the protection and promotion of human rights, particularly by powers which will enable effective cooperation to be established with, or through the presence of, representatives of:

(a) Non-governmental organizations responsible for human rights and efforts to combat racial discrimination, trade unions, concerned social and professional organizations, for example, associations of lawyers, doctors, journalists and eminent scientists;

(b) Trends in philosophical or religious thought;

(c) Universities and qualified experts;

(d) Parliament;

(e) Government departments (if these are included, their representatives should participate in the deliberations only in an advisory capacity).

2. The national institution shall have an infrastructure which is suited to the smooth conduct of its activities, in particular adequate funding. The purpose of this funding should be to enable it to have its own staff and premises, in order to be independent of the Government and not be subject to financial control which might affect its independence.

3. In order to ensure a stable mandate for the members of the national institution, without which there can be no real independence, their appointment shall be effected by an official act which shall establish the specific duration of the mandate. This mandate may be renewable, provided that the pluralism of the institution's membership is ensured.

Methods of operation

Within the framework of its operation, the national institution shall:

(a) Freely consider any questions falling within its competence, whether they are submitted by the Government or taken up by it without referral to a higher authority, on the proposal of its members or of any petitioner;

(b) Hear any person and obtain any information and any documents necessary for assessing situations falling within its competence;

(c) Address public opinion directly or through any press organ, particularly in order to publicize its opinions and recommendations;

(d) Meet on a regular basis and whenever necessary in the presence of all its members after they have been duly concerned;

(e) Establish working groups from among its members as necessary, and set up local or regional sections to assist it in discharging its functions;

(f) Maintain consultation with the other bodies, whether jurisdictional or otherwise, responsible for the promotion and protection of human rights (in particular, ombudsmen, mediators and similar institutions);

(g) In view of the fundamental role played by the non-governmental organizations in expanding the work of the national institutions, develop relations with the non-governmental organizations devoted to promoting and protecting human rights, to economic and social development, to combating racism, to protecting particularly vulnerable groups (especially children, migrant workers, refugees, physically and mentally disabled persons) or to specialized areas.

Additional principles concerning the status of commissions with quasi-jurisdictional competence

A national institution may be authorized to hear and consider complaints and petitions concerning individual situations. Cases may be brought before it by individuals, their representatives, third parties, non-governmental organizations, associations of trade unions or any other representative organizations. In such circumstances, and without prejudice to the principles stated above concerning the other powers of the commissions, the functions entrusted to them may be based on the following principles:

(a) Seeking an amicable settlement through conciliation or, within the limits prescribed by the law, through binding decisions or, where necessary, on the basis of confidentiality;

(b) Informing the party who filed the petition of his rights, in particular the remedies available to him, and promoting his access to them;

(c) Hearing any complaints or petitions or transmitting them to any other competent authority within the limits prescribed by the law;

(d) Making recommendations to the competent authorities, especially by proposing amendments or reforms of the laws, regulations and administrative practices, especially if they have created the difficulties encountered by the persons filing the petitions in order to assert their rights.

source: http://www2.ohchr.org/english/law/parisprinciples.htm, © 1993, United Nations. Reprinted with the permission of the United Nations.

Appendix 2

The NHRIs: Mandate Excerpts and Contact Information

note: The excerpts from the mandates all focus on the nature of the institution created, its powers, and its jurisdiction. For more detailed information on the composition of the NHRI, its relationship to government, and a more complete list of its activities and complaint procedure (where applicable), please see the complete document listed for each case study.

1. Bosnia-Herzegovina

The Human Rights Ombudsman of Bosnia and Herzegovina
Marsala Tita 7
BA 7100 Bosnia and Herzegovina
Phone: +387 33 666 005/6
Fax: +387 666 004/7
E-mail: ombudsman@ohro.ba
Website: http://www.ohro.ba

Excerpts from Mandate

I. Nature

Article 1

1. The Human Rights Ombudsman of Bosnia and Herzegovina is an independent institution set up in order to promote good governance and the rule of law and to protect the rights and liberties of natural and legal persons, as enshrined in particular in the Constitution of Bosnia and Herzegovina and the international treaties appended thereto, monitoring to this end the activity of the institutions of Bosnia and Herzegovina, its entities, and the District of Brčko, in accordance with the provisions of the present Law.

II. Powers and Jurisdiction

Article 2

1. The Institution shall consider cases involving the poor functioning of, or violations of human rights and liberties committed by, any government body.

2. The Institution shall act either on receipt of a complaint or *ex officio*.

3. The Institution may undertake general investigations.

4. The Institution may recommend appropriate individual and/or general measures.

5. The Institution shall not consider cases concerning decisions, facts or events prior to 15 December 1995.

Article 6

1. An Ombudsman may refer cases of alleged human rights violations to the highest judicial authorities of Bosnia and Herzegovina competent in human rights matters, pursuant to the rules concerning appeals to these authorities, whenever he or she finds that this is necessary for the effective performance of his or her duties.

source: Law on the Human Rights Ombudsman on Bosnia & Herzegovina, http://www.legislationline.org/legislation.php?tid=160&lid=3025&less=false

2. The Czech Republic

Czech Republic Ombudsman
Ombudsman Judr. Otakar Motejl
Údolní 39
602 00 Brno
Czech Republic
Phone: +420 0 542542 777
Fax: +420 0 542542 772
E-mail: kancelar@ochrance.cz
Website: http://www.ochrance.cz

Excerpts from Mandate

Part One

General Provisions

§1

(1) The Public Defender of Rights (hereinafter referred to as "the Defender") works to defend persons in relation to the actions of authorities and other institutions listed in this Law, should such actions be inconsistent with the law, in contradiction to the principles of a democratic legal state and good administration, and also in the event of inaction by these authorities, thereby contributing to the defense of fundamental rights and freedoms.

(2) The scope of activity of the Defender under clause 1 applies to ministries and other administrative authorities having competence over the entire territory of the Czech Republic, administrative authorities subject to such authorities, the Czech National Bank when acting as an administrative authority, the Council for Radio and Television Broadcasting, bodies of municipal authorities when performing state administration, as well as the Czech Police, Czech Army, Castle Guard, the Czech Prison Service unless specified otherwise below, to facilities performing custody, imprisonment, protective or institutional care, protective therapy as well as to public medical insurance organizations (hereinafter referred to as "Authority").

(3) The Defender systematically visits places where there are or may be located persons whose freedom is restricted by public authority, or as a result of their dependence on care provided, to strengthen protection of such persons against torture, or cruel, inhumane and degrading treatment, or punishment or other mistreatment.

(4) The scope of activity of the Defender under clause 3 applies to

   a. facilities performing custody, imprisonment, protective or institutional care, or protective therapy;

   b. other places where there are or may be located persons whose freedom is restricted by public authority, especially police cells, facilities for holding foreigners and asylum facilities;

   c. places where there are or may be located persons whose freedom is restricted as a result of dependence on the care provided, especially social care institutes and other facilities providing similar care, medical facilities and facilities providing social/legal protection of children (hereinafter referred to as "Facilities").

Part Two

Activities of the Defender

§9

The Defender acts

   a. On the basis of a Complaint filed by a person or entity (hereinafter referred to as "Complaint") addressed to his/her person,

   b. On the basis of a Complaint addressed to a Member of the Chamber of Deputies or a Senator, who has passed the said Complaint to the Defender,

   c. On the basis of a Complaint addressed to either of the Houses of Parliament, which has passed the said Complaint to the Defender, or

   d. On his/her own initiative.

§10

(1) Anyone has the right to address the Defender with a written Complaint in matters that are in his/her sphere of competence under §1, clauses 1 and 2; such a Complaint may be entered verbally into a record.

source: Czech Republic: Law of 8th December 1999 on the Public Defender of Rights, http://www.ochrance.cz/en/ombudsman/zakon.php.

3. Denmark

The Danish Institute for Human Rights
Executive Director Mr. Morten Kjaerum
Strandgade 56
1401 Copenhagen K.
Denmark
Phone: +45 326 98888
Fax: +45 326 98800
E-mail: center@humanrights.dk
Website: http://www.humanrights.dk

Excerpts from Mandate

Chapter 1

Establishment and objective

Section 1. For the purpose of strengthening research, analysis and information activities in Denmark relating to international matters, these being understood as the areas of foreign affairs, security and development policy, conflict, holocaust, genocide and politically motivated mass killings, as well as human rights at home and abroad, a Danish Center for International Studies and Human Rights is established.

Subsection 2. The Center comprises the following independent units:

1) The Institute for International Studies, including the activities so far incumbent upon the Danish Institute of International Affairs, the Center for Development Research and the Copenhagen Peace Research Institute. The previous activities of the Danish Center for Holocaust and Genocide Studies comprise a special section in the Institute.

2) The Danish Institute for Human Rights, including the activities of the Danish Center for Human Rights to date.

Section 2. The Institute for International Studies works for the achievement of its objective by the following:

1) To undertake, promote and coordinate independent research on international affairs.

2) To conduct analyses and statements upon request from Parliament, the government or on its own initiative, as well as to follow international development with a view to assessing the foreign and security policy situation in a broad political and economic context, including the position of Denmark in relation to development policy issues. Unless otherwise decided in each individual case, the aforementioned analyses and statements fall within the sphere of responsibility of the Board of the Institute.

3) To communicate research results, analyses and knowledge and to carry out documentation and information activities, including library, on international affairs.

4) To participate in research education in collaboration with other research institutions, including the enhancement of research capacity in developing countries as well as to undertake supplementary education for the users of the Institute.

5) To function as a link between Danish and international research environments within the sphere of work of the Institute.

Subsection 2. The Danish Institute for Human Rights shall in the execution of its activities take its outset in the human rights recognized at any given time by the international society, including in particular those laid down in the United Nations Universal Declaration, conventions adopted by the United Nations and the Council of Europe, and the civil rights contained in the Danish Constitution.

The Institute shall work to strengthen research and information relating to human rights in times of peace and under armed conflict, in particular:

1) To carry out an independent and autonomous Danish research effort in the area of human rights.

2) To advise Parliament and the government on Denmark's obligations in the area of human rights.

3) To conduct and promote education at all levels in relation to human rights, including public information.

4) To promote equal treatment of all persons without discrimination on the basis of race or ethnic origin, including the provision of assistance to victims of discrimination to have their complaints dealt with, with due regard for the rights of the victims, the associations, the organizations and other legal entities, to initiate independent analyses on discrimination and to publish reports and to make recommendations on issues relating to discrimination.

5) To provide information on human rights to volunteer organizations, researchers, public authorities and the interested public.

6) To ensure modern publicly accessible library and documentation facilities relating to human rights.

7) To support volunteer organizations and others in collecting human rights documentation.

8) To promote the coordination between and assisting the volunteer organizations' work in the area of human rights.

9) To support and strengthen Nordic and other international cooperation in the area of human rights.

10) To contribute to the implementation of human rights domestically as well as internationally.

source: Act Governing the Establishment of the Danish Center for International Studies and Human Rights, http://www.humanrights.dk/About+us/Founding+law

4. Germany

Deutsches Institut für Menschenrechte (German Institute for Human Rights)
Zimmerstraße 26/27
D-10969 Berlin
Germany
Phone: +49 30 259 359-0
Fax: +49 30 259 359-59
E-mail: No general e-mail address; see web page for e-mail form.
Website: http://www.institut-fuer-menschenrechte.de/webcom/show_article.php/_c-635/_nr-1/_lkm-653/i.html.

Excerpts from Mandate

Preamble

All states and societies worldwide are required to give high priority to protecting and promoting human rights, as called for emphatically in the Paris Principles adopted by the United Nations General Assembly in 1993 which called for the establishment of independent national human rights institutions (Resolution 48/134).

The Committee of Ministers of the Council of Europe in 1997 likewise recommended the establishment of independent national institutions for the promotion of human rights (Recommendation R (97) 14). The aim is to safeguard and develop the comprehensive system of protection that has evolved in Council of Europe member states on the basis of the European Convention on the Protection of Human Rights and Fundamental Freedoms. National human rights institutes are intended to make an important contribution towards achieving this aim.

Conscious of its responsibility for policies to protect human rights in Germany and abroad, the German Federal Parliament (Deutscher Bundestag) resolved unanimously on 7 December 2000 to establish an independent German Institute for Human Rights (Bundestag Printed Paper 14/4801). As an institution of civil society in relation to existing governmental and non-governmental institutions, it is to play an important role as a mediator and catalyst and to support and interlink the work of those institutions.

I. General Provisions

§2

Aims and Tasks

1. The Association shall inform on the situation of human rights in Germany and abroad and contribute toward the prevention of human rights violations and towards the promotion and protection of human rights.

2. The Association shall realize its aims by carrying out the following tasks in particular:

   (a) Information and documentation:
   It shall keep an internet-based record of existing databases with the aim of improving access to information for members of parliament, government departments, non-governmental organizations, scientists, journalists, legal practitioners and the interested public. In addition it shall provide access to JURIS [Juristisches Informationssystem für die Bundesrepublik Deutschland/legal information system for the Federal Republic of Germany] and provide computer based access to library networks in Germany. It is also planned to set up a specialist presence library with a collection of fundamental works, treaties, case law, resolutions of international human rights protection bodies and parliamentary resolutions on human rights. . . .

   (b) Research:
   The Institute's research shall contribute towards developing competences for human rights work. Prompt publication of studies that can be used to work out strategies to prevent, avoid and cope with situations that violate human rights will be especially helpful in furthering this aim. . . .

   (c) Policy advice:
   The Institute's practice-oriented focus will enable it, inter alia, to advise representatives of politics and society on human rights issues and to recommend strategies for action. It may do this on its own initiative or by request. Academics and politicians should engage in continuous dialogue and exchanges of views on human rights issues. Events organized by the Human Rights Institute can assist this dialogue.

   (d) Human rights-related educational work in Germany:
   Human rights-related educational work is to be carried out primarily by providing second-line support to other institutions. The Institute can be involved, inter alia, by way of

   • Its establishment as a national coordinating centre for human rights education in line with United Nations guidelines set out in Document A/52/469 Addendum 1,

- Drawing up teaching programs and materials for human rights education in sensitive areas such as police authorities, prison services and psychiatric establishments,
- Drawing up ideas for school curricula,
- Involvement in developing competences in human rights-related issues and themes for experts engaged in civil conflict resolution,
- Human rights-related events, seminars and symposia.

(e) International cooperation:
The Institute will be active abroad if this is required in order to properly fulfill its responsibilities and in order to exchange experience and knowledge on human rights. Possible areas of work are in the field of civil society and government administration, focusing mainly on collaboration with existing government and non-government agencies. Simultaneously, the Institute's international work will consist of interaction with other comparable institutions abroad and of content-related support and monitoring of the EU, the Council of Europe, the OSCE and UN human rights mechanisms.

(f) Promotion of dialogue and cooperation in Germany.

source: Statutes of the German Institute for Human Rights (revised version dated November 29, 2006), http://www.institut-fuer-menschenrechte.de/webcom/show_article.php/_c-636/_nr-7/i.html.

5. Northern Ireland

Northern Ireland Human Rights Commission
Chief Commissioner Professor Monica McWilliams
Temple Court
39 North Street
Belfast, BT1 1 NA
Northern Ireland, U.K.
Phone: +44 28 90243987
Fax: +44 28 90247844
E-mail: information@nihrc.org
Website: http://www.nihrc.org

Excerpts from Mandate

The Commission was created by Section 68 of the Northern Ireland Act 1998, in compliance with a commitment made by the British Government in the Belfast (Good Friday) Agreement of 10 April 1998.

Section 68

The Northern Ireland Human Rights Commission

(1) There shall be a body corporate to be known as the Northern Ireland Human Rights Commission.

(2) The Commission shall consist of a Chief Commissioner and other Commissioners appointed by the Secretary of State.

(3) In making appointments under this section, the Secretary of State shall as far as practicable secure that the Commissioners, as a group, are representative of the community in Northern Ireland.

Section 69

The Commission's functions

(1) The Commission shall keep under review the adequacy and effectiveness in Northern Ireland of law and practice relating to the protection of human rights.

(2) The Commission shall, before the end of the period of two years beginning with the commencement of this section, make to the Secretary of State such recommendations as it thinks fit for improving—

   (a) its effectiveness;

   (b) the adequacy and effectiveness of the functions conferred on it by this Part; and

   (c) the adequacy and effectiveness of the provisions of this Part relating to it.

(3) The Commission shall advise the Secretary of State and the Executive Committee of the Assembly of legislative and other measures which ought to be taken to protect human rights—

   (a) as soon as reasonably practicable after receipt of a general or specific request for advice; and

   (b) on such other occasions as the Commission thinks appropriate.

(4) The Commission shall advise the Assembly whether a Bill is compatible with human rights—

   (a) as soon as reasonably practicable after receipt of a request for advice; and

   (b) on such other occasions as the Commission thinks appropriate.

(5) The Commission may—

   (a) give assistance to individuals in accordance with section 70; and

   (b) bring proceedings involving law or practice relating to the protection of human rights.

(6) The Commission shall promote understanding and awareness of the importance of human rights in Northern Ireland; and for this purpose it may undertake, commission or provide financial or other assistance for—

(a) research; and

(b) educational activities.

(7) The Secretary of State shall request the Commission to provide advice of the kind referred to in paragraph 4 of the Human Rights section of the Belfast Agreement.

(8) For the purpose of exercising its functions under this section the Commission may conduct such investigations as it considers necessary or expedient.

(9) The Commission may decide to publish its advice and the outcome of its research and investigations.

source: Northern Ireland Act of 1998 (Good Friday Agreement), Sections 68–69 (establishing the Northern Ireland Human Rights Commission and its mandate), http://www.opsi.gov.uk/Acts/acts1998/ukpga_19980047_en_7#pt7-pb1-l1g68.

Notes

Chapter 1

1. See Ishay, *History of Human Rights*; and Lauren, *Evolution of Human Rights*.

2. Quotation from my conversations with Larry Minear over the past fifteen years.

3. For the purpose of this book, *local* (as in "local political context") is used interchangeably with *domestic* and *national*.

4. United Nations Commission on Human Rights, *Report of the Secretary General*.

5. Office of the United Nations High Commissioner for Human Rights, *Fact Sheet No. 19*; International Council on Human Rights Policy, *Performance and Legitimacy*, 5; Reif, "Building Democratic Institutions," 11–13; Parlevliet, *National Human Rights Institutions*, 3.

6. See Reif, "Building Democratic Institutions."

7. Cardenas, "Adaptive States," 5.

8. Baylis, "Minority Rights," 66.

9. See Tsekos, "Human Rights Institutions in Africa." There are now NHRIs across all regions. For a comprehensive list of NHRIs, see http://www.nhri.net.

10. Cardenas, "Emerging Global Actors," 35.

11. United Nations World Conference on Human Rights, *Vienna Declaration*, Article 36.

12. Doorenspleet, "Reassessing the Three Waves." See also Office of the United Nations Office of the High Commissioner for Human Rights, *Fact Sheet No. 19.*

13. Parlevliet, *National Human Rights Institutions*, 7.

14. Recent examples of NHRIs developed as part of a peace agreement mandate include El Salvador (1992), Rwanda (1993), Bosnia-Herzegovina (1995), Northern Ireland (1998), Sierra Leone (1999) (still under establishment), and Afghanistan (2004). The peace agreement following Guatemala's conflict (1996) called for the strengthening and broadening of the mandate of an already existing institution.

15. Recent examples include Afghanistan and Iraq.

16. See United Nations Security Council, *Establishment of UN Transitional Administration in East Timor*, para. 8.

17. See Bell, *Peace Agreements*. In her book, Bell develops this observation with reference to peace agreements and democratic and human rights institutions.

18. South Asia Human Rights Documentation Center, *National Human Rights Institutions in the Asia Pacific Region*.

19. See Ishay, *History of Human Rights*. See also Ishay, *Human Rights Reader*.

20. See Mertus, "Prospects for National Minorities."

21. See Forsythe, *Human Rights in International Relations*.

22. See Morsink, *Universal Declaration of Human Rights*, 400.

23. Blanton, "Foreign Policy in Transition?"

24. Donnelly, *International Human Rights*, 13–16. See also D. C. Thomas, *Helsinki Effect*, 312; and Dunne and Wheeler, *Human Rights in Global Politics*, 350.

25. Bouvier, *Globalization of U.S.-Latin American Relations*, 272.

26. Jackson, *Global Covenant*, 112.

27. Compare Mertus, *United Nations and Human Rights*, with Gallagher, "Making Human Rights Treaty Obligations a Reality."

28. See Risse et al., *Power of Human Rights*, 334; and Landman, *Studying Human Rights*, 178.

29. Keck and Sikkink, *Activists Beyond Borders*.

30. See, for example, Article 2 of the International Covenant on Civil and Political Rights (ICCPR), 1966, UN document A/6316 (entered into force March 23, 1976); Convention for the Elimination of All Forms of Discrimination Against Women, adopted December 18, 1979, UN document 1249 UNTS 13 (entered into force September 3, 1981).

31. Universal Declaration of Human Rights (http://www.udhr.org/UDHR/default .htm).

32. United Nations World Conference on Human Rights, *Vienna Declaration*, pt. I, ch. III.

33. United Nations General Assembly, *Report of the Secretary General*.

34. See, generally, Danish Institute for Human Rights, *National Human Rights Institutions*.

35. In 1991, after the first major United Nations meeting on NHRIs was held, other transnational gatherings on NHRIs were held in Tunis, Tunisia (1993), Manila, Philippines (1995), Merida, Mexico (1997), Marrakesh, Morocco (2000), and Cairo, Egypt (2005). Regional workshops were also carried out in Europe, Africa, and the Asia-Pacific region. Plans to bring NHRIs to the Middle East are currently being developed.

36. United Nations World Conference on Human Rights, *Vienna Declaration*, Article 36.

37. See Lord, "United Nations Commissioner for Human Rights," 329; Ramcharan, *United Nations High Commissioner*.

38. The International Coordinating Committee has also developed best practices for NHRIs. See http://www.nhri.net.

39. "Principles Relating to the Statutes and Functioning of National Institutions," G.A. Res. 48/134, U.N. ESCOR, Annex (1993) (reprinted in United Nations, *National Human Rights Institutions: Handbook*); Commission on Human Rights Research, 1992/

54, Annex, UN ESCOR, Supp. 22, E/1992/22, ch. II, sec. A (1992). Also, UN document A/48/134 Annex (1993). The Paris Principles were drafted at the first International Workshop on National Institutions, held in Paris in 1991, which was then endorsed by the United Nations in 1993.

40. See Coordinating Committee of National Human Rights Institutions, *Rules of Procedure*, adopted April 15, 2000, and amended April 13, 2002 (http://www.nhri .net/2007/ICCProcedureEng2006.pdf).

41. See, for example, Matshekga, "Toothless Bulldogs?"

42. All the NHRIs in the present study have been awarded an A, except for the Czech ombudsman office, which has not been graded.

43. See http://www.nhri.net.

44. International Council on Human Rights Policy, *Human Rights Standards*.

45. United Nations Human Rights Council, "Information for National Human Rights Institutions."

46. The activities of the Asia Pacific Forum include "information exchanges; training and development for commission members and staff; development of joint positions on issues of common concern; sharing expertise; periodical regional meetings; specialist regional seminars on common themes and needs; [and] responding promptly and effectively to requests from other national institutions to investigate violations of the human rights of their nationals present in a country that has a national institution" (Mission of Asia Pacific Forum, http://www.asiapacificforum.net/about/mission.html). All participants in the forum are required to be independent national institutions that conform with the Paris Principles.

47. For examples from Africa, see Murray, *Role of National Human Rights Institutions*.

48. Reif, "Building Democratic Institutions"; Gallagher, "Making Human Rights Treaty Obligations a Reality"; Pinheiro and Baluarte, "National Strategies."

49. See Lord, "National Human Rights Institutions"; Cardenas, "State Institutions for Human Rights"; and Kumar, "NHRIs in South Asia."

50. See, for example, Human Rights Watch, *Protectors or Pretenders*; International Council on Human Rights Policy, *Performance and Legitimacy*; Pinheiro and Baluarte, "National Strategies"; and Howe and Johnson, *Restraining Equality*.

51. See Ramcharan, *Protection Role*.

52. See publications of the Danish Institute for Human Rights. In particular, see Pohjolainen, *Evolution of National Human Rights Institutions*; and Lindsnaes et al., *National Human Rights Institutions*.

53. Murray, *Role of National Human Rights Institutions*.

54. The leading how-to text is United Nations, *National Human Rights Institutions: Handbook*.

55. As sociolegal theorist John Flood observes, "If we want to know how organizations attempt to create a culture . . . we need narrative because these things are contested, ambiguous and inchoate." Flood, "Socio-Legal Ethnography," 47.

56. See, for example, Murray, *Role of National Human Rights Institutions*; and Human

Rights Watch, *Protectors or Pretenders*. This is not to suggest that only European scholars write about African NHRIs. See, for example, Okafor and Agbakwa, "On Legalism."

57. Pragmatic considerations that contributed to the case selection include my own familiarity with the countries in question, the strength of my contacts in each area, and my award of a Fulbright grant (which supported research in Denmark in particular).

58. Commission Nationale Consultative des Droits de l'Homme (National Consultative Commission on Human Rights), http://www.cncdh.fr/.

59. Greek National Commission for Human Rights, http://www.nchr.gr.

60. Office of the Ombudsman, Spain, http://www.defensordelpueblo.es/Index.asp.

61. Office of the Ombudsman, Portugal, http://www.provedor-jus.pt/.

62. For a good classification of types of NHRIs, see Cardenas, "Emerging Global Actors," 35.

63. For a good illustration of this technique, see Pickering, *Peacebuilding in the Balkans*, 189–191.

Chapter 2

1. Østergaard, "Danish National Identity."

2. Arter, *Democracy in Scandinavia*, 158–159, 270–273.

3. Some critics suggest that "a characteristic of being Danish is unwillingness to go to extremes" and that "the drawback of equality [in Denmark] is mediocrity." Zarrehparvar and Hildebrandt, "Discrimination in Denmark," 45–46.

4. As noted in this chapter, the DIHR was once known as the Danish Center for Human Rights (DCHR).

5. Denmark's first constitution was adopted in 1849. Important amendments were introduced in 1866 and 1915. The current constitution dates from June 5, 1953.

6. For further historical analysis, see Jespersen, *History of Denmark*; and Lauring, *History of Denmark*.

7. See Givens, *Voting Radical Right*, 136.

8. *Encyclopedia of the Nations*, s.v. "Denmark: Political Background."

9. As presented on the respective parliaments' web pages: "Stortingsvalg" [Storting Election], Stortinget, http://www.stortinget.no/om_stortinget/forfatningen/stortings valg.html; and "Vilka kommer in i riksdagen?" [Who Will Be Elected to the Riksdagen?], Sveriges Riksdag, http://www.riksdagen.se/templates/R_Page____1536.aspx.

10. "Oppløsningsrett" [The Right to Dissolve Parliament] (a comparative discussion of the parliamentary mechanism), *Kommunal-og regionaldepartementet* (Norwegian Ministry of Local Government and Regional Development), http://www.regjeringen .no/nb/dep/krd/dok/NOUer/2001/NOU-2001-03/20/5.html?id=363364#note3. The alternative to holding an election is for the government chief to resign.

11. See Borre and Andersen, *Voting*, 18–19.

12. Between 1995 and 2007 six new parties were created from factions of already existing parties. For a brief history of the political party system, see "Politiske partier," Folketinget, November 28, 2007, http://www.ft.dk/UserFiles/1FD5DDEF-92B4-4032 -A4C4-71B53FFFAB2D/Informationsark/politiske_partier.pdf.

13. See "Kort beskrivelse" [Short Description (of Folkebevaegelsen)], http://www.folkebevaegelsen.dk/visartikel.php?artikelnr=775.

14. See "Arbejdsprogram" [Work Program (for Junibevaegelsen)], http://www.j.dk/index.php/juni/baggrund/C31/.

15. "Kort beskrivelse."

16. See their own comments at "Frihed 2000 (FRI)," Folketinget, http://www.folketinget.dk/BAGGRUND/00000035/00479365.htm.

17. "Analyse: Valgets hotte emner" [Analysis: The Hot Topics of the Election], Danish Broadcasting Corporation (DR) (Denmark's public, license-financed media corporation), October 24, 2007, http://www.dr.dk/Nyheder/Temaer/Politik%20temaer/2007/Valg/2007/08/17/101758.htm.

18. See Sidmore-Hess, "Danish Party System."

19. See Givens, *Voting Radical Right*, 133.

20. Givens, *Voting Radical Right*, 133.

21. "Lov om ændring af udlændingeloven og ægteskabsloven med flere love" [Law on Change of the Danish Aliens Act, the Act on Marriage, and Other Laws], Retsinformation.dk (a law database managed by the Danish Ministry of Justice), https://www.retsinformation.dk/Forms/R0710.aspx?id=28895.

22. "Lov om ændring."

23. "Lov om ændring."

24. On October 24, 2007, Rasmussen announced that new elections for the Folketinget would be held because of the major reforms that the government had suggested. The suggestions included a "quality reform" of the public sector, a strategy for increasing the workforce, a climate and energy plan, a finance bill for 2008, and a seven-year economic strategy (to be finished in 2015). The articulated rationale behind holding new elections was that political disputes should be identified and diffused so that political parties can work in peace on the reforms without speculating on elections. There were no substantial changes for the government as a result of the election; Rasmussen made a few changes to his cabinet, and the governing coalition of the Liberal Party and the Conservative People's Party remained the largest groups in the parliament. Their ability to form a majority together with the Danish People's Party on a case-by-case basis thus remained intact. Although the Liberal Party lost six of their seats in parliament, they remained the largest party. The Danish Social Liberal Party suffered the biggest loss, and the Socialist People's Party gained the most seats. Anders Fogh Rasmussen, "Statsminister Anders Fogh Rasmussens udtalelse af særlig karakter onsdag den 24. oktober 2007 (jf. Folketingets forretningsorden, §19, stk. 3)" [Prime Minister Anders Fogh Rasmussen's Statement of Particular Character, Wednesday, October 24, 2007], Statsministeriet (Prime Minister's Office), October 24, 2007, http://www.stm.dk/index/dokumenter.asp?o=2&n=0&d=2914&s=1; "Her er Foghs nye regering" [This Is Fogh's New Government], Danish Broadcasting Corporation, http://www.dr.dk/Nyheder/Politik/2007/11/23/083052.htm.

25. Interviews with political analysts by author, Copenhagen, October 2006.

26. Givens, *Voting Radical Right*, 145.

27. Haahr, "Between Scylla and Charybdis."

28. Ministry of the Interior and Health (Denmark), "New Denmark."

29. Dansk Indutri, "Danish Confederation of Industries."

30. Larsen, "Municipal Size and Democracy."

31. Municipal Trust of Denmark (DKK), "KL Concerned."

32. Axel Pihl-Andersen and Henrik Vinther Olesen, "Countries Must Borrow for Reforms," *Jyllands-Posten,* January 3, 2006.

33. That Denmark has been active in debates on the definition of torture does not imply that all human rights advocates view the country's contribution in a positive light. In the discussions over the definition of torture, Denmark has worked hard to distinguish torture from inhumane treatment; in so doing, Denmark has suggested that the prohibition against torture is absolute but that, at the same time, in some cases inhumane treatment is permissible. Many human rights advocates are dismayed that Denmark opened the door for inhumane treatment. Interviews with human rights advocates by author, Copenhagen, November 2006.

34. See, for example, Pohjolainen, *Evolution of National Human Rights Institutions;* and Lindsnaes et al., *National Human Rights Institutions.*

35. Incorporation would make the treaty part of Danish law in its original form. Birgitte Olsen reminds us that treaties can also be implemented through active or passive transformation. See Olsen, "Incorporation and Implementation."

36. As of this writing the European Convention on Human Rights (ECHR) is the only human rights convention to be incorporated into Danish legislation.

37. Olsen, "Incorporation and Implementation," 228.

38. Interview with DIHR staff by author, Copenhagen, November 2006.

39. Interview with DIHR staff by author, Copenhagen, November 2006.

40. United Nations Committee on the Rights of the Child, *Consideration of Reports.*

41. United Nations Committee on the Rights of the Child, *Consideration of Reports.*

42. United Nations Human Rights Committee, *Concluding Observations of the Committee: Denmark,* para. 15.

43. United Nations Human Rights Committee, *Concluding Observations of the Committee: Denmark,* para. 16.

44. United Nations Human Rights Committee, *Concluding Observations: Denmark.*

45. United Nations Human Rights Committee, *Concluding Observations: Denmark.*

46. United Nations Human Rights Committee, *Concluding Observations: Denmark.*

47. Hans Otto-Sano, interview by author, Copenhagen, November 2006.

48. Henrik Rothe, interview by author, Copenhagen, November 2006.

49. Rothe, interview by author, Copenhagen, November 2006.

50. Rita Roca, interview by author, Copenhagen, November 2006.

51. Tina Klejs Jensen, interview by author, Copenhagen, November 2006.

52. Interview with social workers by author, Copenhagen, November 2006.

53. Nye, *Introducing Denmark,* 32.

54. Nye, *Introducing Denmark,* 32.

55. Koch, "Protection of Socioeconomic Rights," 405. See also Koch, "Political Rights."

56. Because human rights claims are usually brought by individuals against the state, they are said to have vertical effect. Two areas in which claims are said to have horizontal effect (because claims may be between private parties) are the right to assembly and freedom of expression under the ECHR. See Olsen, "Incorporation and Implementation," 240.

57. Despite these significant advances in the area of disability, substantial accusations have arisen in recent years pointing out the inadequacy of disability policies and practices in Denmark. Part of the problem stems from the general lack of willingness of Danish lawmakers to enact laws prohibiting specific forms of discrimination against people with disabilities. The lack of appropriate legislation in this area has drawn particular international attention. The UN Committee on the Rights of the Child, for example, criticized the Danish government in 2005 for not having a uniform policy for ensuring rights for children with disabilities. See Højsteen, "More UN Criticism."

58. Dane Age Association, "Ældre patienter bliver svigtet" [Older Patients Neglected].

59. The basis for this bill of rights would be national minimum standards for care for the elderly (e.g., at least one bath a week, healthier food) and a complaints board. Danish Social Democrats, "Clear Rights for the Elderly."

60. U.S. Department of State, Bureau of Democracy, Human Rights, and Labor, *Denmark.*

61. See European Commission Against Racism and Intolerance, "Third Report on Denmark." See also the remarks of the editor-in-chief of *Skara Rosen* (the Swedish newspaper of the Social Democrats) at http://www.socialdemokraterna.se/upload/webbforalla/ak/skara/dokument/skararosen/skararosen_05_02.pdf.

62. This is an ongoing issue that is still being widely reported; see, for instance, "Denmark Busts Alleged Plot to Kill Cartoonists," *Der Spiegel*, February 12, 2008, http://www.spiegel.de/international/europe/0,1518,534704,00.html; and "Danish Muhammad Cartoon Reprinted," *BBC*, February 14, 2008, http://news.bbc.co.uk/2/hi/europe/7242258.stm.

63. For an overview of the most dramatic events during the first three months of 2006, see "Muhammed-krisen dag for dag" [The Muhammed Crisis Day by Day], Danish Broadcasting Corporation, March 26, 2006, http://www.dr.dk/Nyheder/Temaer/Oevrige_temaer/2006/Tegninger/Artikler/kronologi1.htm.

64. "Muhammed-krisen dag for dag."

65. See, for instance, the prime minister's New Year's address for the government's view on freedom of expression, http://www.statsministeriet.dk/Index/dokumenter.asp?o=6&n=0&h=6&t=14&d=2468&s=2. The court's decision was appealed, only to be upheld by the Director of Public Prosecutions. See his press release at http://www.rigsadvokaten.dk/media/bilag/pressemeddelelse_engelsk_endelig.pdf.

66. Ministry of Foreign Affairs of Denmark, "Official Response."

67. "Danske varer sælger igen i Mellemøsten" [Danish Goods Sold Again in Middle East], Danish Broadcasting Corporation, September, 3, 2007, http://www.dr.dk/Nyheder/Penge/2007/09/03/054124.htm; "Muhammedkrisen kostede to milliarder i eksport" [The Muhammed Crisis Cost Two Billion in Exports], Danish Broadcasting

Corporation, February 4, 2007, http://www.dr.dk/Nyheder/Penge/2007/02/04/111521 .htm.

68. Flemming Rose, "Kommentar: DR støtter Ellemanns løgn" [Commentary: DR Supports Elleman's Lies], *Jyllands-Posten*, January 13, 2008, http://jp.dk/kultur/article 1229181.ece.

69. Jacob Mollerup, "Muhammed-sagen år 3: Hårdt JP-angreb på DR" [The Muhammed Case Year 3: Jyllands-Posten Gives Hard Blow to DR], Danish Broadcasting Corporation, January 14, 2008, http://www.dr.dk/OmDR/Lytternes_og_seernes_redaktoer/ Klummer/2008/0114144224.htm.

70. "Murder Plot Against Danish Cartoonist," *Jyllands-Posten*, February 12, 2008, http://jp.dk/uknews/article1263133.ece. The authorities' immediate response was to decide to deport the Tunisians, but according to Christoffer Badse at the DIHR, this would be illegal in the aftermath of a recent European Court of Human Rights judgment. According to the judgment, Italy would be in breach of Article 3 of the European Convention on Human Rights if Nassim Saadi, a terror suspect, were to be deported to Tunisia. See "Ny dom understøtter torturfare i Tunesien" [New Judgment Affirms Danger of Torture in Tunisia], *DIHR*, February 29, 2008, http://menneskeret.dk/Nyheder/ ARKIV/Nyheder+2008/Ny+dom+underst%c3%b8tter+torturfare+i+Tunesien; European Court of Human Rights, "Grand Chamber Judgment."

71. "Mange aviser trykker Muhammed-tegning" [Many Newspapers Print Muhammed Drawing], *Berlingske Tidende* (one of Denmark's major newspapers), February 13, 2008, http://www.bt.dk/article/20080213/pcindland/802130342/.

72. "Uklart om ny Muhammed-krise er undervejs" [Unclear Whether New Muhammed Crisis Is Under Way], *Jyllands-Posten*, February 22, 2008, http://jp.dk/udland/ article1275479.ece. A few days after Møller's statement, however, the Sudanese government decided to boycott Danish goods. See "Sudan boykotter officielt danske varer" [Sudan Officially Boycotts Danish Goods], *Jyllands-Posten*, February 25, 2008, http:// jp.dk/udland/article1277993.ece.

73. "Bislev Mejeri skruer ned for productionen" [Bislev Dairy Reduces Production], *Arla Foods*, February 27, 2008, http://www.arlafoods.dk/appl/HJ/HJ201AFD/HJ201D01 .NSF/O/8609706CA61E05A2C12573FC004BEA48.

74. "Muhammed-tegninger koster jobs i Bislev" [Muhammed Drawings Cost Jobs in Bislev], Danish Broadcasting Corporation, February 27, 2008, http://www.dr.dk/ Regioner/Nord/Nyheder/Nordjylland/2008/02/27/150627.htm?rss=true&regional.

75. Erik André Andersen, interview by author, Copenhagen, October 2006.

76. Ministry of Foreign Affairs, "Capacity Assessment."

77. Birgit Lindnaes, interview by author, Copenhagen, November 2006.

78. Lindnaes, interview by author, Copenhagen, November 2006.

79. Interview with DIHR staff by author, Copenhagen, November 2006.

80. Morten Kjaerum, interview by author, Copenhagen, November 2006.

81. Kjaerum, interview by author, Copenhagen, November 2006.

82. European Network Against Racism, "Deplorable Action."

83. The Danish Institute for Human Rights, founded by the act on establishment of

the Danish Center for International Studies and Human Rights on June 6, 2002, carries forth the mandate vested in the Danish Center for Human Rights.

84. The board included one of the highest ranking businessmen in all of Denmark, Mads Oulisen, who was the CEO of Novo Nordesk.

85. Kjaerum, interview by author, Copenhagen, November 2006.

86. Morten Kjaerum explained that the decision to promote a "broader face" of the DIHR led some to the impression that the crisis of 2001 had diminished the public profile of the organization. "They have the idea that if they don't speak to the Executive Director, they don't speak to the organization," he explained. On close inspection of newspaper clippings of all references to the DIHR, he claimed, one can see no discernible decrease in press coverage. According to Kjaerum, 80 percent of Danes are aware of the DIHR. Kjaerum, interview by author, Copenhagen, November 2006.

87. European Union antidiscrimination legislation, with its two directives—the race and employment directives, widely referred to simply as Article 13—became effective in Denmark on May 28, 2003, and April 7, 2004, respectively. See European Commission, "Implementation of Anti-Discrimination Directives."

88. United Kingdom Government Equalities Office, "EU Article 13."

89. See Danish Institute for Human Rights, "National Department," http://human rights.dk/about+us/organisation/national+++department; and Danish Institute for Human Rights, "Forskningsafdelingen—1. Diskrimination og ligebehandling" [The Research Department—1. Discrimination and Equal Treatment (stating that the DIHR has "a special mandate to promote equal treatment of all regardless of ethnicity and race")], http://menneskeret.dk/om+os/organisation+og+personale/forskning -+afdelingen.

90. Complaints Committee for Ethnic Equal Treatment, http://www.klagekomite .dk/?ID=289&AFD=1.

91. Birgitte Kofod Olsen, interview by author, Copenhagen, November 2006.

92. See the MIA-Prize website at http://www.miapris.dk.

93. See United Nations Committee on the Rights of the Child, *Concluding Observations: Denmark.*

94. United Nations Committee on the Rights of the Child, *Concluding Observations: Denmark.*

95. Danish Institute for Human Rights, "Partners," http://humanrights.dk/ international/partners+and+donors/partners.

96. Lone Lindholt, interview by author, Copenhagen, October 2006.

97. See Danish Institute for Human Rights, "Geographical Regions," http://human rights.dk/international/geographical+regions. See, for example, "Activities in Tanzania," http://www.humanrights.dk/international/geographical+regions/africa/ countries/tanzania/activities+in+tanzania; "Malawi," http://humanrights.dk/inter national/geographical+regions/africa/countries/malawi; "The Balkans," http://human rights.dk/international/geographical+regions/europe+and+central+asia/regional/ the+balkans; "Kyrgyzstan," http://humanrights.dk/International/Geographical+Regions/ Europe+and+Central+Asia/Countries/Kyrgyzstan/Partners+and+Activities; and

"Tajikistan," http://humanrights.dk/International/Geographical+Regions/Europe +and+Central+Asia/Countries/Tajikistan/Partners+and+Activities.

98. Danish Institute for Human Rights, "The Balkans."

99. Danish Institute for Human Rights, "Nepal," http://humanrights.dk/Inter national/Geographical+Regions/Asia/Countries/Nepal/Partners+and+Activities.

100. Danish Institute for Human Rights, "Activities in Tanzania."

101. Olsen, interview by author, Copenhagen, November 2006; Danish Institute for Human Rights, *Annual Report 2005*, 11.

102. Ida Elisabeth Koch, interview by author, Copenhagen, November 2006.

103. Council of Europe, *European Social Charter*.

104. United Nations Committee on Economic, Social, and Cultural Rights, *Concluding Observations: Denmark* (1999); United Nations Committee on Economic, Social, and Cultural Rights, *Concluding Observations: Denmark* (2004).

105. Collection of information on file with author.

106. United Nations Committee on Economic, Social, and Cultural Rights, *Concluding Observations: Denmark* (1999).

107. Gupta et al., "Swimming Upstream."

108. Interview with DIHR staff by author, Copenhagen, November 2006.

109. See Nour and Thisted, "When We Are Equal."

110. Nour and Thisted, "When We Are Equal," 27.

111. Green, "Work Culture."

112. Interview with DIHR staff by author, Copenhagen, November 2006.

113. Olsen, interview by author, Copenhagen, November 2006.

114. Nour and Thisted, *Diversity in the Workplace*, 321.

115. Interview with DIHR staff by author, Copenhagen, November 2006.

116. Olsen, interview by author, Copenhagen, November 2006.

117. R. R. Thomas, "Managing Diversity," 311.

118. CABI, "For Democracy's Sake," 5.

119. CABI, "For Democracy's Sake," 5.

120. CABI, "For Democracy's Sake," 5.

121. Kjaerum, interview by author, Copenhagen, November 2006.

Chapter 3

1. These high degrees of segregation are obvious in housing, education, and employment in the jurisdiction. See Murtagh, *Politics of Territory*.

2. "The protection and vindication of the human rights of all" is one of the stated priorities of the major peace accord signed in Northern Ireland in 1998, the Good Friday Agreement. CAIN, *Agreement*, Declaration of Support, 2. See further discussion in this chapter.

3. Colin Harvey has made a powerful argument for the link between human rights and democratic renewal in Northern Ireland. See Harvey, *Human Rights*.

4. Harvey, "Building Bridges." See also Mageean and O'Brien, "From Margins to the Mainstream."

5. Hall, "Justice for All."

6. See Aoláin, *Politics of Force*.

7. For an analysis of the segregation, see Murtagh, *Politics of Territory*. For a perspective on how to improve community relations in the long-term, see Hughes et al., *Community Relations*.

8. McGarry and O'Leary, *Explaining Northern Ireland*, 171– 213.

9. For different perspectives on Northern Ireland history, compare Darby, "Conflict in Northern Ireland"; Dixon, *Northern Ireland*; Hennessey, *Northern Ireland Peace Process*; McKittrick, *Making Sense of the Troubles*; Tonge, *Northern Ireland*; and Ruane and Todd, *Dynamics of Conflict*.

10. A finding confirmed by the Cameron Commission, a body appointed by the Northern Ireland government in March 1969 to report, inter alia, on the causes of disturbances in the six counties in 1968–1969, justified many of the grievances then felt by the Catholics, in particular, those concerned with the allocation of housing, local authority appointments, limitations on local electoral franchise, and deliberate manipulation of ward boundaries and electoral areas. See CAIN, *Cameron Report*.

11. For a full account of historical origins and relationship to contemporary manifestation of the conflict, see Foster, *Modern Ireland*.

12. For an overview of these initiatives, see Hadfield, *Constitution of Northern Ireland*.

13. See CAIN, "Cost of the Troubles Study."

14. IRA Ceasefire Statement, August 31, 1994. Reprinted in the appendix to Cox et al., *Farewell to Arms*. For IRA origins and development up to the contemporary peace process, see English, *Armed Struggle*.

15. Combined Loyalist Military Command Ceasefire Statement, October 13, 1994. Reprinted in appendix to Cox et al., *Farewell to Arms*.

16. In December 1993 the British and Irish governments made a joint commitment to convene talks among democratically mandated parties on the future of Northern Ireland upon the cessation of paramilitary violence. CAIN, "Joint Declaration on Peace." This event was widely regarded as the beginning of the peace process that led to the Good Friday Agreement. See, for example, Bell, *Peace Agreements*.

17. CAIN, *Agreement*.

18. Nationalists (predominantly Catholics) seek to unify the island of Ireland.

19. "Unionist" refers to the majority of Northern Irish citizens who support the current constitutional status of Northern Ireland within the United Kingdom.

20. Good Friday Agreement, "Constitutional Issues," 1(iii). This was a reiteration of earlier commitments made by the British government in the Northern Ireland Constitution Act of 1973 and the Anglo-Irish Agreement of 1985.

21. Good Friday Agreement, "Validation, Implementation and Review," 2.

22. Good Friday Agreement, "Strand Two."

23. Good Friday Agreement, "Prisoners."

24. Good Friday Agreement, "Strand One."

25. Farry, *Northern Ireland*, 2.

26. United Kingdom Parliament, *Northern Ireland Act 1998*.

27. The Ulster Unionist Party formed all Northern Ireland governments from 1921 to 1972 and has traditionally had strong links to the British Conservative Party.

28. The Social Democratic and Labour Party was established in 1970. The party website (http://www.sdlp.ie) contains an account of its history, origins, and current policies.

29. Sinn Féin had been traditionally excluded from attempts to negotiate a political settlement in Northern Ireland. However, since the IRA cease-fire of 1994, Sinn Féin has gathered popular support and has participated in all major peace negotiations in the jurisdiction. As of this writing, it is the largest nationalist political party in Northern Ireland.

30. Good Friday Agreement, "Democratic Institutions in Northern Ireland," 5.a.

31. For one account of the IRA and decommissioning, see Coogan, *IRA*.

32. For a fascinating take on the Northern Ireland style of politicism, see Purdie, *Politics in the Street.*

33. Loyalism constitutes a more militant and populist form of Unionism.

34. "Stone Held over Stormont Attack," *BBC News Online*, November 24, 2006, http://news.bbc.co.uk/2/hi/uk_news/northern_ireland/6181994.stm.

35. See St. Andrews Agreement, Annex D.

36. See Sinn Féin press release, "Motion Passed by the Sinn Féin Ard Fheis," January 28, 2007, http://www.sinnfeinonline.com/news/3189.

37. Democratic Unionist Party, "Getting It Right: Manifesto 2007," http://www.dup.org.uk/.

38. See welcome page of website of the Northern Ireland Assembly, http://www.niassembly.gov.uk.

39. St. Andrews Agreement, Annex D.

40. Democratic Unionist Party press release, "NIO Engaged in Wishful Thinking—Dodds," January 14, 2008, http://www.dup.org.uk.

41. Orla Ryan, "Northern Ireland's Economic Fears," *BBC News Online*, June 22, 2001, http://news.bbc.co.uk/2/hi/business/1402261.stm.

42. "Regional GDP per Capita in the EU25," *Eurostat*, January 25, 2005, http://europ.eu/rapid/pressReleasesAction.do?reference=STAT/05/13&format=HTML&aged=0&language=en&guiLanguage=en.

43. Northern Ireland Executive, "Economic Performance Briefing," January 25, 2006, http://www.nics.gov.uk/briefjan06.pdf.

44. Northern Ireland Executive, "European Sustainable Competitiveness Programme." Statistics in this section are all taken from this report.

45. Northern Ireland Executive, "European Sustainable Competitiveness Programme."

46. Hanvey et al., *Report on Labour Market Dynamics.*

47. Hanvey et al., *Report on Labour Market Dynamics.*

48. Hanvey et al., *Report on Labour Market Dynamics.*

49. Hanvey et al., *Report on Labour Market Dynamics.*

50. Hanvey et al., *Report on Labour Market Dynamics.*

51. The positions of the respective political parties and their concerns are expressed in the Transitional Assembly debate by the Committee on the Preparation for Government's discussion of the Northern Ireland Human Rights Consortium, August 11, 2006, http://www.niassembly.gov.uk/theassembly/Plenary/p060811.htm.

53. See Finucane, *Cory Collusion Report.*

53. Bell, "Dealing with the Past," 1095.

54. Human Rights First, "Human Rights Defenders."

55. Human Rights First, "Human Rights Defenders."

56. Testimony of Elisa Massimino, Washington Director, Human Rights First, "Hearing on Northern Ireland and Human Rights: Update on the Cory Collusion Inquiry Reports Before the United States House of Representatives Committee on International Relations Subcommittee on Africa, Global Human Rights and International Operations," March 16, 2005, http://www.humanrightsfirst.org/defenders/hrd _n_ireland/HIRC-collusion-031605.pdf.

57. Committee on the Administration of Justice, "War on Terror."

58. French and Campbell, "Fear of Crime."

59. See Lysaght and Basten, "Violence."

60. Jarman, *Demography.*

61. CAIN, "Violence."

62. Jarman, *No Longer a Problem.*

63. For government statistics on hate crimes, see Northern Ireland Affairs Committee, *Hate Crime.*

64. Northern Ireland Affairs Committee, *Hate Crime.* For firsthand accounts of children, see Connolly and Healy, "Children and Conflict."

65. "Victim's Family Reject IRA Offer," *BBC News Online*, March 9, 2005, http://news.bbc.co.uk/2/hi/uk_news/northern_ireland/4330445.stm.

66. David Teather and Angelique Chrisafis, "McGuinness Warns McCartney Sisters," *Guardian Online*, March 15, 2005, http://politics.guardian.co.uk/northernireland assembly/story/0,9061,1437913,00.html.

67. "Victim's Family Reject IRA Offer."

68. "Murder 'Lost' Seat for Sinn Féin," *BBC News Online*, March 10, 2005, http://news.bbc.co.uk/2/hi/uk_news/northern_ireland/4532073.stm.

69. Henry MacDonald, "Grieving Sisters Square Up to IRA," *Guardian Online*, February 13, 2005, http://www.guardian.co.uk/Northern_Ireland/Story/0,,1411855,00.html.

70. Harvey McGavin, "McCartney Murder Case: Man Charged," *Independent Online*, June 4, 2005, http://news.independent.co.uk/uk/ulster/article224337.ece.

71. Brian Lavery, "IRA Turncoat Is Murdered in Donegal," *New York Times Online*, April 5, 2006, http://select.nytimes.com/search/restricted/article?res=F50913FF3B540C768CDDAD0894DE404482.

72. "UK Spy's Murder Threatens Peace," *CNN Online*, April 5, 2006, http://www.cnn.com/2006/WORLD/europe/04/05/nireland-shooting/index.html?eref=sitesearch.

73. Northern Ireland Independent Monitoring Commission, *Seventeenth Report.*

74. Northern Ireland Independent Monitoring Commission, *Seventeenth Report*, para. 2.3–2.4, 2.8, and 2.17–2.18.

75. Northern Ireland Independent Monitoring Commission, *Seventeenth Report*, para. 2.13–2.14.

76. Northern Ireland Independent Monitoring Commission, *Seventeenth Report*, para. 2.22.

77. Northern Ireland Independent Monitoring Commission, *Seventeenth Report*, para. 3.4–3.5.

78. CAIN, *Agreement*.

79. See Northern Ireland Human Rights Commission, http://www.nihrc.org.

80. The Good Friday Agreement also called for establishment of a new statutory Equality Commission to replace the four equality bodies that then existed (the Fair Employment Commission, the Equal Opportunities Commission, the Commission for Racial Equality, and the Disability Council). The reconfigured commission thus has a general mandate to advance equality, promote equality of opportunity, encourage good relations, and challenge discrimination through promotion, advice, and enforcement. Assistance by the NIHRC ranges from giving advice to arranging for legal representation in some cases. The NIHRC also has a wide range of powers to ensure compliance with the legislation, including powers of inquiry and investigation. In addition, the Good Friday Agreement provided for a statutory obligation on all public bodies to promote equality of opportunity in specified areas and parity of esteem between the two main communities. See Good Friday Agreement, "Strand One, Safeguards." This was implemented through the Northern Ireland Act of 1998, sec. 75. See, generally, Livingstone, "Northern Ireland Human Rights Commission."

81. Northern Ireland Human Rights Commission, *Progressing a Bill of Rights*.

82. See Smith, "Drafting Process."

83. For example, the NIHRC was involved in the drafting of a new United Nations treaty on people with disabilities. See Northern Ireland Human Rights Commission, "Addendum."

84. Northern Ireland Human Rights Commission, *Tackling Violence at Home*.

85. Northern Ireland Human Rights Commission, *Response to Prison Consultation*.

86. Northern Ireland Human Rights Commission, *Response to the Northern Ireland Prison Service's Policy*.

87. Northern Ireland Human Rights Commission, *Single Equality Bill*.

88. See, for example, Letter to Secretary of State for Northern Ireland on the ratification of Optional Protocol to the UN Convention Against Torture, January 1, 2004 (on file with author); and Northern Ireland Human Rights Commission, *Examination of the 6th Report*.

89. See United Nations Committee on Economic, Social, and Cultural Rights, *Concluding Observations of the CESCR*.

90. United Nations Committee on Economic, Social, and Cultural Rights, *Concluding Observations of the CESCR*.

91. See, for example, McGleenan, *Investigating Deaths*.

92. Northern Ireland Human Rights Commission, *Evaluation of Human Rights Training*.

93. The NIHRC, for example, has encouraged dialogue on counterterrorism tactics. See Northern Ireland Human Rights Commission, *Countering Terrorism*.

94. Interviews with NIHRC staff members by author, Belfast, October 2006.

95. See discussion of the scope of this divide in Cross-Party Working Group on Religious Hatred, *Tackling Religious Hatred*.

96. Cross-Party Working Group on Religious Hatred, *Tackling Religious Hatred*.

97. Sonya Sceats, interview by author, London, October 2006.

98. Ciarán Ó Mailain, interview by author, Belfast, October 2006.

99. Recent discussion among political parties in the Preparation for Government Committee referred to the imbalance of the "first commission," especially from the DUP. See the Committee on the Preparation of Government's discussion of the Northern Ireland Human Rights Consortium, August 11, 2006, http://www.niassembly.gov .uk/theassembly/Plenary/p060811.htm.

100. For an account of the origins and development of the CAJ in the divisive Northern Ireland political environment, see Whelan, "Challenge of Lobbying."

101. For a description of the efforts by the Independent Commission on Policing for Northern Ireland to distance itself from the CAJ in order to avoid allegations of bias, see O'Rawe, "Transitional Policing Arrangements," 1043.

102. See the debate in the Northern Ireland Assembly on the motion that the Human Rights Commission had failed to discharge its remit: Northern Ireland Assembly, Minutes of Proceedings, Monday, September 21, 2001, http://www.niassembly.gov.uk/ minutes/pdf/2001-2002MOP.pdf. Ulster Unionist politician Dr. Birnie charged, "Persons with a CAJ background continue to have a disproportionate representation on the Northern Ireland Human Rights Commission" (Northern Ireland Assembly, Minutes of Proceedings [continued], Tuesday, September 25, 2001, http://www.niassembly.gov.uk/ record/reports/010925b.htm).

103. Interview with NIHRC board members by author, Belfast, October 2006.

104. See Smith, "Unique Position."

105. Christine Bell, interview by author, Derry, Northern Ireland, October 2006.

106. Maggie Beirne, interview by author, Belfast, October 2006.

107. Brice Dickson, interview by author, Belfast, October 2006.

108. Brian Burdekin, interview by author, Lund, Sweden, November 2006.

109. See James, "Northern Ireland."

110. Other factors contributing to the resignations were the Holy Cross case and the dispute over the use of the word *communities* over *minorities*.

111. Anne Smith, interview by author, Derry, Northern Ireland, October 2006.

112. Christine Bell, interview by author, Derry, October 2006.

113. See Cadwallader, *Holy Cross*.

114. *Report Submitted by Katarina Tomaševski, Special Rapporteur, Pursuant to Commission on Human Rights Resolution 2002/23*. United Nations Economic and Social

Council, E/CN.4/2003/9/Add.2, January 21, 2003, http://www.right-to-education.org/content/unreports/unreport10prt1.html.

115. Joint Committee on Human Rights, "Memorandum from Madden and Finucane."

116. "In the Matter of an Application by 'E' for Judicial Review," [2004] NIQB 35 (N.Ir.), http://www.courtsni.gov.uk/NR/rdonlyres/1475F1C5-0646-4639-BFB5-14E4D5705A1E/0/j_j_KERF4184.htm.

117. Smith, "Unique Position," 936.

118. Dickson, interview by author, Belfast, October 2006. Dickson's chronology of the Holy Cross case, dated 2003 (on file with author).

119. See Joint Committee on Human Rights, *Fourteenth Report*, para. 14.

120. Smith, "Unique Position," 937.

121. Northern Ireland Human Rights Commission, *Making a Bill of Rights*.

122. See Meehan, "Northern Ireland Bill of Rights."

123. Emphasis added. The full text of the Good Friday Agreement can be found at http://members.fortunecity.com/irish_history_and_more/today/good_friday/full_text.html.

124. The positions of the respective political parties and their concerns are expressed in the Transitional Assembly debate by the Committee on the Preparation of Government's discussion of the Northern Ireland Human Rights Consortium, August 11, 2006, http://www.niassembly.gov.uk/theassembly/Plenary/p060811.htm.

125. Deasúin Ó Donghaile, "The Battle for Rights," *Irish Democrat*, January 30, 2007, http://www.irishdemocrat.co.uk/news/2007/the-battle-for-rights/.

126. Donghaile, "Battle for Rights."

127. Donghaile, "Battle for Rights."

128. This remains a disputed area. See, for example, House of Lords, "Northern Ireland: Bill of Rights," February 19, 2008, http://www.theyworkforyou.com/wrans/?id=2008-02-19a.46.9.

129. Donghaile, "Battle for Rights."

130. Alliance Party, "NIHRC."

131. The draft provisions are much longer and more encompassing than represented here; this list is designed to provide only a sampling. See Northern Ireland Human Rights Commission, *Submission to the Roundtable*.

132. Northern Ireland Human Rights Commission, *Making a Bill of Rights*.

133. Northern Ireland Human Rights Commission, *Making a Bill of Rights*.

134. See Smith, "Drafting Process."

135. Northern Ireland Human Rights Commission, *Opening the Door*.

136. Interview with NIHRC staff by author, Belfast, October 2006.

137. Northern Ireland Human Rights Commission, "Case Work."

138. Northern Ireland Human Rights Commission, "Case Work."

139. Interview with NIHRC staff by author, Belfast, October 2006.

140. For a comprehensive account (and critique) of these dynamics, see McCrudden, "Consociationalism."

141. Livingstone, "Need for a Bill of Rights," 269, 283.

142. Livingstone, "Need for a Bill of Rights," 269, 283.

143. McCrudden, "Consociationalism."

144. Patrick Yu, interview by author, Belfast, October 2006.

145. Yu, interview by author, Belfast, October 2006.

146. Yu, interview by author, Belfast, October 2006.

147. Analysis on this section draws heavily from Bell, *Peace Agreements*.

148. Northern Ireland Human Rights Commission, *Enhancing the Rights*.

149. Northern Ireland Human Rights Commission, *Women's Rights*.

150. Northern Ireland Human Rights Commission, *Young People's Rights*.

151. Davidson et al., *Connecting Mental Health*.

153. Jim Deery, interview by author, Belfast, October 2006.

153. See Hosking, *Northern Ireland Human Rights Commission*. The NIHRC was given more general power by the Northern Ireland Act of 1998 (NIA 1998) to conduct "such investigations as it considers necessary or expedient . . . for the purpose of exercising its functions." Northern Ireland Act, 1998, c. 47, § 69(8) (Eng.), http://www.opsi.gov.uk/acts/acts1998/80047-j.htm.

154. Smith, interview by author, Derry, Northern Ireland, October 2006.

155. For example, see Fair Employment and Treatment (Northern Ireland) Order 1998, art. 11; Sex Discrimination (Northern Ireland) Order 1976, art. 57; Race Relations (Northern Ireland) Order 1997, art. 46. The ECNI has different powers depending on whether the investigation is formal or informal.

156. Justice and Security (Northern Ireland) Act of 2007, http://www.opsi.gov.uk/acts/acts2007/ukpga_20070006_en_1.

Chapter 4

1. See Andjelic, *Bosnia-Herzegovina*; and Noel, *Bosnia*, 364. See also Carmichael, *Ethnic Cleansing*, 224; and Donia and Fine, *Bosnia and Hercegovina*, 318.

2. See Weine, *When History Is a Nightmare*, 259. See also Sells, *Bridge Betrayed*, 260; Rohde, *Endgame*, 464; and Klejda, "On Bosnia's Borders."

3. Kjell Arild Nilsen, "102,000 Killed in Bosnia NTB," *Norwegian News Agency*, November 14, 2004, http://grayfalcon.blogspot.com/2004/11/bosnia-death-toll-revealed.html. See also Tabeau and Bijak, "War-Related Deaths."

4. United Nations High Commission for Refugees, "Internally Displaced Number Drops." See also Dahlman and Tuathail, "Legacy of Ethnic Cleansing."

5. See United Nations Committee Against Torture, "Committee Against Torture Begins Review."

6. See Reliefweb, *Country Profiles from Eastern Europe*.

7. See Riedlmayer, *Destruction of Cultural Heritage*.

8. Note that although the three signatories to the Dayton Agreement—Bosnia's president Alija Izetbegovic, Yugoslavia's president Slobodan Milosevic, and Croatia's president Franjo Tudjman—were accepted by the international community as legitimate representatives of the warring factions, many of the people in the region dis-

agreed. See Stewart, "International Community." See also Søberg, "Empowering Local Elites."

9. Cushman and Mestrovic, *This Time We Knew*, 296.

10. Office of the High Representative and EU Representative, *General Framework Agreement*, Annex 3, Article II, 4. See also Bose, *Bosnia After Dayton*, 352. See, generally, Issacharoff, "Constitutionalizing Democracy"; and Chandler, "Democracy Paradox." See also Beriker-Atiyas and Demirel-Pegg, "Analysis of Integrative Outcomes."

11. For a solid account of this structure and its implications, see Bose, *Bosnia After Dayton*.

12. See Ramet, *Balkan Babel*, 280–281.

13. See Kumar, *Divide and Fall*, 121.

14. See Friedman, *Bosnia and Herzegovina*.

15. Francis Boyle, the American attorney who was counsel for Bosnia before the World Court, has called Dayton a "nihilistic carve-up" that sacrifices Bosnia "on the altars of the Great Powers." Boyle, *Negating Human Rights*, 1.

16. Borden and Hedl, "How the Bosnians Were Broken."

17. Yordán, "Resolving the Bosnian Conflict," 150.

18. See Belloni, *State Building*, 44–46.

19. Petrovic, *Peace in Our Times*.

20. The country consists of 137 municipalities, of which 74 are in the Federation of Bosnia and Herzegovina and 63 are in Republika Srpska. Municipalities also have their own local government and are typically based around the most significant city or place in the region. As such, many municipalities have a long tradition and history with their present boundaries.

21. For an early account of the complete crisis in Republika Srpska, see Dyker and Vejvoda, *Yugoslavia and After*, 111–114.

22. Brčko was claimed during the Dayton mediation. See Arbitral Tribunal for Dispute over Inter-Entity Boundary in Brčko Area, *Federation of Bosnia and Herzegovina v. The Republika Srpska*.

23. Commission on Security and Cooperation in Europe, *Briefing*.

24. Gallagher, *Balkans in the New Millennium*, 133.

25. Kaus and Whyte, *Internationals*.

26. For controversies over implementation, see Cousens and Cater, "Towards Peace in Bosnia."

27. Austermiller, "Mediation," 132.

28. Gallagher, *Balkans in the New Millennium*, 132.

29. Office of the High Representative and EU Representative, *OHR Mission Implementation Plan*.

30. Office of the High Representative and EU Special Representative, Mandate of the OHR. These powers were given to the High Representative by the Peace Implementation Council, at a conference in Bonn in 1997 and are referred to as the Bonn Powers.

31. Bieber, *Post-War Bosnia*, 59.

32. Gallagher, *Balkans in the New Millennium*, 141.

33. Gallagher, *Balkans in the New Millennium*, 138.

34. Human Rights Watch, "Hopes Betrayed."

35. See Colum Lynch, "Misconduct, Corruption by UN Mission Mar Bosnia Mission," *Washington Post*, May 29, 2001. See also Julie Poucher Harbin, "Bosnia: UN Handover Causing Concern," *Reliefweb*, December 23, 2002, http://www.reliefweb.int/rw/rwb.nsf/AllDocsByUNID/d0c8ab9e0c6b8451c1256c9b005ac865.

36. Bieber, *Post-War Bosnia*, 34.

37. Bieber, *Post-War Bosnia*, 34.

38. See International Crisis Group, *Bosnia's Precarious Economy*.

39. Bieber reports that in 2003, 62.2 percent of the population earned less than 500 KM per month (225 Euros) and only 0.6 percent earned more than 2,000 KM monthly. Bieber, *Post-War* Bosnia, 35.

40. Pickering, *Peacebuilding in the Balkans*, 38.

41. *Encyclopedia of the Nations*, s.v. "Bosnia-Herzegovina, Economy."

42. *Encyclopedia of the Nations*, s.v. "Bosnia Herzegovina, Domestic Policy."

43. World Bank, *Bosnia and Herzegovina: Country Brief 2006*, http://web.worldbank.org/WBSITE/EXTERNAL/COUNTRIES/ECAEXT/BOSNIAHERZEXTN/0,,contentMDK:20629017~menuPK:362034~pagePK:141137~piPK:141127~theSitePK:362026,00.html.

44. *Encyclopedia of the Nations*, s.v. "Bosnia-Herzegovina, Economy."

45. Belloni, *State Building*, 100.

46. *Encyclopedia of the Nations*, s.v. "Bosnia Herzegovina, Domestic Policy."

47. *Encyclopedia of the Nations*, s.v. "Bosnia Herzegovina, Domestic Policy."

48. *Encyclopedia of the Nations*, s.v. "Bosnia Herzegovina, Domestic Policy."

49. World Bank, *Bosnia-Herzegovina*.

50. *Encyclopedia of the Nations*, s.v. "Bosnia-Herzegovina, Economy."

51. World Bank, *Bosnia-Herzegovina*.

52. World Bank Group, "Bosnia and Herzegovina."

53. World Bank Group, "Bosnia and Herzegovina."

54. Adeyi, "Priorities."

55. Adeyi, "Priorities."

56. U.S. Agency for International Development, "2001 NGO Sustainability Index."

57. Leban, "Faith-Based NGOs."

58. SPAI, "Empowering Civil Society."

59. Human Rights Watch, "World Report 2007."

60. Human Rights Watch, "World Report 2007."

61. Human Rights Watch, "World Report 2007."

62. U.S. Department of State, Bureau of Democracy, Human Rights, and Labor, *Country Reports: Bosnia and Herzegovina*. See also U.S. Congress, *U.N. and the Sex Slave Trade*. For background information, see Benedek, *Human Rights*, 272. See also Chandler, *Bosnia*, 239.

63. United Nations Committee on Economic, Social, and Cultural Rights, *Reports Submitted by States Parties*.

64. See discussion in Pickering, *Peacebuilding in the Balkans*, 34–39.

65. Amnesty International, "Bosnia and Herzegovina."

66. Belloni, *State Building*, 67.

67. Dino Abazović, interview by author, Sarajevo, October 2006.

68. Reif, "Building Democratic Institutions."

69. See Constitution of the Federation of Bosnia and Herzegovina, http:// 72.14.209.104/search?q=cache:jXAglOdVytcJ:www.ohr.int/ohr-dept/legal/oth-legist/ doc/fbihconstitution.doc+constitution+of+the+federation+of+bosnia+and+herzego vina&hl=en&gl=us&ct=clnk&cd=1.

70. Bosnia and Herzegovina, Federation Constitution, Article II (Human Rights and Fundamental Freedoms), Annex. The three ombudsmen are to be composed of one Bosnian, one Croat, and one "other." Bosnia and Herzegovina, Federation Constitution, at Article II.B.1(1).

71. Bosnia and Herzegovina, Federation Constitution, Article II.B.2(1).

72. Bosnia and Herzegovina, Federation Constitution, Article II.B.5. See also Article II.B.3.

73. See Bosnia and Herzegovina, Federation Constitution, Articles II.B.6–8.

74. See Ombudsman of the Federation of Bosnia and Herzegovina, *Annual Report, 1996* (on file with author).

75. See Bosnia and Herzegovina, Federation Constitution, Article IV(2) and IV(4).

76. Aoláin, "Fractured Soul."

77. Emir Kaknjasević, interview by author, Sarajevo, September 2006.

78. Enes Hašić, interview by author, Banja Luka, September 2006.

79. Boris Topić, interview by author, Banja Luka, September 2006.

80. See Framework Agreement, Annex 6 (Agreement on Human Rights), Article XIV.

81. See Framework Agreement, Annex 6 (Agreement on Human Rights), Article V(1)–V(3). Complaints can be made by a party, a person, an NGO, or a group of individuals. The complainant also has the option of specifying that her complaint be heard directly by the Chamber, bypassing the Ombudsman. See Framework Agreement, Annex 6 (Agreement on Human Rights), Article V(1).

82. Bosnia and Herzegovina Human Rights Ombudsman, Rules of Procedure, Rule 18, reprinted in Bosnia and Herzegovina Human Rights Ombudsman, *Annual Report 1999* (hereafter Rules of Procedure).

83. Ombudsman Information Network, "Bosnia and Herzegovina."

84. See Framework Agreement, Annex 6 (Agreement on Human Rights), Articles V(4), V(6), and V(7); see also Rules of Procedure, Rules 18(3) and 20(3).

85. See Framework Agreement, Article V(7); Rules of Procedure, Rule 23.

86. For the workings of the Human Rights Chamber, see Dakin, "Islamic Community," 247–249.

87. Human Rights Chamber for Bosnia and Herzegovina, *Annual Report.*

88. Dino Abazović, interview by author, Sarajevo, September 2006.

89. Srđan Dizdarević, interview by author, Sarajevo, September 2006.

90. Zivanovic, "Human Rights," 69.

91. The name of the law was Law on the Human Rights Ombudsman of Bosnia and Herzegovina. The same law extended the termination date for the Human Rights Chamber to 2003. http://www.legislationline.org/legislation.php?tid=160&lid=3025.

92. Some important differences exist between the state ombudsman's office and the entity ombudsman's office. One difference, which would emerge later as a key problem in merger efforts, was that the Republika Srpska entity-level body had one commissioner and two deputy commissioners, whereas the Federation Commission and the state-level body had three commissioners.

93. Topić, interview by author, Banja Luka, September 2006.

94. Sladana Marić, interview by author, Banja Luka, September 2006.

95. Ahmed Zilic, interview by author, Sarajevo, September 2006.

96. Zivanovic, "Human Rights," 7.

97. Nedim Ademović, interview by author, Sarajevo, October 2006.

98. Zivanovic, "Human Rights," 70.

99. See web page of Venice Commission, http://www.venice.coe.int.

100. OSCE Mission to Bosnia and Herzegovina, *Ten Years OSCE Mission to Bosnia and Herzegovina*. See especially pp. 53–54 for a description of state and entity ombudsmen.

101. Human Rights Ombudsman of Bosnia and Herzegovina, *Annual Report 2004* (English language hard copy on file with author; Web version not available). See also Ombudsman of Republika Srpska, Human Rights Protector, *Annual Report 2005* (hard copy on file with author; Web version not available).

102. Observation based on author's individual and collective interviews with Federation ombudsmen, Sarajevo, October 2006.

103. Example provided to author during interview with Republika Srpska ombudsman staff, Banja Luka, October 2006.

104. Organization for Security and Cooperation in Europe, "Promoting and Protecting."

105. Organization for Security and Cooperation in Europe, "Promoting and Protecting."

106. Courdesse and Hemingway, "Human Rights-Based Approach."

107. Interview by author, Sarajevo, October 2006.

108. Zivanovic, "Human Rights," 80.

109. United Nations Commission on Human Rights, *Question of the Violation.*

110. United Nations Commission on Human Rights, *Question of the Violation.*

111. Information drawn from annual reports and other publications as well as from interviews with staff by author in Banja Luka in September 2006.

112. Office of the Human Rights Defender (Republika Srpska), *Annual Report 2005*, May 2006.

113. Information drawn from annual reports and other publications as well as from interviews with staff by author in Banja Luka in September 2006.

114. Office of the Federation Ombudsman, *Annual Report 2005*, May 2006, 6.

115. Information drawn from annual reports and other publications as well as from interviews with staff by author in Banja Luka in September 2006.

116. Office of the Human Rights Ombudsman of Bosnia and Herzegovina, *Annual Report 2005*, May 2006, 6.

117. Interview with staff by author, Banja Luka, October 2006.

118. Chandler, *Peace Without Politics*, 192; Fischer, *Peacebuilding*, 200.

119. Belloni, *State Building*, 115.

Chapter 5

1. Discalla, *Twentieth Century Europe*, 259.

2. Leff, *Czech and Slovak Republics*, 43.

3. See Rothschild, *East Central Europe*, 86–87; Prypr, "Czechoslovak Economic Development."

4. See, generally, Mamatey and Luza, *History of the Czechoslovak Republic*.

5. See Shawcross, *Dubček*.

6. See Remington, *Winter in Prague*. See also Globalsecurity.org, "Soviet Invasion."

7. Leff, *Czech and Slovak Republics*, 28.

8. Leff, *Czech and Slovak Republics*, 28. See also discussion of national character in Stone and Strouhal, *Czechoslovakia*.

9. Jiri Kopal, interview by author, Brno, November 2006.

10. Ramet, *Rock Music*.

11. Dvoráková, "Civil Society," 136.

12. Dvoráková, "Civil Society," 136.

13. Kopecký and Barnfield, "Charting the Decline," 78

14. See Skilling, *Charter 77*.

15. See "Country Briefing: The Czech Republic," *The Economist*, February 14, 2007, http://www.economist.com/countries/CzechRepublic/profile.cfm?folder=History%20in%20brief.

16. See, generally, Wheaton and Zdenek, *Velvet Revolution*.

17. See Whipple, *After the Velvet Revolution*.

18. Blahoz et al., "Czech Political Parties," 123.

19. See Hanley, "Blue Velvet."

20. Czech Social Democratic Party, "Brief History," http://www.cssd.cz/english-version.

21. European Greens, "The Charter of the European Greens: European Green Party Guiding Principles," October 14, 2006, http://www.europeangreens.org/cms/default/rubrik/9/9341.the_charter_of_the_european_greens@en.htm.

22. Dvoráková, "Civil Society," 140.

23. It was not until 1995 that the law on the organization of benefit to public was enacted, and the law on foundations was enacted in 1997. Dvoráková, "Civil Society," 137.

24. To take one recent illustration, just before the fall 2006 elections, Vladimir Dolezal, a member of parliament for the opposition right-of-center Civic Democratic Party gave up his mandate and all his political functions after he was accused of accepting an 800,000 crown bribe (more than US$32,000) in return for a promise to clear

the way for construction on municipal plots. All the while Dolezal protested his innocence. At the same time, Michal Kraus, a member of Parliament for the ruling Social Democrats, is alleged to have invested tens of thousands of dollars in a business deal in the West African country of Ghana. Dita Asiedu, "Corruption Scandals Mushrooming in Czech Politics Ahead of General Elections," *Radio Praha*, November 1, 2006, http://www.radio.cz/en/article/74607.

25. Asiedu, "Corruption Scandals."

26. Ministry of Foreign Affairs of the Czech Republic, "Development After November 1989."

27. U.S. Department of State, Bureau of European and Eurasian Affairs, *Background Note*.

28. Hrdlickova, *Czech Republic Exporter Guide*.

29. Czech Republic Official Website, "Economy, Business, Science."

30. U.S. Department of State, Bureau of Europe and Eurasian Affairs, *Background Note*.

31. U.S. Department of State, Bureau of European and Eurasian Affairs, *Background Note*.

32. U.S. Department of State, Bureau of European and Eurasian Affairs, *Background Note*.

33. London Chamber of Commerce and Industry, *Czech Republic*.

34. London Chamber of Commerce and Industry, *Czech Republic*.

35. Vachudova, *Europe Undivided*, 197.

36. Vachudova, *Europe Undivided*, 197.

37. Vachudova, *Europe Undivided*, 197.

38. See, generally, Palouš, *Human Rights*.

39. Bayefsky.com, "United Nations Human Rights Treaties."

40. Ministry of Foreign Affairs of the Czech Republic, *Report on the Foreign Policy*.

41. Ministry of Foreign Affairs of the Czech Republic, *Report on the Foreign Policy*.

42. Article 10 of the Czech constitution stipulates that all ratified and published international treaties on human rights and fundamental freedoms, to which the Czech Republic has acceded, are immediately binding and take precedence over the law.

43. Constitutional Law 2/1993 Coll. introduces the Charter of Fundamental Rights and Liberties. The Czechoslovak Federal Assembly originally adopted the charter on January 9, 1991.

44. Law 150/2002 Coll., on Judicial Review of Administrative Acts.

45. Blahoz et al., "Czech Political Parties," 131.

46. Interview with Public Defender staff by author, Brno, October 2006.

47. Baršová, "Enhancing the Effectiveness," 20.

48. Havelková, "Public Awareness."

49. Havelková, "Public Awareness."

50. Until 2000, the commissioner was also the head of two additional government bodies: the Council for National Minorities and the Council for Roma Community Affairs. Since 2000, the commissioner has been executive vice-chair of the two bodies.

51. Robert Cholensky, interview by author, Brno, October 2006.

52. Baršová, "Enhancing the Effectiveness," 24.

53. Baršová, "Enhancing the Effectiveness," 24.

54. Monika Landmanova, interview by author, Prague, October 2006.

55. U.S. State Department, Bureau of Democracy, Human Rights, and Labor, *Czech Republic*. See also Czech Helsinki Committee, *Human Rights Report 2005*.

56. Dita Asiedu and Alexis Rosenzweig, "The Roma in Czech Politics," *Radio Praha*, June 1, 2001, http://www.radio.cz/en/article/79538.

57. "U.N. Committee Criticizes Czech Republic for Approach to Romanies," *Prague Daily Monitor*, April 8, 2007.

58. European Roma Rights Center and Vzájemné Soužití, *Written Comments*.

59. The National Party also rejects the concept of registered partnership and speaks of homosexuality as a disease.

60. "Czech Republic: Hate Crimes," Legislationline, http://www.legislationline.org/?jid=14&less=false&tid=218.

61. See Amnesty International, "Czech Republic." See also Council of Europe, European Commission Against Racism and Intolerance, *Draft Third Report*.

62. See Kurti, "Emergence."

63. For one of the latest reports on discrimination against Roma in education, see Human Rights Watch, "Roma Children."

64. Human Rights Watch, "Roma Children."

65. Human Rights Watch, "Roma Children."

66. Human Rights Watch, "Roma Children."

67. See, for example, Štamberková, *Implementing the Policy*.

68. The Czech Republic has still not been able to enact a special antidiscrimination law in which gender equality is specified. The antidiscrimination law was rejected by the Czech Parliament. People who believe they have been harmed in the field of equal opportunities can ask the Czech Ombudsman for help. The movement pushing for reform calls itself "Jsme Obcane!" ("We are citizens!").

69. Marksova-Tominova, *Gender Equality*.

70. Monika Landmanova, interview by author, Prague, September 2006.

71. Gwendolyn Albert, interview by author, Prague, September 2006.

72. Association for Education and Development of Women, "Overview."

73. Law 349/1999 Coll., on the Public Defender of Rights (hereafter referred to as the Law on the Public Defender of Rights). Office of the Public Defender of Rights, *Law of 8th December 1999*.

74. Office of the Public Defender of Rights, *Czech Public Defender*.

75. Office of the Public Defender of Rights, *Czech Public Defender*.

76. Law 349/1999 Coll., sec. 1(1).

77. Interview with Public Defender lawyer by author, Brno, September 2006.

78. Law 349/1999 Coll., sec. 1(1).

79. Law 349/1999 Coll., sec. 1(1).

80. Office of the Public Defender of Rights, "Powers."

81. The building also saw brief use as a children's hospital.

82. Interviews with staff in Brno and human rights advocates by author, Prague, September 2006.

83. Most of the office furniture was purchased from the workshops of the Prison Service of the Czech Republic in the prison in Mírov. Office of the Public Defender of Rights, "Annual Report."

84. Law 349/1999 Coll., sec. 1(1).

85. See the Office of Public Defender's 2005 annual report, where it notes that dealing with the 43 percent of complaints that fail the Defender's mandate is no less laborious and that it would be wrong to omit them from the Defender's performance.

86. Law 349/1999 Coll., sec. II.

87. The European Roma Rights Center official website is http://www.errc.org.

88. Interview with Romani rights advocates and Defender office staff by author, Brno, November 2006.

89. "Final Statement in the Matter of Sterilizations Performed in Contravention of the Law," December 23, 2005 (for the full text, see http://www.ochrance.cz).

90. Gwendolyn Albert, "UN Demands Results on Racism in the Czech Republic," *Prague Post*, April 7, 2007.

91. Gender Studies, "Who We Are."

92. LIGA (Lidsých Práv), http://www.llp.cz.

93. Interview with law students by author, Brno, September 2006.

94. Interview with law students by author, Brno, September 2006.

95. Interview with law students by author, Brno, September 2006.

96. Gwendolyn Albert, interview by author, Prague, September 2006.

97. Interview with young lawyers by author, Brno, September 2006.

98. See, for example, Baršová, "Enhancing the Effectiveness."

99. Interview with young lawyers by author, Brno, September 2006.

Chapter 6

1. Quoted in Commission on Security and Cooperation in Europe, "Human Rights."

2. The terms *backward thinking* and *forward thinking* are used here to describe thinking that looks more to the past or to the future. The use of the terms *backward* and *forward* is *not* used to express a judgment on the sophistication of the thinking.

3. In the interests of space and because Germany is likely to be more familiar to readers than the other case studies in this book, I do not include a sketch of the German political system here. For more background on German politics and political institutions, see Wende, *History of Germany*; Padgett et al., *Developments in German Politics*; Schmidt, *Political Institutions*; and Roberts, *German Politics Today*.

4. Geiger, "Believing in a Miracle Cure."

5. Müller, *Disenchantment*, 1.

6. Commission on Security and Cooperation in Europe, "Human Rights." See also Schmidt, "Political Costs."

7. Flockton, "German Economy."

8. See Singer, "Politics and Economics."

9. See Commission on Security and Cooperation in Europe, "Human Rights."

10. See http://bundesrecht.juris.de/solzg_1995/ and http://www.bundesfinanz ministerium.de/lang_de/DE/Aktuelles/BMF__Schreiben/Veroffentlichungen__zu __Steuerarten/abgabenordnung/028, templateId=raw,property=publicationFile.pdf.

11. See, generally, Cooke, *Representing East Germany*; and Plock, *East German–West German Relations.*

12. Derek Scally, "Boom Makes Germans Hanker for Old Days; But Ruling Coalition Partner's Bid to Woo Back Voters Could Jeopardise Growth," *Strait Times*, November 3, 2007.

13. Quint, "Constitutional Guarantees," 306.

14. Quint, "Constitutional Guarantees," 306.

15. Library of Congress Country Studies and CIA World Factbook, "Germany."

16. According to figures from the Federal Statistical Office, Germany spent €26.4 billion on social assistance benefits in 2004, almost €10 billion (38 percent of expenditure) of which covered benefits paid to help with living expenses and the remaining €16.4 billion (62 percent) going for assistance in particular circumstances. At the end of 2004 almost 3 million people in Germany were receiving continuous subsistence benefits, and another 1.5 million received shorter term health benefits. Federal Statistical Office of Germany, "Social Security Schemes."

17. Federal Statistical Office of Germany, "Social Security Schemes."

18. Federal Statistical Office of Germany, "Social Security Schemes."

19. See, generally, Rittberger, *German Foreign Policy.*

20. Longhurst, *Germany.*

21. See Karp, "New German Foreign Policy Consensus."

22. Library of Congress Country Studies, *Germany.*

23. See Huelshoff et al., *From Bundesrepublik to Deutschland.*

24. In July 2005, after a long delay, the Ministers of the Interior of the sixteen Länder recommended ratification of the Optional Protocol to the UN Convention Against Torture. The Optional Protocol requires, among other things, an independent monitoring mechanism for detention facilities at the national level. The Bundestag (parliament) ratified the Optional Protocol to the UN Children's Convention on the involvement of children in armed conflicts. Regrettably, it ordered a reservation to be made to allow minors from the age of 17 to join the armed forces. For more on Germany's treaty history, see the UN's treaty database at http://www.unhchr.ch/tbs/doc.nsf/ Statusfrset?OpenFrameSet.

25. See, in general, Lantis, *Strategic Dilemmas.*

26. Nuschler, *Lern und Arbeitsbuch Entwiclkungspoliti.*

27. See Federal Ministry for Economic Cooperation and Development, "The BMZ: Guiding Principles," http://bmz.de/en/issues/index.html.

28. Kinkel, "Statement."

29. See Rudolf, "Myth of the German Way."

30. Some German foreign policy analysts contend that rather than a dramatic break with the past, Germany's actions in Kosovo can be seen as the culmination of a series of incremental steps that began a decade ago. See Berger, "Perfectly Normal Abnormality." See also Friedrich, "Legacy of Kosovo."

31. "Germany Elected to UN Human Rights Council," http://www.germany.info/ relaunch/politics/new/pol_UN_HRC_05_2006.html.

32. See Fedtke, *Protection of Human Rights*.

33. Basic Law for the Federal Republic of Germany, articles 1–19, http://www.bunde stag.de/htdocs_e/parliament/function/legal/germanbasiclaw.pdf.

34. For a good discussion of the impact of these and other policies on East Germans, see Major and Osmond, *Workers' and Peasants' State*.

35. See Stephen Roth Institute for the Study of Contemporary Anti-Semitism and Racism, "Country Studies: Germany."

36. U.S. Department of State, Bureau of Democracy, Human Rights, and Labor, *Germany*.

37. Human Rights Watch, "Germany for Germans."

38. Jamie Smyth, "Surge in Racial Violence in Europe Highlighted in Report," *Irish Times*, August 28, 2007.

39. Kim Murphy, "Ethnic Tension Surfaces in Germany; Immigrant Crime Is a Central Issue in the Hesse State Election, Stirring a Backlash Among Younger Voters," *Los Angeles Times*, January 27, 2008.

40. German Embassy, London, "Reform of Germany's Citizenship."

41. German Federal Ministry of the Interior, "Major Reform Aspects."

42. German Federal Ministry of the Interior, "Major Reform Aspects."

43. Human Rights Watch, "Germany for Germans."

44. Diez, "Opening, Closing."

45. Diez, "Opening, Closing."

46. Diez, "Opening, Closing."

47. See International Crisis Group, *Islam and Identity*.

48. Interviews with civil society activists by author, Berlin, November 2006.

49. Interviews with civil society activists by author, Berlin, November 2006.

50. Wildenthal, "Origins."

51. See Thomas, *Protest Movements*.

52. Olivo, *Creating a Democratic Civil Society*, 63.

53. Torpey, *Intellectuals*, 68.

54. Olivo, *Creating a Democratic Civil Society*, 63.

55. Olivo, *Creating a Democratic Civil Society*, 63.

56. See Keane, *Civil Society*.

57. Riley, *Everyday Subversion*.

58. The term *antipolitics* was popularized by George Konrad, in his *Antipolitics*.

59. Konrad, *Antipolitics*, 15.

60. Olivo, *Creating a Democratic Civil Society*, 1.

61. Olivo, *Creating a Democratic Civil Society*, 1.

62. Olivo, *Creating a Democratic Civil Society*, 2.

63. Karapin, *Protest Politics in Germany*.

64. Federal Ministry for the Environment, *Environmental Protection in Germany*.

65. Jaggard, *Climate Change Politics*.

66. Dubal et al., "Why Are Some Trade Agreements Greener."

67. For a particularly interesting ethnographic examination of environmental activism in Germany, see Berglund, *Knowing Nature*.

68. Interviews with current and former members of Human Rights Forum (Forum Menschenrechte) by author, Berlin, October 2006.

69. For one account of vibrant NGO activity, see Mertus and Goldberg, "Inside/Outside Construct."

70. See United Nations World Conference on Human Rights, *Vienna Declaration*, Article 1(1) (emphasizing the universality, indivisibility, and interconnectedness of all human rights).

71. United Nations World Conference on Human Rights, *Vienna Declaration*, Article 18.

72. United Nations World Conference on Human Rights, *Vienna Declaration*, Article 36.

73. German Institute for Human Rights, *Annual Report 2002*.

74. German Institute for Human Rights, *Annual Report 2002*.

75. German Institute for Human Rights, *Annual Report 2002*.

76. The twelve trustees with voting rights include two Bundestag deputies from the Bundestag's Committee on Human Rights (one each from the Social Democratic Party [SPD] and the Christian Democratic Union [CDU] and Christian Social Union [CSU] parliamentary groups), three representatives of the Human Rights Forum (from Amnesty International, the Diakonisches Werk—a church charity—and the Friedrich Naumann Foundation), the chairperson of the Heinrich Böll Foundation, four representatives of UN organizations (the UNHCR, the Commission on the Status of Women, the Committee on Civil and Political Rights ["Human Rights Committee"], and the Committee on Economic, Social, and Cultural Rights), one journalist, and—last but not least—a representative of the Federal Government Commissioner for Migration, Refugees, and Integration.

77. Jorgensen, *Strategies*.

78. These objectives are also explained in the 2002 annual report of the German Institute for Human Rights.

79. Jorgensen, *Strategies*.

80. Jorgensen, *Strategies*.

81. Frauke Seidensticker, interview by author, Berlin, October 2006.

82. Seidensticker, interview by author, Berlin, October 2006.

83. German Institute for Human Rights, *Annual Report 2002*, 7.

84. MacLean repeated these allegations in interviews with me in Berlin, October 2006.

85. The MacLean statement (in German) can be found on the web page for judges.

See http://bund-laender.verdi.de/fachgruppen/justiz/richterinnen_und_richter_staat
sanwaeltinnen_und_staatsanwaelte/verdikt/data/ver_dikt_1_2003, pp. 13–16.

86. MacLean repeated this allegation in an interview with me in Berlin, October 2006.

87. These observations are made on the basis of computerized searches of media
and are supported by a media clippings file that was kept by a German civil society advocate who prefers to remain anonymous. (File was given to author in October 2006.)

88. Summary of accounts on file with author.

89. *FAZ* has a national distribution, with a daily circulation as of August 2004 of
around 407,000 copies in Germany and 40,000 copies outside the country (for an overall readership of its German and English editions of about 1 million people), http://
www.ketupa.net/faz.htm.

90. Schlagheck, "Human Rights Official Quits."

91. MacLean repeated this allegation in an interview with me in Berlin, October 2006.

92. Schlagheck, "Human Rights Official Quits."

93. German Institute for Human Rights, *Annual Report 2002*, 12.

94. Seidensticker, interview by author, Berlin, October 2006.

95. Heiner Bielefeldt, interview by author, Berlin, October 2006.

96. German Institute for Human Rights, *Annual Report 2004*, 19.

97. German Institute for Human Rights, *Annual Report 2005*.

98. German Institute for Human Rights, *Annual Report 2006*, 28–29.

99. Note that many categories of the Institute's work are not included here purely
because of space limitations. Other areas include work on human rights and development concerns, cultural relativity, and refugee and migrant issues.

100. German Institute for Human Rights, *Annual Report 2003*, 1.

101. The full text of the Völkerstrafgesetzbuch (VStGB) can be found at http://
bundesrecht.juris.de/vstgb/index.html.

102. German Institute for Human Rights, *Annual Report 2005*.

103. Bielefeldt, interview by author, Berlin, October 2006.

104. Arloth and Seidensticker, *ESDP Crisis Management Operations*.

105. Arloth and Seidensticker, *ESDP Crisis Management Operations*.

106. Arloth and Seidensticker, *ESDP Crisis Management Operations*.

107. See Heinz and Arend, *International Fight Against Terrorism*. See also German
Institute for Human Rights, "Diplomatic Assurances."

108. Seidensticker, interview by author, Berlin, October 2006.

109. See the German Institute for Human Rights website, http://www.institut-fuer
-menschenrechte.de/webcom/show_article.php/_c-476/_lkm-653/i.html.

110. Basic Law for the Federal Republic of Germany.

111. Basic Law for the Federal Republic of Germany.

112. Basic Law for the Federal Republic of Germany.

113. Basic Law for the Federal Republic of Germany.

114. German Institute for Human Rights, *Annual Report 2005*.

115. German Institute for Human Rights, *Annual Report 2005*.

116. German Institute for Human Rights, *Annual Report 2005*.

117. See, for example, Spieß, *Die Wanderarbeitnehmerkonvention.* See also Motakef, *Das Menschenrecht.*

118. Shadow reports on file with author.

119. E-mail correspondence and interview with former staff member, German Institute for Human Rights, by author, San Francisco and Pittsburgh, April 2008.

120. German Institute for Human Rights, *Annual Report 2006.*

121. Bielefeldt, interview by author, Berlin, October 2006.

Chapter 7

1. Jelena Subotić, "Hijacked Justice," 28.

2. For a comprehensive overview of Northern Ireland's community and voluntary sector, see Northern Ireland Council for Voluntary Action, *State of the Sector.*

3. See Chapter 2. DIHR director Morten Kjaerum was accused by right-leaning critics of being an "opinion doctor" for allegedly attempting to use his elite position to push ideas onto an otherwise unreceptive public.

4. United Nations Office of the High Commissioner for Human Rights, *Fact Sheet No. 19.* See, in general, Reif, "Building Democratic Institutions," specifically 2–13.

5. Brian Burdekin held the position of the UN special adviser on NHRIs from 1995 to 2004. During this period he undertook 200 missions to 55 countries pressing the NHRI agenda. Brian Burdekin, telephone interview by author, Lund, Sweden, November 2007.

6. See Cardenas, "Emerging Global Actors."

7. Parlevliet, *National Human Rights Institutions,* 7.

8. Lord, "National Human Rights Institutions."

9. See, for example, the critique offered by Human Rights Watch in relation to the proliferation of NHRIs in Africa. Human Rights Watch, *Protectors or Pretenders,* 2.

10. Lord, "National Human Rights Institutions."

11. See, in general, Mertus, *Bait and Switch.*

12. Cardenas, "Adaptive States," 56.

13. See, in general, Commonwealth Secretariat, *National Human Rights Institutions.*

14. Overseas Development Administration, *Note on Enhancing Stakeholder Participation.*

15. Gallagher, *Balkans in the New Millennium,* 186.

16. Bell and Keenan, "Human Rights Nongovernmental Organizations," 334. See also Hadden, "Role of a National Commission."

17. Bell, *Peace Agreements,* 199.

18. Okafor and Agbakwa, "On Legalism," 699.

19. Thio, "Future of National Human Rights Institutions."

20. Kumar, "NHRIs in South Asia," 3.

Bibliography

Adeyi, Olusoji. "Priorities for Medium-Term Development in the Health Sector of Bosnia and Herzegovina." *CMJ Online* 39(3) (1998). http://www.cmj.hr/1998/39/3/9740641.htm.

Aichele, Valentin, and Jakob Schneider. *Soziale Menschenrechte älterer Personen in Pflege.* Berlin: German Institute for Human Rights, 2006. http://files.institut-fuer-menschenrechte.de/488/d51_v1_file_44d9abe25461c_DIMR%20Studie%20Pflege%202%20%20Auflage%2007-08-06.pdf.

Alliance Party. "NIHRC: Progressing a Bill of Rights for Northern Ireland—Alliance Party Response to Consultation Paper by the Northern Ireland Human Rights Commission." August 31, 2004. http://www.allianceparty.org/resources/sites/82.165.40.25-42fa41bb0bef84.24243647/3-Consultations/NIHRC%3A+Progressing+a+Bill+of+Rights+for+NI.html.

Amnesty International. "Bosnia and Herzegovina: Behind Closed Gates—Ethnic Discrimination in Employment." January 26, 2006. http://news.amnesty.org/index/ENGEUR630032006.

———. "Czech Republic." *Amnesty International Report 2007.* http://www.amnesty.org/en/region/europe-and-central-asia/eastern-europe/czech-republic.

———. *National Human Rights Institutions: Amnesty International's Recommendations for Effective Protection and Promotion of Human Rights.* October 1, 2001. http://web.amnesty.org/library/index/ENGIOR400072001.

Andjelic, Nevan. *Bosnia-Herzegovina: The End of a Legacy.* Portland, OR: Frank Cass, 2003.

Aoláin, Fionnuala N. "The Fractured Soul of the Dayton Peace Agreement: A Legal Analysis." *Michigan Journal of International Law* 19(4) (1998): 957–1004.

———. *The Politics of Force: Conflict Management and State Violence in Northern Ireland.* Belfast: Blackstaff Press, 1994.

Arbitral Tribunal for Dispute over Inter-Entity Boundary in Brcko Area. *The Federation of Bosnia and Herzegovina v. The Republika Srpska* (Final Award). 38 I.L.M. 534 (1999). http://www.state.gov/www/regions/eur/bosnia/990305_arbiter_brcko.html.

Arloth, Jana, and Frauke Seidensticker. *The ESDP Crisis Management Operations of the European Union and Human Rights.* Berlin: German Institute for Human Rights, 2007.

Arter, David. *Democracy in Scandinavia: Consensual, Majoritarian, or Mixed?* Manchester, U.K.: Manchester University Press, 2006.

Association for Education and Development of Women (ATHENA). "Overview of Gender Equality Issues in the Czech Republic." http://www.gender-equality.webinfo .lt/results/czech.htm.

Austermiller, Steven. "Mediation in Bosnia and Herzegovina: A Second Application." *Yale Human Rights and Development Law Journal* 9 (2006): 132–165.

Baršová, Andrea. "Enhancing the Effectiveness of the Non-Judicial Human Rights Protection Mechanisms in the Czech Republic." 2003. http://www.policy.hu/barsova/ final_research_paper.pdf.

Bayefsky.com. "The United Nations Human Rights Treaties: Czech Republic." February 27, 2007. http://www.bayefsky.com/pdf/czechrepublic_t1_ratifications.pdf.

Baylis, Elena A. "Minority Rights, Minority Wrongs." *UCLA Journal of International and Foreign Affairs* 10(1) (2005): 66–140.

Bell, Christine. "Dealing with the Past in Northern Ireland." *Fordham International Law Journal* 26(4) (2003): 1095–1147.

———. *Peace Agreements and Human Rights.* New York: Oxford University Press, 2005.

Bell, Christine, and Johanna Keenan. "Human Rights Nongovernmental Organizations and the Problem of Transition." *Human Rights Quarterly* 26(2) (2004): 330–374.

Belloni, Robert. *State Building and International Intervention in Bosnia.* New York: Routledge, 2007.

Benedek, Wolfgang. *Human Rights in Bosnia and Herzegovina After Dayton: From Theory to Practice.* The Hague: Martinus Nijhoff, 1999.

Berger, Thomas U. "A Perfectly Normal Abnormality: German Foreign Policy After Kosovo and Afghanistan." *Japanese Journal of Political Science* 3(2) (2002): 173–193.

Berglund, Eva K. *Knowing Nature, Knowing Science: An Ethnography of Local Environmental Activism.* Cambridge, U.K.: White Horse Press, 1998.

Beriker-Atiyas, Nimet, and Tijen Demirel-Pegg. "An Analysis of Integrative Outcomes in the Dayton Peace Negotiations." *International Journal of Conflict Management* 11(4) (2000): 358–378.

Bieber, Florian. *Post-War Bosnia: Ethnicity, Inequality, and Public Sector Governance.* New York: Palgrave, 2006.

Blahoz, Joseph, Lubomir Brokll, and Zdenka Mansfeldová. "Czech Political Parties and Cleavages After 1989." In *Cleavages, Parties, and Voters: Studies from Czech Republic, Hungary, Poland, and Romania*, edited by Kay Lawson, Andrea Rommele, and Georgi Karasimeionov, 123–140. Westport, CT: Praeger, 1999.

Blanton, Shanon Lindsay. "Foreign Policy in Transition? Human Rights, Democracy, and U.S. Arms Exports." *International Studies Quarterly* 49(4) (2005): 647–668.

Borden, Anthony, and Drago Hedl. "How the Bosnians Were Broken: Twenty-One Days at Dayton." *War Report* 39 (1996). http://www.iwpr.net/index.php?apc_state =henoarchive_warreport_index.html&s= o&o=archive_warreport_39.html.

Borre, Ole, and Jørgen Goul Andersen. *Voting and Political Attitudes in Denmark*. Aarhus, Denmark: Aarhus University Press, 1997.

Bose, Sumantra. *Bosnia After Dayton: Nationalist Partition and International Intervention*. New York: Oxford University Press, 2002.

Bouvier, Virginia M. *The Globalization of U.S.-Latin American Relations: Democracy, Intervention, and Human Rights*. Westport, CT: Praeger, 2002.

Boyle, Francis. *Negating Human Rights in Peace Negotiations*. Helsinki: Domovina Net, 1996.

Burdekin, Brian. "Human Rights Commissions." In *Human Rights Commissions and Ombudsman Offices: National Experiences Throughout the World*, edited by Kamal Hossain, Leonard F. M. Besselink, Haile Selassie, and Edmond Volker, 801–808. Boston: Martinus Nijhoff, 2001.

CABI (Center for Aktiv BeskæftigelsesIndsats [Danish National Center for Employment Initiatives]). "For Democracy's Sake." In *A Diverse Public Sector Labor Market— How?* Aarhus, Denmark: CABI, October 2006 (in Danish).

Cadwallader, Anne. *Holy Cross: The Untold Story*. Belfast: Brehon Press, 2004.

CAIN (Conflict Archive on the Internet). *The Agreement: Agreement Reached in the Multi-Party Negotiations*, April 10, 1998. http://cain.ulst.ac.uk/events/peace/docs/ agreement.htm.

———. *Cameron Report: Disturbances in Northern Ireland*. Belfast: Her Majesty's Stationery Office, 1969. http://cain.ulst.ac.uk/hmso/cameron.htm.

———. "The Cost of the Troubles Study." http://cain.ulst.ac.uk/cts/index.html.

———. "Joint Declaration on Peace: Downing Street Declaration." December 15, 1993. http://cain.ulster.ac.uk/events/peace/docs/dsd151293.html

———. "Violence: Draft List of Deaths Related to the Conflict in 2006." 2006. http:// cain.ulst.ac.uk/issues/violence/deaths2006draft.htm.

Cardenas, Sonia. "Adaptive States: The Proliferation of National Human Rights Institutions." Working Paper T-01-04. Carr Center for Human Rights, n.d. http://www .ksg.harvard.edu/cchrp/Web%20Working%20Papers/Cardenas.pdf.

———. "Emerging Global Actors: The United Nations and National Human Rights Institutions." *Global Governance* 9(1) (2003): 23–42.

———. "State Institutions for Human Rights: Latin America in Comparative Perspective." Paper presented at the annual meeting of the International Studies Association 48th Annual Convention, February 27, 2007.

Carmichael, Cathie. *Ethnic Cleansing in the Balkans*. Oxford, U.K.: Routledge, 2002.

Chandler, David. *Bosnia: Faking Democracy After Dayton*. London: Pluto Press, 2000.

———. "The Democracy Paradox." *Current History* 100(644) (March 2001): 114–120.

———. *Peace Without Politics? Ten Years of State-Building in Bosnia*. Oxford, U.K.: Routledge, 2005.

Chiongson, Rea A., Gilbert V. Sembrano, and Patricia-Provido Dehlma, eds. *National Human Rights Institutions in the Asia-Pacific: A Source Book.* Manila: Working Group for an ASEAN Human Rights Mechanism, 2001.

Commission on Security and Cooperation in Europe. *Briefing: Brčko and the Future of Bosnia.* December 10, 1996. SU document Y.SE 2:B 73. http://www.csce.gov/index.cfm?FuseAction=UserGroups.Home&ContentRecord_id=193&ContentType=H,B&ContentRecordType=B&UserGroup_id=62&Subaction=Hearings&CFID=14714891&CFTOKEN=43444418.

———. "Human Rights and Democratization in United Germany." December 1993. http://home.snafu.de/tilman/krasel/germany/csce.html.

Committee on the Administration of Justice. "War on Terror: Lessons from Northern Ireland." January 2008. http://www.caj.org.uk/Front%20page%20pdfs/Terror%20summary_12pp%20pages.pdf.

Commonwealth Secretariat. *National Human Rights Institutions: Best Practice.* London: Commonwealth Secretariat, 2001.

Connolly, Paul, and Julie Healy. "Children and Conflict in Northern Ireland: The Experiences and Perspectives of 3–11 Year Olds." Belfast: Office of the First Minister and Deputy First Minister, 2004.

Coogan, Tim Pat. *The IRA: A History.* Hampshire, U.K.: Palgrave Macmillan, 2002.

Cooke, Paul. *Representing East Germany Since Unification: From Colonization to Nostalgia.* Oxford, U.K.: Berg, 2005.

Council of Europe. *European Agreement on Transfer of Responsibility for Refugees.* Strasbourg, October 16, 1980. http://conventions.coe.int/treaty/en/Treaties/html/107.htm.

———. *European Social Charter.* http://www.coe.int/T/E/Human_Rights/Esc/.

Council of Europe, European Commission Against Racism and Intolerance. *Third Report on the Czech Republic.* December 5, 2003. Council of Europe, Strasbourg, 2004. http://www.policy.hu/olmazu/migration_reports/ECRI%20Report%20on%20Czech%20Republic.pdf.

Courdesse, Laure-Anne, and Sarah Hemingway. "A Human Rights-Based Approach to Development in Practice: Some Lessons Learned from the Rights-Based Municipal Assessment and Planning Project in Bosnia and Herzegovina." Paper presented at the Conference, "Winners and Losers from Rights-Based Approaches to Development," February 21–22, 2005. http://www.sed.manchester.ac.uk/research/events/conferences/winnersandloserspapers.htm.

Cousens, Elizabeth, and Charles Cater. "Towards Peace in Bosnia: Implementing the Dayton Accords." Occasional Paper Series, August 2001. New York: International Peace Academy.

Cox, Michael, Adrian Guelke, and Fiona Stephen, eds. *A Farewell to Arms? Beyond the Good Friday Agreement.* Manchester: Manchester University Press and Palgrave, 2006.

Cross-Party Working Group on Religious Hatred. *Tackling Religious Hatred: Report of Cross-Party Working Group on Religious Hatred.* Edinburgh: Office of the Scottish Executive, December 5, 2002. http://www.scotland.gov.uk/Publications/ 2002/12/15892/14531.

Cushman, Thomas C., and Stjepan G. Mestrovic, eds. *This Time We Knew: Western Responses to Genocide in Bosnia.* New York: New York University Press, 1996.

Czech Helsinki Committee. *Human Rights Report 2005.* http://www.helcom.cz/search .php?rsvelikost=sab&rstext=all-phpRS-all&rstema=96.

Czech Republic Official Website. "Economy, Business, Science." http://www.czech.cz/ en/economy-business-science/general-information/economy-development-and -potential/economic-history/development-after-november-1989/. Updated regularly, last checked July 2008.

Czech Statistics Office. "Results of Elections." http://www.volby.cz/index_en.htm.

Dahlman, Carl, and Gearóid Ó Tuathail. "The Legacy of Ethnic Cleansing: The International Community and the Returns Process in Post-Dayton Bosnia-Herzegovina." *Political Geography* 24(5) (June 2005): 569–599.

Dakin, Brett. "The Islamic Community in Bosnia and Herzegovina v. The Republika Srpska: Human Rights in a Multi-Ethnic Bosnia." *Harvard Human Rights Journal* 15 (Spring 2002): 245–267.

Dane Age Association. "AEldre patienter bliver svigtet." October 27, 2006. http://www .aeldresagen.dk/newspage.asp?id=58F48CA6-DD5A-4040-86B1-2A13D6A 112D2.

Danish Centre for Human Rights. "National Human Rights Institutions Implementing Human Rights." Copenhagen: Danish Centre for Human Rights, 2003.

Danish Institute for Human Rights. *National Human Rights Institutions: Articles and Working Papers.* Copenhagen: Danish Institute for Human Rights, 2000.

Danish Ministry of Foreign Affairs. *Capacity Assessment of the Danish Centre for Human Rights: Final Report.* June 2002. http://www.humanrights.dk:81/upload/ application/606dbc7f/capacity.pdf.

Danish Social Democrats. "Clear Rights for the Elderly." September 7, 2006. http:// socialdemokratiet.dk/default.aspx?site=vaerloese&func=article.view&id=162599.

Dansk Indutri. "The Danish Confederation of Industries." Press release, April 27, 2004. http://www.di.dk/DI/Presse/Pressemeddelelser/Regeringens+strukturudspil .htm.

Darby, John. "Conflict in Northern Ireland: A Background Essay." In *The Facets of Conflict in Northern Ireland*, edited by Seamus Dunn. Hampshire, U.K.: Palgrave Macmillan, 1995.

Davidson, G., M. McCallion, and M. Potter. *Connecting Mental Health and Human Rights.* Belfast: Northern Ireland Human Rights Commission, December 2003.

Dickson, Brice. "The Contribution of Human Rights Commissions to the Protection of Human Rights." *Public Law* 272 (2003): 272–285.

Diez, Thomas. "Opening, Closing: Securitisation, the War on Terror, and the Debate About Migration in Germany." Paper presented at the MIDAS/SWP Workshop on Security and Migration, Berlin, Germany, March 9, 2006. http://www.midas .bham.ac.uk/Berlin%20Paper%20Diez%2020060307.pdf.

Discalla, Spencer M. *Twentieth Century Europe: Politics, Society, and Culture*. New York: McGraw-Hill, 2004.

Dixon, Paul. *Northern Ireland: The Politics of War and Peace*. Hampshire, U.K.: Palgrave Macmillan, 2001.

Donia, Robert J., and John V. A. Fine. *Bosnia and Hercegovina*. New York: Columbia University Press, 1995.

Donnelly, Jack. *International Human Rights: Dilemmas in World Politics*, 3rd ed. New York: Westview Press, 2006.

Doorenspleet, R. "Reassessing the Three Waves of Democratization." *World Politics* 52(3) (2000): 384–406.

Dubal, Veena Jung Lah, Ian Monroe, and Martha Roberts. "Why Are Some Trade Agreements 'Greener' Than Others?" *Earth Island Journal* 16(4) (2001–2002). http://www.earthisland.org/journal/index.php/eij/article/why_are_some_trade_agreements_greener_than_others/.

Dunne, Tim, and Nicholas J. Wheeler, eds. *Human Rights in Global Politics*. New York: Cambridge University Press, 1999.

Dvoráková, Vladímír. "Civil Society in the Czech Republic: 'Impulse 99' and 'Thank You, Time to Go.'" In *Uncivil Society? Contentious Politics in Post-Communist Europe*, edited by Petr Kopecký and Cas Mudde, 134–156. London: Routledge, 2007.

Dyker, D. A., and I. Vejvoda. *Yugoslavia and After: A Study in Fragmentation, Despair, and Rebirth*. New York: Longman, 1996.

Encyclopedia of the Nations, s.v. "Bosnia Herzegovina, Domestic Policy." 2007. http://www.nationsencyclopedia.com/World-Leaders-2003/Bosnia-Herzegovina-DOMESTIC-POLICY.html.

———, s.v. "Bosnia-Herzegovina, Economy." 2007. http://www.nationsencyclopedia.com/Europe/Bosnia-and-Herzegovina-ECONOMY.html.

———, s.v. "Denmark: Political Background." 2007. http://www.nationsencyclopedia.com/World-Leaders-2003/Denmark-POLITICAL-BACKGROUND.html.

English, Richard. *Armed Struggle: A History of the IRA*. Oxford, U.K.: Oxford University Press, 2003.

European Commission. *European Commission Report (2002): Czech Republic*. 2002. http://www.fifoost.org/tschechien/EU_czech_2002/node21.php.

———. "Implementation of Anti-Discrimination Directives into National Law." April 2005. http://ec.europa.eu/employment_social/fundamental_rights/legis/lgms_en.htm.

European Commission Against Racism and Intolerance. *Third Report on Denmark*. Strasbourg: European Commission Against Racism and Intolerance, May 16, 2006. http://www.coe.int/t/e/human_rights/ecri/1%2Decri/2%2Dcountry%2Dby%2Dcountry_approach/denmark/Denmark%20third%20report%20-%20cri06-18.pdf.

European Court of Human Rights. "Grand Chamber Activity Report 2007." Registry of the European Court of Human Rights, Strasbourg, 2008. http://www.echr.coe.int/NR/rdonlyres/FF7C4EB6-C3A4-4A4E-AB32-17D4A4A99BCF/0/2007Grand_Chamber_activity_report.pdf.

European Network Against Racism (ENAR). "Deplorable Action on the Part of the Danish Government." Press release, March 6, 2002. http://www.no-racism.net/MUND/archiv/maerz2/aussendung090302.htm.

European Roma Rights Center and Vzájemné Soužití. *Written Comments of the European Roma Rights Centre and Vzájemné Soužití Concerning the Czech Republic, for Consideration by the United Nations Committee on the Elimination of Racial Discrimination at Its 70th Session.* December 12, 2006. http://www.errc.org/db/02/C8/m000002C8.pdf.

Farry, Stephen. *Northern Ireland: Prospects for Progress in 2006?* Special Report 173. Washington, DC: United States Institute of Peace, September 2006.

Federal Ministry for the Environment. *Environmental Protection in Germany.* Berlin: Federal Ministry for the Environment, 1992.

Federal Ministry of the Interior. "Questions and Answers About the German Nationality Law." Updated 2008. http://www.bmi.bund.de/cln_028/nn_148248/SiteGlobals/Forms/EN/Suche__en/serviceSucheFormular,templateId=processForm.html?resourceId=148676&input_=&pageLocale=en&searchEngineQueryString=german+nationality+law&submit=search&sortString=-score&searchArchive=2&searchIssued=0&path=%2FSites%2FBMI%2FInternet%2F&maxResults=5000.8

Federal Statistical Office of Germany. "Social Security Schemes: Public Assistance." December 15, 2005. http://www.destatis.de/themen/e/thm_sozial.htm.

Fedtke, Jorg. *The Protection of Human Rights in German and English Law.* New York: Routledge, 2008.

Finucane, Patrick. *Cory Collusion Report.* London: Stationery Office, 2004. http://www.nio.gov.uk/cory_collusion_inquiry_report_(with_appendices)_pat_finucane.pdf.

Fischer, Martina, ed. *Peacebuilding and Civil Society in Bosnia-Herzegovina: Ten Years After Dayton.* Hamburg, Germany: Lit Verlag, 2005.

Flockton, Christopher. "The German Economy Since 1989–90: Problems and Prospects." In *Germany Since Unification: The Development of the Berlin Republic,* 2nd ed., edited by Klaus Larres, 63–87. New York: Palgrave Macmillan, 2001.

Flood, John. "Socio-Legal Ethnography." In *Theory and Method in Socio-Legal Research,* edited by Reza Banakar and Max Travers, 33–48. Oxford, U.K.: Hart, 2007.

Forsythe, David P. *Human Rights in International Relations.* New York: Cambridge University Press, 2000.

Foster, R. F. *Modern Ireland, 1600–1972.* London: Penguin, 1989.

French, B., and P. Campbell. "Fear of Crime in Northern Ireland: Findings from the 2001 Northern Ireland Crime Survey." *Research and Statistical Bulletin* 5 (2002). http://www.nio.gov.uk/fear_of_crime_in_northern_ireland_findings_from_the_2001_ni_crime_survey.pdf.

Friedman, Franci. *Bosnia and Herzegovina: A Polity on the Brink.* New York: Routledge, 2004.

Friedrich, Wolfgang-Uwe, ed. "The Legacy of Kosovo: German Politics and Policies in the Balkans." *German Issues* 22 (2000). http://www.aicgs.org/documents/legacy_of_kosovo.pdf.

Gallagher, Anne. "Making Human Rights Treaty Obligations a Reality: Working with New Actors and Partners." In *The Future of UN Human Rights Treaty Monitoring*, edited by Philip Alston and James Crawford, 201–228. Cambridge, U.K.: Cambridge University Press, 2000.

Gallagher, Tom. *The Balkans in the New Millennium: In the Shadow of War and Peace*. New York: Routledge, 2005.

Geiger, Till. "Believing in a Miracle Cure: The Economic Transition Process in Germany and East-Central Europe." In *Germany Since Unification: The Development of the Berlin Republic*, 2nd ed., edited by Klaus Larres, 74–202. New York: Palgrave Macmillan, 2001.

Gender Studies. "Who We Are." http://www.en.genderstudies.cz/.

German Embassy, London. "Reform of Germany's Citizenship and Nationality Law." n.d. http://www.london.diplo.de/Vertretung/london/en/06/other__legal__matters /Reform__Germanys__citizenship__seite.html.

German Federal Ministry of the Interior. "Major Reform Aspects of the German Nationality Law." http://www.bmi.bund.de/cln_028/nn_148248/SiteGlobals/Forms/ EN/Suche__en/serviceSucheFormular,templateId=processForm.html?resourceId =148676&input_=&pageLocale=en&searchEngineQueryString=german+nation ality+law&submit=search&sortString=-score&searchArchive=2&searchIssued =0&path=%2FSites%2FBMI%2FInternet%2F&maxResults=5000.

German Institute for Human Rights. *Annual Report 2002*. Berlin: German Institute for Human Rights, 2003. http://files.institut-fuer-menschenrechte.de/488/d7_v1 _file_408cd3ea5d3eb_Annual%20Report%202002.pdf.

———. *Annual Report 2003*. Berlin: German Institute for Human Rights, 2004. http://files.institut-fuer-menschenrechte.de/488/d31_v1_file_411c76fe6b063 _DIMR_2004_Jahresbericht_2003.pdf.

———. *Annual Report 2004*. Berlin: German Institute for Human Rights, 2005. http:// www.institut-fuer-menschenrechte.de/webcom/show_shop.php/_c-488/ _nr-40/i.html.

———. *Annual Report 2005*. Berlin: German Institute for Human Rights, 2006. http:// files.institut-fuer menschenrechte.de/488/d53_v1_file45081e6eaccd1_IUS-015 _DIMR_JB05_RZ_WWW_ES.pdf.

———. *Annual Report 2006*. Berlin: German Institute for Human Rights, 2007. http://files.institut-fuer-menschenrechte.de/488/d69_v1_file_46efb25702233 _IUS-035_DIMRJB06_RZ_ANSICHT_ES.pdf.

———. "Diplomatic Assurances and the Extradition of Suspected Terrorists." Paper presented at the session of the Council of Europe's Working Group on Human Rights, December 5–7, 2005.

Givens, Terri E. *Voting Radical Right in Western Europe*. New York: Cambridge University Press, 2005.

Globalsecurity.org. "Soviet Invasion of Czechoslovakia." n.d. http://www.globalsecurity .org/military/world/war/czechoslovakia2.htm.

Green, Tristin K. "Work Culture and Discrimination." *California Law Review* 93(3) (2005): 623–684.

Gupta, Nabanita Datta, Ronald Oaxaca, and Nina Smith. "Swimming Upstream, Floating Downstream: Comparing Women's Relative Wage Progress in the United States and Denmark." *Industrial and Labor Relations* 59(2) (2006): 243–266.

Haahr, Jens Henrik. "Between Scylla and Charybdis: Danish Party Policies on European Integration." In *Denmark's Policy Towards Europe After 1945: History, Theory, and Options*, edited by Hans Branner and Morten Kelstrup, 305–322. Odense, Denmark: Odense University Press, 2000.

Hadden, T. "The Role of a National Commission in the Protection of Human Rights." In *Human Rights Commissions and Ombudsman Offices*, edited by K. Hossain, Leonard F. M. Besselink, Haile Selassie, and Edmond Volker, 791–799. The Hague: Martinus Nijhoff, 2001.

Hadfield, Bridget. *Constitution of Northern Ireland*. Belfast: SLS Legal Publications, 1989.

Hall, Julia A. "Justice For All? An Analysis of the Human Rights Provisions of the 1998 Northern Ireland Peace Agreement." *Human Rights Watch* 10(3) (D), April 1998. http://www.hrw.org/reports98/nireland/.

Hanley, Seán. "Blue Velvet: The Rise and Decline of the New Czech Right." In *Centre-Right Parties in Post-Communist East-Central Europe*, edited by Aleks Szcerbiak and S. Hanley, 8–54. New York: Routledge, 2006.

Hanvey, Eric, Iain McNicoll, Richard Marsh, and Fabian Zuleeg. *Report on Labour Market Dynamics, Phase One: A Descriptive Analysis of the Northern Ireland Labour Market*. Belfast: Office of the First Minister and Deputy Prime Minister, November 2005. http://www.ofmdfmni.gov.uk/phase1.pdf.

Harvey, Colin. "Building Bridges? Protecting Human Rights in Northern Ireland." *Human Rights Law Review* 1(2) (2001): 243–264.

Harvey, Colin, ed. *Human Rights, Equality, and Democrat Renewal in Northern Ireland*. Oxford, U.K.: Hart, 2001.

Havelková, Hana. "Public Awareness of Civil Society and Human Rights After 1989." *Patrin Web Journal*, February 22, 1999. http://www.geocities.com/~patrin/czech-public-aware.htm.

Heinz, Wolfgang, and Jan-Michael Arend. *The International Fight Against Terrorism and the Protection of Human Rights*. Berlin: German Institute for Human Rights, 2005.

Hennessey, Thomas. *The Northern Ireland Peace Process*. New York: Palgrave Macmillan, 2001.

Højsteen, Signe. "More UN Criticism of the Danish Government's Policies." *DSI Nyhedsbrev*, December 4, 2005. http://www.handicap.dk/dsi-nyhedsbrev/nyhedsbrev-4-2005/kap-19.

Howe, Robert Brian, and David Johnson, eds. *Restraining Equality: Human Rights Commissions in Canada*. Toronto: Toronto University Press, 2000.

Hrdlickova, Petra. *Czech Republic Exporter Guide Annual Report: 2006.* GAIN Report EZ6012. Washington, DC: USDA Foreign Agricultural Service, October 3, 2006. http://www.fas.usda.gov/gainfiles/200610/146249191.doc.

Huelshoff, Michael, Andrei S. Markovits, and Simon Reich, eds. *From Bundesrepublik to Deutschland: German Politics After Unification.* Ann Arbor: University of Michigan Press, 1993.

Hughes, Joanne, Caitlin Donnelly, Gillian Robinson, and Lizanne Dowds. *Community Relations in Northern Ireland: The Long View.* Belfast: ARK, March 2003. http://www.ark.ac.uk/publications/occasional/occpaper2.PDF.

Human Rights Chamber for Bosnia and Herzegovina. *Annual Report: Bosnia and Herzegovina.* Sarajevo: Human Rights Chamber, March 1998. http://wwwuser.gwdg.de/~ujvr/hrch/98annrep.html.

Human Rights First. "Human Rights Defenders in Northern Ireland: Rosemary Nelson." http://www.humanrightsfirst.org/defenders/hrd_n_ireland/hrd_northern_irland.htm.

Human Rights Ombudsman of Bosnia and Herzegovina. *Annual Report 2004.* Banja Luka and Sarajevo, 2005.

Human Rights Watch. "Germany for Germans: Xenophobia and Racist Violence in Germany." April 1995. http://www.hrw.org/reports/1995/Germany.htm.

———. "Hopes Betrayed: Trafficking of Women and Girls to Post-Conflict Bosnia and Herzegovina for Forced Prostitution." *Bosnia and Herzegovina* 14(9) (November 2002). http://www.hrw.org/reports/2002/bosnia/.

———. *Protectors or Pretenders? Government Human Rights Commissions in Africa.* New York: Human Rights Watch, 2001.

———. "Roma Children Denied Equal Education." November 2007. http://hrw.org/english/docs/2007/11/14/czech17329.htm.

———. "Roma in the Czech Republic: Foreigners in Their Own Land." June 1996. http://hrw.org/reports/1996/Czech.htm.

———. "World Report 2007: Bosnia and Herzegovina, Events of 2006." n.d. http://hrw.org/englishwr2k7/docs/2007/01/11/bosher14773.htm.

International Council on Human Rights Policy. *Human Rights Standards: Learning from Example.* Versoix, Switzerland: ICHRP, 2006.

———. *Performance and Legitimacy: National Human Rights Institutions.* Versoix, Switzerland: ICHRP, 2004.

International Council on Human Rights Policy and Office of the High Commissioner for Human Rights. *Assessing the Effectiveness of National Human Rights Institutions.* 2005. http://www.ichrp.org/en/projects/125?theme=15.

International Crisis Group. *Bosnia's Precarious Economy: Still Not Open for Business.* Europe Report 115. Brussels: Crisis Group, August 7, 2001. http://www.crisisgroup.org/home/index.cfm?id=1494&l=1.

———. *Islam and Identity in Germany.* Europe Report 181. Brussels: Crisis Group, March 14, 2007. http://www.crisisgroup.org/home/index.cfm?l=1&id=4693.

Ishay, Micheline R. *The History of Human Rights: From Ancient Times to the Globalization Era*. Berkeley: University of California Press, 2004.

———. *The Human Rights Reader: Major Political Essays, Speeches, and Documents from the Bible to the Present*. New York: Routledge, 1997.

Issacharoff, Samuel. "Constitutionalizing Democracy in Fractured Societies." *Journal of International Affairs* 58 (2004): 73–93.

Jackson, Robert. *The Global Covenant: Human Conduct in a World of States*. New York: Oxford University Press, 2000.

Jaggard, Lyn. *Climate Change Politics in Europe: Germany and the International Relations of the Environment*. London: Tauris Academic Studies, 2007.

James, Steve. "Northern Ireland: Human Rights Redefined on Sectarian Lines." International Committee of the Fourth International, August 20, 2003. http://www.wsws.org/articles/2003/aug2003/nire-a20.shtml.

Jarman, Neil. *Demography, Development, and Disorder: Changing Patterns of Interface Areas*. Belfast: Institute for Conflict Research, July 2004. http://www.conflictresearch.org.uk/documents/Interface_Paper.pdf.

———. *No Longer a Problem? Sectarian Violence in Northern Ireland*. Belfast: Institute for Conflict Research, March 2005. http://www.community-relations.org.uk/consultation_uploads/OFMDFM_-_Sectarian_Violence.pdf.

Jespersen, Knud J. V. *A History of Denmark*. New York: Palgrave Macmillan, 2004.

Joint Committee on Human Rights. *Joint Committee on Human Rights: Fourteenth Report*. London: United Kingdom Parliament, 2003. http://www.parliament.the-stationery-office.com/pa/jt200203/jtselect/jtrights/132/13205.htm.

———. "Memorandum from Madden and Finucane, Solicitors." In *Joint Committee on Human Rights: Written Evidence*. London: United Kingdom Parliament, November 24, 2002. http://www.publications.parliament.uk/pa/jt200203/jtselect/jtrights/132/132we13.htm.

Jorgensen, Rikke Frank. *Strategies for National Human Rights Work: The German Institute for Human Rights*. Copenhagen: Danish Human Rights Institute, June 2, 2004.

Karapin, Roger. *Protest Politics in Germany: Movements on the Left and Right Since the 1960s*. University Park: Pennsylvania State University Press, 2007.

Karp, Regina Cowen. "The New German Foreign Policy Consensus." *Washington Quarterly* 29(1) (Winter 2005–2006): 61–82.

Kaus, Gerald, and Nicholas Whyte. *The Internationals and the Balkans: Time for a Change*. Balkan Crisis Report 505. London: Institute for War and Peace Reporting, July 2004.

Keane, John, ed. *Civil Society and the State: New European Perspectives*. New York: Verso, 1988.

Keck, Margaret, and Kathryn Sikkink. *Activists Beyond Borders*. Ithaca, NY: Cornell University Press, 1998.

Kinkel, Klaus. "Statement on the German Cabinet's Approval of the 'Fourth German Government Report on Its Human Rights Policy in Foreign Relations.'"

Washington, DC: German Embassy, October 29, 1997. http://www.germany
.info/relaunch/politics/speeches/102997.html.

Klejda, Mulaj. "On Bosnia's Borders and Ethnic Cleansing: Internal and External Factors." *Nationalism and Ethnic Politics* 11(1) (Spring 2005): 1–24.

Koch, Ida Elisabeth. "Political Rights: A Hermeneutic Perspective." *International Journal of Human Rights* 10(4) (2006): 17–41.

———. "The Protection of Socioeconomic Rights as Human Rights in Denmark." In *Justiciability of Economic and Social Rights*, edited by Fons Cooms, 405–430. Antwerp, Belgium: Intersentia, 2006.

Konrad, George. *Antipolitics: An Essay*, translated by Richard E. Allen. New York: Harcourt Brace Jovanovich, 1984.

Kopecký, Petr, and Edward Barnfield. "Charting the Decline of Civil Society: Explaining the Changing Roles and Conceptions of Civil Society in East and Central Europe." In *Democracy Without Borders: Transnationalisation and Conditionality in New Democracies*, edited by Jean Grugrel, 76–91. London: Routledge, 1999.

Kumar, C. Raj. "National Human Rights Institutions: Good Governance Perspectives on Institutionalization of Human Rights." *American University International Law Review* 19(2) (2003): 259–300.

———. "NHRIs in South Asia: Identifying the Need for Focusing on the Implementation of ESC Rights." Paper presented at the annual meeting of the International Studies Association 48th Annual Convention, February 28, 2007. http://convention2.allacademic.com/one/isa/isa07/index.php?click_key=1&PHPSESSID=a32bd3e05e6c4ec9be16bccb51c58b82.

Kumar, Radha. *Divide and Fall? Bosnia in the Annals of Partition.* New York: Verso, 1997.

Kurti, Laszlo. "The Emergence of Postcommunist Youth Identities in Eastern Europe from Communist Youth, to Skinheads to National Socialist." In *Nation and Race: The Developing of Euro-American Racist Subcultures*, edited by Jeffrey Kaplan and Tore Bjorgo, 175–201. Boulder, CO: Westlaw, 1998.

Landman, Todd. *Studying Human Rights.* New York: Routledge, 2006.

Lantis, Jeffrey S. *Strategic Dilemmas and the Evolution of German Foreign Policy Since Unification.* Westport, CT: Praeger, 2002.

Larsen, Christians Albrecht. "Municipal Size and Democracy: A Critical Analysis of the Argument on Proximity Based on Denmark." *Scandinavian Political Studies* 25(4).

Lauren, Paul Gordon. *The Evolution of Human Rights: Visions Seen.* Philadelphia: University of Pennsylvania Press, 1998.

Lauring, Palle. *A History of Denmark.* Rochester, MN: Nordic Books, 1986.

Leban, Mojca. "Faith-Based NGOs in Bosnia and Herzegovina." *The International Journal of Not-for-Profit Law* 6, no. 1 (September 2003). http://www.icnl.org/JOURNAL/vol6iss1/rel_lebanprint.htm.

Lees, Charles. *The Red-Green Coalition in Germany: Politics, Personalities, and Power.* Manchester, U.K.: Manchester University Press, 2000.

Leff, Carol Skalnik. *The Czech and Slovak Republics: Nation Versus State.* Boulder, CO: Westview Press, 1997.

Library of Congress Country Studies. *Germany: Foreign Reaction to Reunification.* August 1995. http://lcweb2.loc.gov/cgi-bin/query/r?frd/cstdy:@field(DOCID+de0145).

Library of Congress Country Studies and CIA World Factbook. "Germany: Social Welfare, Health Care, and Education." Republished by Photius Coutsoukis, 2004. http://www.photius.com/countries/germany/society/germany_society_social _welfare_heal~1364.html.

Lindsnaes, Birgit, Lone Lindholt, and Kristine Yigen, eds. *National Human Rights Institutions: Articles and Working Papers.* Copenhagen: Danish Institute for Human Rights, 2000.

Livingstone, Stephen. "The Need for a Bill of Rights in Northern Ireland." *Northern Ireland Legal Quarterly* 52 (2001): 269–285.

———. "The Northern Ireland Human Rights Commission." *Fordham International Law Journal* 22 (1999): 1465–1498.

London Chamber of Commerce and Industry. *The Czech Republic: Euro Info Centre Country Profile April 2006.* London: Euro Info Centre, April 2006. http://www .londonchamber.co.uk/docimages/1128.doc.

Longhurst, Kerry. *Germany and the Use of Force: The Evolution of Germany Security Policy 1990–2003 (Issues in German Politics).* Manchester, U.K.: Manchester University Press, 2005.

Lord, Janet E. "National Human Rights Institutions and International Human Rights Implementation: New Darlings of the International Human Rights System?" Paper presented at the annual meeting of the International Studies Association 48th Annual Convention, February 28, 2007.

———. "The United Nations Commissioner for Human Rights: Challenges and Opportunities." *Loyola of Los Angeles International and Comparative Law Journal* 17(2) (1995): 329–364.

Lysaght, Karen, and Anne Basten. "Violence, Fear and 'The Everyday': Negotiating Spatial Practice in Belfast." In *The Meanings of Violence*, edited by Elizabeth Stanko, 224–244. New York: Routledge, 2003. Also available at http://www.qub.ac.uk/ c-star/pubs/Violence%20fear%20and%20the%20everyday.pdf.

Mageean, P., and M. O'Brien, "From Margins to the Mainstream: Human Rights and the Good Friday Agreement." *Fordham International Law Journal* 22 (1999): 1499–1538.

Major, Patrick, and Johnathan Osmond, eds. *The Workers' and Peasants' State: Communism and Society in East Germany Under Ulbricht 1945–71.* Manchester, U.K.: University of Manchester, 2002.

Mamatey, Victor, and Radomir Luza, eds. *A History of the Czechoslovak Republic.* Princeton, NJ: Princeton University Press, 1973.

Markovitz, Andrei S., and Philip S. Gorski. *The German Left: Red, Green, and Beyond.* Oxford, U.K.: Polity Press, 1993.

Marksova-Tominova, Michaela. *Gender Equality and EU Accession: The Situation in the*

Czech Republic. Rio de Janeiro: International Gender and Trade Network, November 8, 2003. http://www.igtn.org/page/459/1/.

Matshekga, J. "Toothless Bulldogs? The Human Rights Commission of Uganda and South Africa: A Comparison of their Independence." *African Human Rights Law Journal* 2(1) (2002): 68–91.

McCrudden, Chris. "Consociationalism, Equality, and Minorities in the Northern Ireland Bill of Rights: The Inglorious Role of the OSCE High Commissioner for National Minorities." In *Judges, Transition, and Human Rights Cultures*, edited by John Morison, Kieran McEvoy, and Gordon Anthony. Oxford, U.K.: Oxford University Press, 2007.

McGarry, John, and Brendan O'Leary. *Explaining Northern Ireland: Broken Images.* Oxford, U.K.: Blackwell, 1995.

McGleenan, Tony. *Investigating Deaths in Hospitals in Northern Ireland: Does the System Comply with the European Convention on Human Rights?* Belfast: Northern Ireland Human Rights Commission, 2004.

McKittrick, David. *Making Sense of the Troubles: The Story of the Conflict in Northern Ireland.* Chicago: New Amsterdam Books, 2002.

Meehan, Michael. "Towards a Northern Ireland Bill of Rights." *Liverpool Law Review* 23(1) (January 2001): 33–56.

Mertus, Julie A. *Bait and Switch: Human Rights and U.S. Foreign Policy*, 2nd ed. New York: Routledge, 2008.

———. "Prospects for National Minorities Under the Dayton Accords: Lessons From History—The Inter-War Minorities Schemes and the 'Yugoslav Nations.'" *Brooklyn Journal of International Law* 23 (1998): 793–832.

———. *The United Nations and Human Rights.* New York: Routledge, 2006.

Mertus, Julie, and Pamela Goldberg. "The Inside/Outside Construct and a Perspective on Women's Human Rights After Vienna." *New York University Journal of International Law and Politics* 26 (1994): 201–226.

Ministry of Foreign Affairs of Denmark. "Capacity Assessment of the Danish Centre for Human Rights: Final Report," June 2002. http://humanrights.palermo.magenta-aps.dk/upload/application/606dbc7f/capacity.pdf.

———. "Official Response by the Danish Government to the UN Special Rapporteurs." January 24, 2006. http://www.um.dk/NR/rdonlyres/00D9E6F7-32DC-4C5A -8E24-F0C96E813C06/0/060123final.pdf.0.

Ministry of Foreign Affairs of the Czech Republic. "Development After November 1989." Czech Republic Official Website. http://www.nihrc.org/dms/data/NIHRC/attachments/dd/files/29/169.pdfz.

———. *Report on the Foreign Policy of the Czech Republic.* 2000. http://www.czech embassy.org/wwwo/mzv/?ido=9080&idj=2&amb=1&ikony=&trid=1&prsl= &pocc1=.

Ministry of the Interior and Health, Denmark. "The New Denmark: A Simple Public Sector Close to the Citizen." Proposal paper published in April 2004 (on file with author).

Morsink, Johannes. *The Universal Declaration of Human Rights: Drafting, Origins, and Intent*. Philadelphia: University of Pennsylvania Press, 2000.

Motakef, Mona. *Das Menschenrecht auf Bildung und der Schutz vor Diskriminierung: Exklusionsrisiken und Inklusionschancen*. Berlin: German Institute for Human Rights, 2006. http://files.institut-fuer-menschenrechte.de/488/d50_v1_file_4472c 3f75f94b_IUS-010_S_RAB_RZAnsicht_ES.pdf.

Müller, Birgit. *The Disenchantment with Market Economics: East Germans and Western Capitalism*. Oxford, U.K.: Berghahn Books, 2007.

Municipal Trust of Denmark (DKK). "KL (The National Association of Local Authorities in Denmark) Concerned About the Economics Behind the Municipal Reform." *Det Kommunale Kartel*, January 12, 2005 (in Danish). http://www.dkk.dk/index.asp?ArtikelNr=5609.

Murray, Rachel. *The Role of National Human Rights Institutions at the Regional and International Levels: The Experience of Africa*. London: Hart, 2007.

Murtagh, Brendan. *The Politics of Territory: Policy and Segregation in Northern Ireland*. Basingstoke, England: Palgrave, 2000.

Noel, Malcolm. *Bosnia: A Short History*. New York: New York University Press, 1994.

Northern Ireland Affairs Committee. *"Hate Crime": The Draft Criminal Justice (Northern Ireland) Order 2004*. London: Stationery Office, 2004.

Northern Ireland Council for Voluntary Action. *State of the Sector*. Belfast: NICVA, 2002.

Northern Ireland Executive. "Economic Performance Briefing." January 25, 2006. http://www.nics.gov.uk/briefjan06.pdf.

———. "The European Sustainable Competitiveness Programme for Northern Ireland 2007–2013." October 4, 2007. http://www.detini.gov.uk/cgi-bin/downdoc?id=3417.

Northern Ireland Human Rights Commission. "Addendum from Northern Ireland Human Rights Commission on the Draft Paper Arising from a Meeting in Stockholm on 21–22 June 2004 Concerning the Draft Comprehensive and Integral International Convention on the Protection and Promotion of the Rights and Dignity of Persons with Disabilities." Belfast: Northern Ireland Human Rights Commission, 2004. http://www.un.org/esa/socdev/enable/rights/nonhricontrib aug04.doc.

———. *Annual Report and Financial Accounts*. Belfast: Northern Ireland Human Rights Commission, 2007. http://www.nio.gov.uk/northern_ireland_human_rights _commissions_seventh_annual_report_2005_-_2006.pdf.

———. "Case Work." Belfast: Northern Ireland Human Rights Commission, 2007. http://www.nihrc.org/index.php?page=res_details&category_id=24.

———. *Countering Terrorism and Protecting Human Rights*. Belfast: Northern Ireland Human Rights Commission, September 2004.

———. *Enhancing the Rights of Older People in Northern Ireland*. Belfast: Northern Ireland Human Rights Commission, November 2001.

———. *An Evaluation of Human Rights Training for Student Police Officers in the Police*

Service of Northern Ireland. Belfast: Northern Ireland Human Rights Commission, November 2002.

———. *Examination of the 6th Report by the United Kingdom Under the International Covenant on Civil and Political Rights List of Issues: Submission by the Northern Ireland Human Rights Commission.* Belfast: Northern Ireland Human Rights Commission, October 2007.

———. *Making a Bill of Rights for Northern Ireland.* Belfast: Northern Ireland Human Rights Commission, September 2001. http://cain.ulst.ac.uk/issues/law/bor/borconsult.htm.

———. *Opening the Door to Health.* Belfast: Northern Ireland Human Rights Commission, December 2000. http://www.simoncommunity.org/filestore/documents/Opening_the_Door_to_Health.pdf.

———. "The Powers of the Northern Ireland Human Rights Commission." Consultation Paper. Belfast: Northern Ireland Human Rights Commission, February 7, 2006.

———. *Progressing a Bill of Rights: An Update.* Belfast: Northern Ireland Human Rights Commission, April 2004.

———. *Response to Prison Consultation on Options for the Accommodation of Immigration Detainees.* Belfast: Northern Ireland Human Rights Commission, March 1, 2004.

———. *Response to the Northern Ireland Prison Service's Policy on Self Harm and Suicide Prevention Management.* Belfast: Northern Ireland Human Rights Commission, March 1, 2004.

———. *A Single Equality Bill for Northern Ireland: Response to the Office of First Minister and Deputy First Minister's Discussion Paper.* Belfast: Northern Ireland Human Rights Commission, November 1, 2004.

———. *Submission to the Roundtable on a Bill of Rights for Northern Ireland.* Belfast: Northern Ireland Human Rights Commission, May 2006. http://www.nihrc.org/dms/data/NIHRC/attachments/dd/files/51/RoundtablefinalMay2006.doc.

———. *Tackling Violence at Home: Response to the Government's Proposals on Domestic Violence at Home.* Belfast: Northern Ireland Human Rights Commission, January 1, 2004.

———. *Women's Rights in a Bill of Rights for Northern Ireland: Report of a Consultative Conference.* Belfast: Northern Ireland Human Rights Commission, May 2002.

———. *Young People's Rights in a Bill of Rights for Northern Ireland: Report of Conference of Senior Schools.* Belfast: Northern Ireland Human Rights Commission, May 2002.

Northern Ireland Independent Monitoring Commission. *Seventeenth Report of the Independent Monitoring Commission.* London: Stationery Office, 2007.

Nour, Susanne, and Lars Nelleman Thisted. "When We Are Equal, But Not the Same." In *Diversity in the Workplace,* edited by Susanne Nour and Lars Nelleman Thisted, 18–44. Copenhagen: Borsens Forlag, 2005.

Nour, Susanne, and Lars Nellemann Thisted, eds. *Diversity in the Workplace.* Copenhagen: Bøsens Forlag, 2005.

Nuschler, Fran. *Lern und Arbeitsbuch Entwiclkungspoliti.* Bonn: Dietz, 1995.

Nye, David. *Introducing Denmark and the Danes.* Odense: University of Southern Denmark Press, 2006.

Office of the High Representative and EU Representative. *General Framework Agreement for Peace in Bosnia and Herzegovina.* December 14, 1995. http://www.ohr.int/dpa/default.asp?content_id=371.

———. "Mandate of the OHR." Undated, but updated 2008. http://www.ohr.int/ohr-info/gen-info/#2.

———. *OHR Mission Implementation Plan 2006–2007.* May 25, 2006. http://www.ohr.int/ohr-info/ohr-mip/default.asp?content_id=37241.

Office of the Public Defender of Rights. *Czech Public Defender of Rights.* http://www.ochrance.cz/en/ombudsman/obecne.php.

———. *Law of 8th December 1999 on the Public Defender of Rights.* http://www.ochrance.cz/en/ombudsman/zakon.php.

———. "The Powers of the Czech Public Defender of Rights." http://www.ochrance.cz/en/pomoc/.

———. "The Public Defender of Rights' Annual Report on Activities During the Year of 2001: Summary." 2002. http://www.ochrance.cz/en/dokumenty/dokument.php?back=/cinnost/index.php&doc=98.

Okafor, Obiora Chinedu, and Shedrack C. Agbakwa. "On Legalism, Popular Agency, and 'Voices of Suffering': The Nigerian Human Rights Commission." *Human Rights Quarterly* 24 (2002): 662–720.

Olivo, Christiane. *Creating a Democratic Civil Society in Eastern Germany: The Case of the Citizen Movements and Alliance 90.* New York: Palgrave, 2001.

Olsen, Birgitte Kofod. "Incorporation and Implementation of Human Rights in Denmark." In *International Human Rights Norms in the Nordic and Baltic Countries,* edited by Martin Scheinin, 227–250. The Hague: Martinus Nijhoff, 1996.

Ombudsman Information Network. "Bosnia and Herzegovina, Human Rights Ombudsman of Bosnia and Herzegovina." http://www.anticorruption.bg/ombudsman/eng/readnews.php?id=4468&lang=en&t_style=tex&l_style=default.

Ombudsman of Republika Srpska, Human Rights Protector. *Annual Report 2005.* Banja Luka, 2006.

O'Rawe, Mary. "Transitional Policing Arrangements in Northern Ireland: The Can't and Won't of the Change Dialectic." *Fordham International Law Journal* 26(4) (2003): 1015–1073.

Organization for Security and Cooperation in Europe. "Promoting and Protecting Economic and Social Rights." http://www.oscebih.org/human_rights/social_rights.asp.

OSCE Mission to Bosnia and Herzegovina. *Ten Years OSCE Mission to Bosnia and Herzegovina.* Sarajevo: OSCE, March 2006. http://www.oscebih.org/documents/OSCE10Years.pdf.

Østergaard, Uffe. "Danish National Identity: Between Multinational Heritage and Small State Nationalism." In *Denmark's Policy Towards Europe After 1945: History, Theory, and Options*, edited by Hans Branner and Morten Kelstrup, 139–184. Odense, Denmark: Odense University Press, 2000.

Overseas Development Administration. *Note on Enhancing Stakeholder Participation in Aid Activities.* April 1995. http://www.euforic.org/gb/stake2.htm#part1.

Padgett, Stephen, William E. Paterson, and Gordon Smith, eds. *Developments in German Politics 3.* Basingstoke, England: Palgrave Macmillan, 2003.

Palouš, Martin. *Human Rights with Respect to Foreign Policy.* Prague: Czech Helsinki Committee, 1999. http://www.helcom.cz/en/view.php?cisloclanku=2003062001.

Parlevliet, Michelle. *National Human Rights Institutions and Peace Agreements: Establishing National Institutions in Divided Societies.* Versoix, Switzerland: ICHPR, 2006.

Petrovic, B. *Peace in Our Times: Details of the Dayton Peace Accord.* Helsinski: Domovina Net, 1995.

Pickering, Paula M. *Peacebuilding in the Balkans: The View from the Ground Floor.* Ithaca, NY: Cornell University Press, 2007.

Pinheiro, Paulo Sergio, and David Carlos Baluarte. "National Strategies: Human Rights Commissions, Ombudsmen, and National Action Plans." Human Development Report 2000 Background Paper. New York: United Nations Development Program, 2000. http://hdr.undp.org/en/reports/global/hdr2000/papers/paulo%20sergio%20pinheiro%20.pdf.

Plock, Ernest D. *East German–West German Relations and the Fall of the GDR.* Boulder, CO: Westview, 1992.

Pohjolainen, Anna-Elina. *The Evolution of National Human Rights Institutions: The Role of the United Nations.* Copenhagen: Danish Institute for Human Rights, 2006.

Prypr, Zora B. "Czechoslovak Economic Development in the Interwar Period." In *History of the Czechoslovak Republic,* edited by Victor Mamatey and Radomir Luza, 188–215. Princeton, NJ: Princeton University Press, 1973.

Purdie, Bob. *Politics in the Street: The Origins of the Civil Rights Movement in Northern Ireland.* Belfast: Blackstaff Press, 1990.

Quint, Peter E. "The Constitutional Guarantees of Social Welfare in the Process of German Unification." *American Journal of Comparative Law* 47(2) (1999): 303–326.

Ramcharan, Bertrand. *The Protection Role of National Human Rights Institutions.* Leiden, Netherlands: Brill Academic, 2005.

———. *The United Nations High Commissioner for Human Rights: The Challenges of International Protection.* The Hague: Martinus Nijhoff, 2002.

Ramet, Sabrina. *Balkan Babel: The Disintegration of Yugoslavia from the Death of Tito to the War for Kosovo,* 3rd ed. Boulder, CO: Westview, 1999.

Ramet, Sabrina, ed. *Rock Music and Politics in Eastern Europe and the Soviet Union.* Boulder, CO: Westview, 1994.

Reif, Linda. "Building Democratic Institutions: The Role of National Human Rights Institutions in Good Governance and Human Rights Protection." *Harvard Human Rights Journal* 13 (Spring 2000): 1–70.

Reliefweb. *Country Profiles from Eastern Europe: Azerbaijan, Bosnia and Herzegovina, and Kosovo.* 2001. http://www.reliefweb.int/library/documents/2002/wcrwc -easterneurope-apr.pdf.

Remington, Robin, ed. *Winter in Prague: Documents on Czechoslovak Communism in Crisis.* Cambridge, MA: MIT Press, 1969.

Reporters Without Borders. "Spectre of Martin O'Hagan's Unsolved Murder Refuses to Fade as Press Freedom Takes a Back Seat on the Road to Peace in Northern Ireland." September 29, 2006. http://www.rsf.org/print.php3?id_article=19011.

Rhode, David. *Endgame: The Betrayal and Fall of Srebrenica—Europe's Worst Massacre Since World War II.* New York: Westview, 1998.

Riedlmayer, András J. *Destruction of Cultural Heritage in Bosnia-Herzegovina, 1992–1996: A Post-War Survey of Selected Municipalities.* Cambridge, MA: András J. Riedlmayer, 2002. http://hague.bard.edu/reports/BosHeritageReport-AR.pdf.

Riley, Kerry Kathleen. *Everyday Subversion: From Joking to Revolting in the German Democratic Republic.* East Lansing: Michigan State University Press, 2007.

Risse, Thomas, Stephen C. Ropp, and Kathryn Sikkink. *The Power of Human Rights: International Norms and Domestic Change.* New York: Cambridge University Press, 1999.

Rittberger, Volker, ed. *German Foreign Policy Since Unification: Theories and Case Studies (Issues in German Politics).* Manchester, U.K.: Manchester University Press, 2001.

Roberts, Geoffrey K. *German Politics Today.* Manchester, U.K.: Manchester University Press, 2000.

Rothschild, Joseph. *East Central Europe Between the Two World Wars.* Seattle: University of Washington Press, 1974.

Ruane, Joseph, and Jennifer Todd. *The Dynamics of Conflict in Northern Ireland.* New York: Cambridge University Press, 2003.

Rudolf, Peter. "The Myth of the German Way." *Survival* 47(1) (2005): 133–152.

Ruhl, Stefan. "Study on Racist Violence of the German National Focal Point." Bamberg, Germany: European Forum for Migration Studies, September 2002. http://www .efms.uni-bamberg.de/pdf/Racial_Violence_Raxen3.pdf.

Schlagheck, Carol. "Human Rights Official Quits: Percy MacLean Clashed with Institute's Board over His Focus on Abuses in Germany." Frankfurter Allgemeine Zeitung, 2002. http://aitel.hist.no/~walterk/wkeim/files/FAZ-PercyMacLean.htm (article on file with author).

Schmidt, Manfred G. "The Political Costs of Unification." *West German Politics* 14(4) (1992): 1–15.

———. *Political Institutions in the Federal Republic of Germany.* New York: Oxford University Press, 2003.

Schneider, Jakob. *Die Justiziabilität wirtschaftlicher, sozialer und kultureller Rechte.* Berlin: German Institute for Human Rights, 2004. http://files.institut-fuer -menschenrechte.de/488/d16_v1_file_40a3523de385e_Schneider_2004.pdf.

Sells, Michael A. *The Bridge Betrayed: Religion and Genocide in Bosnia.* Berkeley: University of California Press, 1998.

Shawcross, William. *Dubček.* New York: Simon and Schuster, 1990.

Sidmore-Hess, Daniel. "The Danish Party System and the Rise of the Right in the 2001 Parliamentary Election." *International Social Science Review* 78(3/4) (2003): 89–110.

Singer, Otto. "The Politics and Economics of German Unification: From Currency Union to Economic Dichotomy." *German Politics* 1 (1991): 7–94.

Skilling, H. Gordon. *Charter 77 and Human Rights in Czechoslovakia.* London: George Allen & Unwin, 1981.

Smith, Anne. "Access to Intervene: The Northern Ireland Human Rights Commission and the Northern Ireland Act 1998." *European Human Rights Law Review* 4 (2003): 423–436.

———. "The Drafting Process of a Bill of Rights for Northern Ireland." *Public Law* (Autumn 2004): 526–535. http://www.transitionaljustice.ulster.ac.uk//publications/smith-pl-2004.pdf.

———. "The Unique Position of National Human Rights Institutions: A Mixed Blessing?" *Human Rights Quarterly* 28 (2006): 904–946.

Søberg, Marius. "Empowering Local Elites in Bosnia and Herzegovina: The Dayton Decade." *Problems of Post-Communism* 53(3) (May–June 2006): 44–58.

South Asia Human Rights Documentation Center (SAHRDC). *National Human Rights Institutions in the Asia Pacific Region: Report of the Alternate NGO Consultation on the Second Asia-Pacific Regional Workshop on National Human Rights Institutions.* New Delhi: SAHRDC, March 1998.

SPAI (Stability Pact Anti-Corruption Initiative). "Empowering Civil Society in the Fight Against Corruption in South East Europe: Bosnia and Herzegovina Civil Society Assessment Report." 2001. http://topics.developmentgateway.org/civilsociety/rc/filedownload.do?itemId=326374.

Spieß, Katharina. *Die Wanderarbeitnehmerkonvention der Vereinten Nationen.* Berlin: German Institute for Human Rights, 2007. http://files.institut-fuer-menschen rechte.de/488/d61_v1_file_45ec16026c07a_Studie%20Wanderarbeiterkonven tion%202007.pdf.

Štamberková, Jaroslava. *Implementing the Policy of Equal Opportunities of Men and Women on the Labour Market.* Prague: Czech Helsinki Committee, 2001. http://www.helcom.cz/search.php?rsvelikost=sab&rstext=all-phpRS-all&rstema=96.

Stephen Roth Institute for the Study of Contemporary Anti-Semitism and Racism. "Country Studies: Germany." Tel Aviv, Israel: Tel Aviv University, 2004. http://www.tau.ac.il/Anti-Semitism/asw2004/germany.htm.

Stewart, Allison. "The International Community in Bosnia: Enduring Questions of Legitimacy." *Chinese Journal of International Law* 5(3) (November 2006): 753–760.

Stone, Norman, and Eduard Strouhal, eds. *Czechoslovakia: Crossroads and Rises, 1918–1988.* New York: St. Martin's, 1989.

Subotič, Jelena. "Hijacked Justice: Domestic Appropriation of International Norms." Human Rights and Human Welfare Working Paper 28, March 2005. http://www.du.edu/gsis/hrhw/working/2005/28-subotic-2005.pdf.

Tabeau, Ewa, and Jacub Bijak. "War-Related Deaths in the 1992–1995 Armed Conflicts in Bosnia and Herzegovina: A Critique of Previous Estimates and Recent Results." *European Journal of Population* 21(2–3) (June 2005): 187–215.

Thio, Li-ann. "The Future of National Human Rights Institutions: Political and Legal Perspectives—Part One: Panacea, Placebo, or Pawn? A Critical and Empirical Analysis of the Role of Suhakam in the Promotion and Protection of Human Rights in Malaysia." Paper presented at the International Studies Association Convention, Chicago, February 28–March 3, 2007. http://convention3.allacademic.com/one/isa/isa07/index.php?click_key=1&PHPSESSID=4397acb608e8153296b5ca9f10e4c3ea.

Thomas, Daniel Charles. *The Helsinki Effect: International Norms, Human Rights, and the Demise of Communism.* Princeton, NJ: Princeton University Press, 2001.

Thomas, Nick. *Protest Movements in 1960s West Germany: A Social History of Dissent and Democracy.* New York: Berg, 2003.

Thomas, R. Roosevelt, Jr. "Managing Diversity: A Conceptual Framework." In *Diversity in the Workplace: Human Resources Initiatives*, edited by Susan E. Jackson, 306–318. New York: Guilford, 1992.

Tonge, Jonathan. *Northern Ireland: Conflict and Change.* New York: Longman, 2002.

Torpey, John. "The Abortive Revolution Continues: East German Civil-Rights Activists Since Unification." *Theory and Society* 24 (February 1995): 105–134.

———. *Intellectuals, Socialism, and Dissent: The East German Opposition and Its Legacy.* Minneapolis: University of Minnesota Press, 1995.

Tsekos, Mary Ellen. "Human Rights Institutions in Africa." *Human Rights Brief* 9(2) (2002): 21–24.

United Kingdom Government Equalities Office. "EU Article 13 Race and Employment Directive." n.d. http://www.womenandequalityunit.gov.uk/eu_int/article_13.htm.

United Kingdom House of Lords. "Northern Ireland: Bill of Rights." February 19, 2008. http://www.theyworkforyou.com/wrans/?id=2008-02-19a.46.9.

United Kingdom Parliament. *Northern Ireland Act 1998 (Commencement Order No 5) Order 1999.* London: Stationery Office, 1999. https://www.legislation.hmso.gov.uk/si/si1999/19993209.htm.

United Nations. *National Human Rights Institutions: A Handbook on the Establishment and Strengthening of National Institutions for the Promotion and Protection of Human Rights.* Professional Training Series no. 4. New York: United Nations, 1995.

———. "Report of the Second International Workshop on National Institutions for the Promotion and Protection of Human Rights." December 23, 1993, UN document E/CN.4/1994/45.

———. "UN Workshop on Establishing an Iraqi Human Rights Commission in Cyprus." Press release, March 13, 2006. (On file with author).

United Nations Commission on Human Rights. *Question of the Violation of Human Rights and Fundamental Freedoms in Any Part of the World: Situation of Human*

Rights in the Former Yugoslavia. Report of Mr. Jiri Dienstbier, Special Rapporteur, 57th session, January 29, 2001, UN document E/CN.4/2001/47.

———. *Report of the Secretary General on National Institutions for the Promotion and Protection of Human Rights.* 53rd session, February 5, 1997, UN document E/CN.4/1997/41. http://daccessdds.un.org/doc/UNDOC/GEN/G97/104/46/PDF/G9710446.pdf?OpenElement.

United Nations Committee Against Torture. "Committee Against Torture Begins Review of Review of Bosnia and Herzegovina." ReliefWeb, November 8, 2005. http://www.reliefweb.int/rw/rwb.nsf/db900SID/HMYT-6HYQQD?OpenDocument.

United Nations Committee on Economic, Social and Cultural Rights. *Concluding Observations of the CESCR: United Kingdom of Great Britain and Northern Ireland, the Crown Dependencies and the Overseas Dependent Territories.* 28th session, June 5, 2002, UN document E/C.12/1/Add.79.

———. *Concluding Observations of the Committee on Economic, Social, and Cultural Rights: Denmark.* May 14, 1999, UN document E/C.12/1/Add.34.

———. *Concluding Observations of the Committee on Economic, Social and Cultural Rights: Denmark.* 33rd session, December 14, 2004, UN document E/C.12/1/Add.102.

———. *Reports Submitted by States Parties in Accordance with Articles 16 And 17 of the Covenant: Initial Report of Bosnia and Herzegovina.* 35th session, November 21, 2005, UN document E/C.12/2005/SR.41.

United Nations Committee on the Rights of the Child. *Concluding Observations: Denmark.* 40th session, November 23, 2005, UN document CRC/C/DNK/CO/3.

———. *Consideration of Reports Submitted by States Parties Under Article 44 of the Convention.* 40th session, September 30, 2005, UN document CRC/C/15/Add.273.

United Nations General Assembly. *Report of the Secretary General on Strengthening of the United Nations: An Agenda for Further Change.* 57th session, September 9, 2002, UN document A/57/387. http://daccessdds.un.org/doc/UNDOC/GEN/N02/583/26/PDF/N0258326.pdf?OpenElement

United Nations High Commission for Refugees (UNHCR). "Internally Displaced Number Drops in Bosnia and Herzegovina." April 15, 2005. http://www.unhcr.org/news/NEWS/425fd70c4.html.

United Nations Human Rights Committee. *Concluding Observations: Denmark.* 70th session, October 31, 2000, UN document CCPR/CO/70/DNK.

———. *Concluding Observations of the Human Rights Committee: Denmark.* November 18, 1996, UN document CCPR/C/79/Add.68.

United Nations Human Rights Council. "Information for National Human Rights Institutions." 2008. http://www2.ohchr.org/english/bodies/hrcouncil/nhri.htm.

United Nations Office of the High Commissioner for Human Rights. *Fact Sheet No. 19: National Institutions for the Promotion and Protection of Human Rights.* Geneva: United Nations, April 2003. http://www.unhchr.ch/html/menu6/2/fs19.htm.

United Nations Security Council. *Establishment of UN Transitional Administration in East Timor.* 54th session, October 25, 1999, UN document S/RES/1272.

United Nations World Conference on Human Rights. *Vienna Declaration and Programme of Action.* July 12, 1993, UN document A/CONF 157/23.

U.S. Agency for International Development (USAID). "2001 NGO Sustainability Index: Bosnia and Herzegovina." 2002. http://www.usaid.gov/locations/europe_eurasia/dem_gov/ngoindex/2001/bosnia.pdf.

U.S. Congress, House, International Relations Committee, Subcommittee on International Operations and Human Rights. *The U.N. and the Sex Slave Trade in Bosnia: Isolated Case or Larger Problem in the U.N. System?* April 24, 2002.

U.S. Department of State, Bureau of Democracy, Human Rights, and Labor. *Bosnia and Herzegovina: Country Reports on Human Rights Practices, 2005.* March 8, 2006. http://www.state.gov/g/drl/rls/hrrpt/2005/61640.htm.

———. *Czech Republic: Country Reports on Human Rights Practices, 2005.* March 8, 2006. http://www.state.gov/g/drl/rls/hrrpt/2005/61644.htm.

———. *Denmark: Country Reports on Human Rights Practices, 2005.* March 8, 2006. http://www.state.gov/g/drl/rls/hrrpt/2005/61645.htm.

———. *Germany: Country Reports on Human Rights Practices, 2005.* March 8, 2006. http://www.state.gov/g/drl/rls/hrrpt/2005/61650.htm.

U.S. Department of State, Bureau of European and Eurasian Affairs. *Background Note: Czech Republic.* January 2008. http://www.state.gov/r/pa/ei/bgn/3237.htm.

Vachudova, Milda Anna. *Europe Undivided: Democracy, Leverage, and Integration After Communism.* New York: Oxford University Press, 2007.

Weine, Stevan M. *When History Is a Nightmare: Lives and Memories of Ethnic Cleansing in Bosnia-Herzegovina.* New Brunswick, NJ: Rutgers University Press, 1999.

Wende, Peter. *A History of Germany.* New York: Palgrave Macmillan, 2006.

Wheaton, Bernard, and Kavan Zdenek. *The Velvet Revolution: Czechoslovakia, 1988–1991.* Boulder, CO: Westview, 1992.

Whelan, Leo. "The Challenge of Lobbying for Civil Rights in Northern Ireland: The Committee on the Administration of Justice." *Human Rights Quarterly* 14 (1992): 149–170.

Whipple, Tim D. *After the Velvet Revolution: Vaclav Havel and the New Leasers of Czechoslovakia Speak Out.* Lanham, MD: Freedom House, 1991.

Wildenthal, Lora. "The Origins of the West German Human Rights Movement, 1945–1961." Public lecture sponsored by the Human Rights Institute and the German Section of the Department of Modern and Classical Languages, Rice University, April 5, 2004.

World Bank Group, "Bosnia and Herzegovina: New Health Sector Enhancement Project Launched." *Reliefweb,* July 13, 2005. http://www.reliefweb.int/rw/RWB.NSF/db900SID/HMYT-6EAPCC?OpenDocument.

Yordán, Carlos L. "Resolving the Bosnian Conflict: European Solutions." *Fletcher Forum of World Affairs* 47 (Winter/Spring 2003): 147–154.

Zarrehparvar, Mandana, and Steen Hildebrandt. "Discrimination in Denmark." In *Diversity in the Workplace,* edited by Susanne Nour and Lars Nelleman Thisted, 45–70. Copenhagen: Borsens Forlag, 2005.

Zivanovic, Miroslav. "Human Rights in Bosnia and Herzegovina in 2005." In *Regional Human Rights Report 2005*, edited by Belgrade Center for Human Rights. Belgrade: Belgrade Center for Human Rights, 2006.

Interviewees

Dino Abazović, director, Human Rights Center, University of Sarajevo

Nedim Ademović, archivist/registrar, Human Rights Commission, Constitutional Court of Bosnia-Herzegovina

Valentin Aichele, researcher, Economic, Social, and Cultural Rights, German Institute for Human Rights

Gwendolyn Albert, director, League of Human Rights, Brno, Czech Republic

Les Allamby, director, Northern Ireland Law Center

Erik André Andersen, analyst, Research Department, Danish Institute for Human Rights

Robert Archer, executive director, International Council on Human Rights Policy

Daniele Archibugi, professor of innovation, governance, and public policy, Birbeck University, London

Kurt Bassuener, strategic analyst, Political Department, Office of the High Representative

Maggie Beirne, director, Committee on the Administration of Justice, Northern Ireland

Christine Bell, professor of law and former commissioner, Northern Ireland Human Rights Commission

Heiner Bielefeldt, director, German Institute for Human Rights

Widney Brown, senior director, International Law, Policy, and Campaigns, Amnesty International, International Secretariat

Brian Burdekin, visiting fellow, Raoul Wallenberg Institute (Sweden); former special adviser on national institutions to the United Nations High Commissioner for Human Rights (UNHCHR)

Iain Byrne, senior lawyer, Commonwealth, Economic, and Social Rights Programme, InterRights

Karel Černín, advocate, Office of the Public Defender, Brno, Czech Republic

Christine Chinkin, professor of international law, Center for the Study of Human Rights, London School of Economics

Jim Deery, senior consultant, Northern Associates, Belfast

Brice Dickson, professor of law and former chief commissioner, Northern Ireland Human Rights Commission

Srđan Dizdarević, president, Helsinki Committee for Human Rights

Maire Nic Fhionnachtaigh, development/marketing officer, Raidió Fáilte 107.1 FM

Tom Hadden, professor, School of Law, Queen's University, Belfast; and commissioner, Northern Ireland Human Rights Commission

Colin Harvey, professor of human rights law and head of the School of Law, Queen's University, Belfast; current commissioner, Northern Ireland Human Rights Commission

Enes Hašić, ombudsman, Republika Srpska

Mohammad M. Al-Heidari, member of the Iraqi Parliament

Emir Kaknjasević, attorney, Sarajevo

Morten Kjaerum, director general, Danish Center for Human Rights

Ida Elisabeth Koch, senior research fellow, Research Department, Danish Institute for Human Rights

Jiri Kopal, advocate, League of Human Rights

Monika Landmanova, director, Open Society

Lone Lindholt, team leader, Education and Academia, International Department, Danish Institute for Human Rights

Birgit Lindsnaes, director, International Department, Danish Institute for Human Rights

Percy MacLean, judge and former executive director, Northern Ireland Human Rights Commission

Ciarán Ó. Maoláin, head of Legal Services, Policy, and Research, Northern Ireland Human Rights Commission

Sladana Marić, ombudsman, Bosnia and Herzegovina

Mohammad Mahmoud Ould Mohamedou, associate director, Program on Humanitarian Policy and Conflict Research, Harvard University

Aoife Nolan, senior legal officer, Center on Housing Rights and Evictions, Belfast

Birgitte Kofod Olsen, director, National Department, Danish Institute for Human Rights

Catherine O'Rourke, researcher, Transitional Justice Project, Derry

Rita Roca, project manager, Human Rights and Business, Danish Institute for Human Rights

Henrik Rothe, secretary general, Danish Bar Association

Hans-Otto Sano, senior researcher, Research Department, Danish Institute for Human Rights

Sonya Sceats, transition team adviser and human rights training officer, British Institute of Human Rights

Marianne Schulze, human rights consultant, Vienna, Austria

Fraude Seidensticker, deputy director, German Institute for Human Rights

Paddy Sloan, chief executive, Northern Ireland Human Rights Commission

Anne Smith, lecturer in law, Transitional Justice Institute, University of Ulster, Northern Ireland

Chandra Lekha Sriram, chair in Human Rights, School of Law, University of East-London

Boris Topić, advocate, Office of the Human Rights Ombudsman of Bosnia-
Herzegovina

Toby Vogel, Balkan editor, Transitions Online

Patrick Yu, executive director, Northern Ireland Council for Ethnic Minorities

Mandana Zarrehparvar, special adviser, National Department, Danish Institute for Human Rights

Ahmed Žilić, attorney and member of the Advisory Committee, Council of Europe,
Directorate General of Human Rights, Framework Convention for the Protection of National Minorities

Miroslav Živanović, librarian/documentalist, Human Rights Center, University of
Sarajevo

Index

Page numbers followed by *t* indicate tables.